CW01635331

The Merchant Ships of Whitstable

To Peter & Sue
Love & Best Wishes
From Mam & Paul
x x

Prince Consort

The Merchant Ships of Whitstable

by Wallace Harvey

Emprint Publications

Books by the same author:

Whitstable and the French Prisoners of War

The Seasalter Company – A Smuggling Fraternity (1740—1854)

Thomas Clark of Canterbury (1775—1859)

Seasalter and the Mystery of Robinson Crusoe

First Printed 1993

© **WALLACE HARVEY**

All rights reserved. No part of this publication may be reproduced or transmitted in any form or by any means, electronic or mechanical, including photocopy, recording, or any information storage and retrieval system without permission in writing from the publishers.

Hardback ISBN 1 871716 03 9
Paperback ISBN 1 871716 04 7

Typeset in Baskerville 10pt by P & J Curtis

Printed and Published in Great Britain by
Emprint Publications, 9 Harbour Street, Whitstable, Kent CT5 1AG

CONTENTS

Whitstable Ships

One day, while gazing into the clear depths of the river Stour by the Westgate at Canterbury, I was reminded of the meaningful verse published by Isaac Watts in 1719.

"Time like an ever rolling stream
Bears all its sons away
They fly forgotten as a dream
Dies at the opening day."

For some time it had been my ambition to write the story of the golden age of Whitstable ships. My boyhood dreams, before the first Great War had often been enriched by stories of thrilling adventures told by the old mariners of Whitstable, described in the local vernacular as 'having a cuff'. They were stories of triumph over the forces of nature, of visits to foreign ports, of skill in navigating brigs, brigantines, and schooners, over the wild restless seas, and sometimes stories of tragic ship-wreck.

Then the second Great War broke upon us, and with the passage of time so many of those old mariners passed to their eternal rest that there scarcely remained any who could speak of personal knowledge of sailing those ships. As I looked into that steadily flowing stream I experienced an overwhelming desire to commemorate the achievements of those humble men, and in some part record the noble part they played in their day and generation. But it seemed far beyond my powers to adequately do justice to so great a subject. Nevertheless close beside me stood the answer to my doubts, for as I looked at those massive towers of the Westgate I could not help thinking that like the intimidating experiences of life there is a way through them and ways round them.

Obscured by the glamour of the great sailing ships, such as the Colonial Clippers, the Blackwall Frigates, the China Clippers, and the Last of the Windjammers, as has been so ably recorded by Basil Lubbock, the unique part played by the humble mariners of the little seaport of Whitstable in the Industrial Revolution of England is apt to be overlooked.

Moreover as Faversham was the ancient port of registry the fact that the fleet of nearly five hundred Whitstable owned and manned vessels were registered there hides a fascinating story of their history.

Also while the poor uneducated working classes of England stagnated under the age-long manorial system or suffered the slavery of the factories, the poor uneducated mariners of Whitstable, by their mastery of the science of navigation, and experience gained by long voyages, achieved a truly unique world-wide vision far more expansive than the suppressed members of the other working classes.

To being privileged to record even a small record of the achievements of those humble mariners and to listen to the stories of their triumph over the forces of nature imposes an honoured duty to preserve that knowledge for future generations.

Wallace Harvey

Whitstable 1993

17th CENTURY SHIPS OF WHITSTABLE 1662-1698

Records of the early ships which were owned here would seem to have been unkept or to have been lost in the mists of time. For some strange and unexplained reason the earliest records yet found, while they reveal a well-established east coast trade and voyages to Sunderland for coal, yet beyond giving the names of the vessels, the names of the owners and masters, they reveal an all too brief description of the type of cargo carried. Some conception of the size of the vessel may be judged from the fact that it could carry up to 42 chaldrons of coal, a chaldron consisting of 36 bushels.

Some interest may be found in studying particulars of the various owners or the masters of the vessels. For instance Thomas Reynolds, who owned the Anne, the Chance, and the Richard and Margaret, lived at the Three Mariners, (now No. 7–9 Oxford Street) and his son, Richard Reynolds, who married Elizabeth Hayward, 20th February 1670, died of the plague, and was buried in All Saints churchyard 1st January 1688.

Christopher Castle, who owned the Christopher and John, lived at the previous Ship Centurion, (now No. 111 High Street) which was pulled down in 1913.

Thomas Oliver, and Edward Oliver, who owned the Canterbury, and the Goodwill, lived at 17–19 High Street. So we may well wonder if any of the paving stones which were unloaded at Whitstable in 1680 exist and are traceable at the present day, as 6 dozen 'flagg' stones are not easy to hide or destroy.

Moreover it is of interest to learn of Christopher Castle, at that early period, bringing to Whitstable, 2 chests of oranges and lemons, and 6 baskets and 1 bag of lemons.

Twenty-eight ships of the 17th Century

1. ANN
2. BLESSING
3. CANTERBURY
4. CHANCE
5. CHRISTOPHER & JOHN
6. CONSTANT FRIENDS
7. CONTENT
8. ENDEAVOUR
9. FRENCH MERCHANT
10. FRIENDS
11. FRIENDS ADVENTURE
12. FRIENDSHIP
13. FURIOUS ADVENTURE
14. GOODWILL
15. HAPPY RETURNS
16. HOPEFUL ADVENTURE
17. HOPEWELL
18. JAMES
19. JOHN
20. JOHN AND ANN
21. MARY
22. OWNERS ADVENTURE
23. PROVIDENCE
24. RICHARD AND MARGARET
25. SEAWONDER
26. THOMAS
27. WILLIAM
28. WILLIAM AND JOSEPH

"Manifests" of 17th Century Whitstable Ships

ANNE *of Whitstable*

1676

London	Master:	Richard Reynolds Thomas Shaw 30 pigges load of fodder landed at Whitstable	10th November
London	Master:	Richard Reynolds John Pilkington 40 gross pigges quarters and a fodder of lead landed at Whitstable	19th January

BLESSING *of Whitstable*

1680

London	Master:	Robert Poore Richard Foote 21 piggs qtrs fodder of lead 10 bars of iron. Landed at Whitstable	June
London	Master:	Robert Poore 40 bags of wool, 100 pounds in weight. Landed at Whitstable	15th July
London	Master:	Robert Poore Thomas Allen 5 fforrorigne of iron Load qtrs of fodder and half one hog White sugar qtrs 6 – wth 4 bags of hay 2 bundles of charge frames	5th August
London	Master:	John Poore John Selby 40 bags of one hundred weight of wool	25th August

1688

9th July	Master:	Robert Poore Thomas Allen	For London

1692

9th July	Master:	John Ayres Thomas Allen 20 tons copperas	For London	18th July
30th September	Master:	John Ayres Thomas Allen 9 tons copperas	For London	7th Oct.

1698 **CANTERBURY** *of Whitstable*

22nd July	Master:	Edward Oliver	26th July
25th July	Master:	Edward Oliver Thomas Oliver	28th July
30th July	Master:	Edward Oliver Thomas Oliver	2nd August
10th August	Master:	Edward Oliver Thomas Oliver	15th August
26th August	Master:	Edward Oliver Thomas Oliver	29th August
10th September	Master:	Edward Oliver Thomas Oliver	13th September
1st October	Master:	Edward Oliver Thomas Oliver	3rd October
3rd November	Master:	Edward Oliver Thomas Oliver	7th November
19th November	Master:	Edward Oliver Thomas Oliver	22nd November
2nd December	Master:	Edward Oliver Thomas Oliver	6th December
1699			
17th January	Master:	Edward Oliver Thomas Oliver	20th January
1700			
13th January	Master:	Edward Oliver Thomas Oliver	16th January
23rd February	Master:	Edward Oliver Thomas Oliver	26th February
9th March	Master:	Edward Oliver Thomas Oliver	12th March
23rd March	Master:	Edward Oliver Thomas Oliver	26th March
5th April	Master:	Edward Oliver Thomas Oliver	8th April
18th May	Master:	Edward Oliver Thomas Oliver	23rd May
June	Master:	Edward Oliver Thomas Styles	

July	Master:	Edward Oliver Thomas Styles
September	Master:	Edward Oliver Thomas Styles
September	Master:	Thomas Oliver
October	Master:	Edward Oliver
November	Master:	Edward Oliver
December	Master:	Edward Oliver Thomas Oliver
1701		
January	Master:	Edward Oliver Benjamin Baddam
January	Master:	Edward Oliver Thomas Styles
February	Master:	Edward Oliver Thomas Oliver
February	Master:	William Adryan
March	Master:	Edward Oliver
April	Master:	William Adryan
May	Master:	William Adryan Thomas Oliver
May	Master:	William Adryan Edward Oliver
May	Master:	Edward Oliver Thomas Styles
June	Master:	William Adryan Thomas Oliver
July	Master:	Edward Oliver Thomas Styles
August	Master:	Edward Phosier
September	Master:	Robert Argent
September	Master:	Edward Oliver
September	Master:	Thomas Oliver

1680 **CHANCE** *of Whitstable*

Master: Richard Reynolds — 29th May
Thomas Shaw
20 qtrs 2 fodder of lead landed at Whitstable

1688 **CHRISTOPHER AND JOHN** *of Whitstable*

22nd February

Master: Christopher Castle
10 qtrs wheat
20 qtrs oats
40 qtrs malt
42 cwt. bags of hops
1 pad flax
1 bag nails
1 cwt. Canterbury worsted
½ load household goods

2nd March

Master: Christopher Castle — From London
William Clarke
5 barrels soap
19 raw hides
14 cwt. and 1 box woollens, linen, mercery
1 capstan
1 cwt. cheese
7 baskets 30 boxes 1 firkin salt
1 Runlett Cyder
1 bag foreign wool
2 tons grocery
1 barrel steele
2 baskets 2 baggs
1 cwt. iron and brass
1 box apothecary wares
1 sack cotton wick
2 chests oranges and lemons
20 ½ cwts. 1 pair scales
6 baskets 1 box earthenware and glass
6 baskets 1 bag lemons
1 piece ware cloth

7th March

Master: Christopher Castle — For London
Anthony Archer
30 qtrs wheat
20 qtrs malt
50 qtrs oats
20 bags hops
1 cwt. Canterbury worsted
2 pieces Canterbury made stuffs
2 of Cyder
1 box of hats
2 baskets old brass and pewter
½ load household goods
1 bag 1 cwt. wool flocks
2 bags flax
1 basket Canterbury hatts   1 bag Canterbury worsted

1689

6th April	Master:	Christopher Castle John Gillum	For London
30th April		John Gillum	For London
24th May		John Gillum	For London
22nd June		Joseph Roberts	For London
5th July		John Powdalling	For London
20th July		Richard Inns	For London
17th August		Edward Piggott	From London
20th September		Richard Shrubsall	For London
4th October		Richard Shrubsall	
19th November		Thomas Dunkin	

1691

15th January — William Phillpott — For London — R. 22nd January
Anthony Archer
9 qtrs wheat
10 qtrs oats
8 bags English hops
2 sacks flare feede
½ load household goods

12h February — William Phillpott — For London — R. 22nd February
Anthony Archer
40 qtrs wheat
30 qtrs oats
12 bags English hoppes
1 cwt. Canterbury worsted
½ load of household goods

5th March — Master: William Phillpott — From London — 8th March
John Hubbing
2 cheese
12 baskets and box of hatts and haberdashery wares
One butt 2½ one rundlett wine
4 qrts mercury
Woollen ware, haberdashery and linen drapery wares
2 doz bare
1 bundle raw silke
5 boxes apothecary and confectioners wares
One box oyle and caulouring
3 cwt. grocery wares
2 cwt. ironmongers bars

1691 continued

11th March	Master: William Phillpott Anthony Archer 40 qtrs wheat 40 qtrs malt 20 qtrs oats 24 bagges English hops 2 cwt. Canterbury worsted	14th March
	1 cwt. mercery wares From London 1 load of household goods	
	Master: William Phillpott Thomas Browne 3 pipes and 4 pipes canary port wine 5 cwt. cheese 5 firkins butter 1 bundle lead shott 1 paper parcell of haberdashery 2 – 7 boxes leaf weight tobacco 4 ton grocery 1 runlett ayle One bag, one box of apothecary wares 2 basketts of bottles 1 doz. barrels blaking One bundle and 2 doz. brooms and lines More 1 cwt. upholstery 3 barrels soape One parcell new silk 2 parcels Sadlers wares	From London
	1692	
18th January	Thomas Brown 10 qtrs wheat 8 qtrs malt 8 qtrs beans 22 bags hops 8 Canterbury hats 5 cwt. Canterbury worsted 1 load household goods	
26th January	1 cwt. wool flocks 15 qtrs wheat 40 qtrs oats 50 qtrs malt 20 qtrs beans 4 pads English flax 34 bags hops 68 cwt. – 2 cwt. Canterbury worsted 1 load household goods	

1692 continued

15th April Master: William Phillpott From London 21st April
Thomas Shaw
7½ barrels soap
7 pigs of ore fodder
Lead eight bags shott
1 cwt. Woollen drapery and mercury
1 cwt. parcell linen drapery
1 pipe canary 4 hampers bottle wine
1 of brandy
5 cwt. cheese
2 baskets 5 boxes felt caster hatts cases
2 doz. boxes 2 parcells haberdashery
6 ton grocery
3 rundletts ayle
3 bags bottom cotton
3 rundletts ayle one like vinegar
1 paper parcell 4 boxes apothecary wares
1 bundle one parcell – and pork
3 one barrel tarr
1 bag 2 doz. brooms and cork
1 chest oranges and lemons
1 matt glue and 1 doz. blacking
1 basket 1 box earthenware glasses

23rd April Master: William Phillpott
Anthony Archer
10 tons copperas
10 qtrs wheat
2 bags English hopps
½ cwt. worsted
1 small woollen drapery net and ½ load of household goods

10th June Master: William Phillpott 14th June
Robert Jefhs
8 barrels wharf soap
1 pipe Spanish 4 pipes port
1 wine 1 fatt and one rundlett Rhenish wine
2 cwts. woollen drapery
2 boxes casters
2 basketts straw hatts 1 basket 10 small parcells glasses
2 boxes cutt tobacco 2 rest drawers 46 couple salt fish
Bottle cider
2 tons grocery
1 hogshead vinegar
6 Turkey work chairs
1 basket one bore gingerbread
3 boxes apothecary wares

CHRISTOPHER AND JOHN *of Whitstable (continued)*

1692 continued

30th July — Master: William Phillpott, Richard Shrubsol — For London — 1st August

127 qtrs malt 15 qtrs wheat
1 cwt. Canterbury worsteds
3 ton copperas

5 pieces Canterbury made silks and straws — From London
4 cwts. woollen drapery
½ load household goods

6th August — Master: William Phillpott, Thomas Shaw — At London — 9th August

10 pigs lead
4 weights mercury
1 pack 1 weight 1 case 2 trunks woollens
Case (Linen?) drapery
3 cwt. cheese
1 barrel soap 4 boxes tobacco
1 hamper bottles of wine
½ barrel of rum
22 cwt. grocery 7 bags mail
3 parcels of 5, day pair hose
1 body 2 weights leather
1 parcel sadlers wares
1 cart
1 box gingerbread
3 boxes apothecary wares
1 press bed
1 chest 1 basket earthenware
Winder glass
1 ton grocery wares

20th August — Master: William Phillpott, Thomas Shaw — At London — 23rd August

20 pigs lead 1 qtr. fodder lead
3 weights mercury
1 weight linen drapery
1 box haberdashery
1 box apothecary wares
1 pkt. paper
1 hogshead oyle
1 weight poldaris
1 box upholstery
4 boxes confectionary
1 hogshead tobacco
2 weights raw silk
Pottle of oylers wares
2 tons grocery wares

1692 continued

23rd September	Master: William Phillpott Richard Srubsol 5 qtrs wheat 10 qtrs oats 27 bags English hopps ½ cwt. Canterbury worsteds ½ load household goods	For London	
30th September	Master: William Phillpott 20 cwt. lead 1 pack 1 weight linen drapery 1 cask butter 4 casks port wine 2 runlets Rhenish wine 1 barrel cutt tobacco 1 basket flask 1 cog of sturgeon 2 cwt. grocery 1 weight boddyer 2 sacks candle mattes 1 bundle leather 2 cwt. cheese 2 bundles – 4 boxes apothecary ware 2 barrels soap	At London	5th October
7th October	Master: William Phillpott Richard Srubsol 35 bags English hopps ½ load household goods 1 cwt. Canterbury worsted 4 qtrs wheat 5 qtrs oats 10 qrts malt		10th October
20th October	10 qtrs wheat 9 qtrs oats 12 bags hops 10 tons copperas ½ cwt. Canterbury worsted ½ load household goods		24th October
3rd November	10 qtrs wheat 9 qtrs malt 12 bags hops 1 cwt. worsted 1 load household goods		7th November

CHRISTOPHER AND JOHN *of Whitstable*

1692

10th December	Master:	William Phillpott John Townesaid	At London	14th December

5 barrels soap
7 weights 1 bundle woollen drapery, mercery and silk wares
2 pipes 1 hogshead port
2 pipes 1 awrn canary wine
6 firkins butter
6 cwt. cheese
1 ton copperas
16 cwt. grocery
1 parcel haberdashery wares
5 cwt. iron wares
1 box coffee
2 boxes 1 bottle apothecary wares
3 baskets 11 parcels turner wares
1 box honey
1 box painters colouring

1693	Master:	William Phillpott
29th January		Robert Joffer
4th February		D. Wigfall
10th February		John Stott
13th February		Daniel Wigfall
28th February		Richard Shrubsall
3rd March		John Townesend
10th March		Richard Shrubsall
24th March		Richard Shrubsall
1st April		Daniel Wigfall
8th April		Richard Shrubsall
19th May		Thomas Gird
15th June		John Townesend
15th July		Richard Shrubsall
22nd September		Richard Shrubsall
1694	Master:	William Phillpott
6th October		Richard Shrubsall
20th October		Richard Shrubsall
27th October		Thomas Sole
14th December		Richard Shrubsall

1698	
25th June	John Larriman
1st July	John Larriman, Richard Shrubsall
30th July	John Larriman John Harris
18th August	Christopher Castle
3rd September	Christopher Castle
10th September	Christopher Castle Robert Flalshan
1st October	Christopher Castle Matthew Hoult
11th October	John Harris
20th October	Christopher Castle
29th October	Christopher Castle
11th November	Christopher Castle
25th November	Christopher Castle
2nd December	Christopher Castle
22nd December	Christopher Castle
1700	
January	John Larriman
5th January	Christopher Castle
2nd February	John Larriman
17th February	John Larriman
2nd March	John Larriman
15th March	John Larriman
30th March	John Larriman
April	Christopher Castle William Loadbetter
13th April	John Larriman
10th May	John Larriman
June	John Larriman Samuel Loadbetter
August	Christopher Castle
September	Christopher Castle Mathias Hoult
November	Christopher Castle Mathias Hoult
December	Christopher Castle Mathias Hoult

CHRISTOPHER AND JOHN *of Whitstable (continued)*

1701

January	Christopher Castle
February	John Larriman
March	John Larriman
April	John Larriman
May	John Larriman
June	John Larriman
July	John Larriman
August	John Larriman
September	John Larriman

CONSTANT FRIENDS *of Whitstable*

1680

Sunderland	Master: Edward Wright 32 chaldrons of coal	6th July

CONTENT *of Whitstable*

1680

London	Master: James Hart 29 bags of wool landed at Whitstable	18th May
London	Master: James Hart 40 bags of wool gt. 57	15th July
London	Master: James Hart John Selby 37 bags of wool	20th July
London	Master: James Hart John Selby 40 bags of wool one hundred weight	

1688

16th February	Master: James Hart, Richard Shrubsall 20 qtrs wheat 15 qtrs oats 16 bags qtr 32 hundred of English hops 3 tons copperas 3 cwt. Canterbury worsted 4 cwt. 2 baskets of old pewter ½ load of household goods 1 bundle qt. ½ cwt. allum leather	For London 2 bagges of coney skins More 5 ton copperas 2 bags of English hops

1688 continued

21st April	Master: James Hart Henry Waddell 15 qtrs wheat 36 backs of leather 6 tons copperas 1 load of household goods	For London
31st June	Master: James Hart Wheat 20 qtrs oats 10 ton copperas 2 bags of course English wool 6 bags of English hops 3 cwt. Canterbury worsted One woollen drapery returned One piece – ½ load of household goods	For London
17th July	Master: James Hart Wheat 15 qtrs oats 10 tons of copperas 4 doz. English felts household goods 1 cwt. Canterbury worsted	For London
	Master: James Hart 19 qtrs wheat 10 tons copperas 20 backs of leather ½ a Eng. Cyder 2 barrels of English spirits 1 cwt. Canterbury worsted ½ load household goods 6 backs of leather 4 bags of English hops ¼ cwt. English wool	For London
	Master: James Hart Matthew Greenstreet 10 tons copperas 15 qtrs wheat ½ tun of English spirits 20 backs of leather 2 bags – weight 2 cwt. – Canterbury worsted 1 load household goods	For London

CONTENT *of Whitstable (continued)*

1688 continued

Master: James Hart
Henry Waddell
For London

10 tons copperas
12 qtrs wheat
17 qtrs oats
7 backs of leather
2 bags of 3 cwt. Canterbury worsted
2 bags of English hops
½ load of household goods
10 sacks of beans
9 pieces of Canterbury stuff
10 doz. Canterbury hats

Master: James Hart
Henry Waddell
For London

10 tons copperas
15 qtrs wheat
2 hogshead Cyder
12 backs tanned leather
1 cwt. Canterbury worsted
½ load of household goods

Master: James Hart
Richard Shrubshall
For London

30 qtrs Wheat
20 qtrs oats
22 bags qr. 4 cwt. of English hops
35 backs leather
1 hundred and a halfe of course wool
2 cwt. tow
1 load household goods
30 yds of returned serg
4 pieces of plush
1 cwt. Canterbury worsted
6 tons copperas more

1689

13th April	Master:	Richard Dickinson Thomas Simpson	For London
4th May	Master:	Richard Hart Nicholas Simpson	For London
1st June	Master:	Richard Dickinson Nicholas Simpson	From London
6th July	Master:	Richard Dickinson Peter Foremore	From London
11th July	Master:	Richard Dickinson Richard Mount	From London
17th October	Master:	Richard Hart Nicholas Simpson	From London

1676 **ENDEAVOUR** *of Whitstable*

Sunderland	Master: William Pizing 34 chaldrons of coal landed at Whitstable	12th May
1677		
Sunderland	Master: William Pizing 34 chaldrons of coke landed at Whitstable	10th April
Newcastle	Master: William Pizing 35 chaldrons of coal landed at Whitstable	22nd May
Sunderland	Master: William Pizing 34 chaldrons of coal landed at Whitstable	19th June
Sunderland	34 chaldrons of coal landed at Whitstable	12th July
1678		
Sunderland	Master: William Pizing 34 chaldrons of coal landed at Whitstable	24th May
Sunderland	Master: William Pizing 34 chaldrons of coal landed at Whitstable	3rd June
Sunderland	Master: William Pizing 34 chaldrons of coal landed at Whitstable	1st July
Sunderland	Master: William Pizing 34 chaldrons of coal landed at Whitstable	24th July
1680		
Sunderland	34 chaldrons of coal landed at Whitstable	17th May
Sunderland	Master: William Pizing 34 chaldrons of coal landed at Whitstable	6th July
1685		
June 10th	Master: Richard Reynolds For London in ballast 150 qtrs of wheat 30 qtrs oats 10 qtrs of barley 10 qtrs beans	Ret. 16th October
1689		
30th August	Master: W. Phillpott For London Robert Mascall	3rd September
September	Master: W. Phillpott From London Thomas Dunkin	
10th October	Master: W. Phillpott For London Thomas Dunkin	
24th October	Master: W. Phillpott Thomas Oliver	

ENDEAVOUR *of Whitstable (continued)*

1689 continued

8th November — Master: W. Phillpott
Thomas Oliver

1691

21st January — Master: Edward Oliver — For London
Thomas Dunkin
60 qtrs malt
6 qtrs wheat
20 qtrs oats
4 tons copperas
2 bags worsted
1 bag English hops
2 baskets mettlehead pads flax
½ load of household goods

3rd March — Master: Edward Oliver — For London — 8th March
Thomas Dunkin
60 qtrs malt
29 qtrs oats
1 bag English hops
1 bag cony skins
5 qtrs wheat
½ load household goods
1 bag Canterbury worsted
10 of East India Satins
7 of East India flowered silkes
2 of blue calico

1692

Master: John Ayres — From London
George Gooday

1 cwt. pewter
6 parcels of Manchester-ware
2 boxes plates
100 deales 2 boxes apothecary wares
1 basket Scythe stone
One weight one box station wares
2 parcels cotton yarn and candlewick
½ pipe canary
1 buolt upholstery
2 rundletts one bottle ayle
1 rundlett capus
8 doz. brooms
3 boxes household goods and apparel
9 baskets glass bottles
6 boxes felt and woollen hats
1½ – vinegar
1 chest window glass
Coach wheels
5 weights of mercury
Linen drapery wares
1 box cobalt
1 firkin shott
4 casks of 70 gallons English spirits
¼ load turner wares
1 caske coulours
1 rundlett of linseede
1 bundle of corke
1 barrel archovies
43 cwts. grocery wares
More than three butts port
1 butt Rhenish
1 butt Clinch of wine
1 basket hamms and tongues
1 ham of wine
2 boxes hatts

1692 continued

2nd April — Master: Edward Oliver, Thomas Dunkin — For London
25 tons copperas — 10 qtrs wheat
8 bags English hops

5 pieces of course linen cloth — From London
1 white wine — ½ load household goods

30th April — Master: Edward Oliver, Thomas Dunkin — For London — 2nd May
18 tons copperas — 6 qtrs wheat
3 packs Canterbury worsted

½ load household goods — From London
5 pieces serge — 7 pieces norwich goods

23rd May — Master: Edward Oliver, Thomas Dunkin — For London
20 tons copperas
1 great chest)
2 boxes) old books
2 trunks)
1 case)
12 qtrs malt
3 bags Canterbury worsted
½ load household goods

6th August — Master: Edward Oliver, Thomas Dunkin — For London — 8th August
15 tons copperas — 1 basket old pewter
40 qtrs malt — ½ load household goods
6 qtrs wheat — 1 bag English hops
3 packs Canterbury worsted

24th September — Master: Edward Oliver, Matthew Wood — At London — 28th September

8 barrels soap
1 basket pewter
11 weights mercury, haberdashery and linen
2 pipes canary
1 butt cherry
2 port 1 run Tent wine
5 cwt. cheese
5 firkins butter
1 pack, 3 weights, 4 baggs, 1 bundle upholstery
1 doz. chaires
3 weights grocerys
2 parcels Brummy
1 firkin 1 bagg sturgion
2 boxes 1 parcel hats, caps and waistcoats
1 barrel 1 rundlett –
2 boxes apothecary wares
1 sack candlewick
2 chests drawers 1 looking glass
2 hattes 1 case glass 1 box and ½ ton more toys

ENDEAVOUR *of Whitstable (continued)*

1692 continued

7th October	Master: Edward Oliver Thomas Brookes	At London		11th October
	3 butts cherry 1 butt port 1 butt Malligo wine 11 packs one weight 1 baile, one of cellwich drapery, silk worsted and mercury 3 hamp 2 bask. and boutle wine 4 cwt. cheese 2 boxes apothecary wares 1 box books 3 of cells, 1 bundle hese fringe and ticking 6 chairs one couch 1 looking glass 1 pillion 2 baskets More than gingerbread 1 cwt. linen drapery 1 cask tobacco			
14th October	Master: Edward Oliver Thomas Dunkin	For London		17th October
	20 bags hops 3 bags Canterbury worsted		2 baskets old mettle waste Load household goods	
27th October	Master: Edward Oliver Thomas Dunkin	For London		1st November
	24 tons copperas 18 qtrs oates		3 bags Canterbury worsted ½ load household goods	
25th November	15 tons copperas 18 qtrs oats ½ load household goods 3 bags Canterbury worsted 2 packs English flax			28th November
18th December	Master: Thomas Oliver John Wilts & Comp.	At London		20th December

3 pipes canary
1 hamp bottles wine
1 barrel soap
8 bags lead shott
2 weights mercury and woollen drapery
1 rundlett English spirits
4 cwt. grocery

4 boxes apothecary and confectioners wares and salt petre
1 sack candlewick
1 bladder pitch
1 doz. bellivers
1 bundle baskets and candlestick
More than 1 cwt. grocery
1 parcel hose
½ cwt. dyed wool

1693

5th January	Master:	Edward Oliver Joseph King	For London
14th January	Master:	Edward Oliver Matthew Wood	For Whitstable
20th January	Master:	Edward Oliver Thomas Dunkin	For London
20th January	Master:	Edward Oliver Thomas Oliver	For London
2nd February	Master:	Edward Oliver Thomas Dunkin	For London
8th February	Master:	Edward Oliver Thomas Oliver	For London
10th February	Master:	Edward Oliver Thomas Dunkin	For London
11th February	Master:	Edward Oliver Joseph King	For Whitstable
23rd February	Master:	Edward Oliver Thomas Oliver	For London
9th March	Master:	Edward Oliver Thomas Oliver	For London
17th March	Master:	Edward Oliver Thomas Dunkin	For London
23rd March	Master:	Edward Oliver Thomas Oliver	For London
24th March	Master:	Edward Oliver	For Whitstable
1st April	Master:	Edward Oliver Thomas Dunkin	For London
15th April	Master:	Edward Oliver Thomas Dunkin	For London
21st April	Master:	Edward Oliver Thomas Oliver	For London
26th April	Master:	Edward Oliver Thomas Dunkin	For London
5th May	Master:	Edward Oliver Thomas Oliver	For London
11th May	Master:	Edward Oliver Thomas Dunkin	For London

ENDEAVOUR *of Whitstable (continued)*

1693 continued

18th May	Master:	Edward Oliver Thomas Oliver	For London
1st June	Master:	Edward Oliver	For Whitstable
2nd June	Master:	Edward Oliver Thomas Oliver	For London
10th June	Master:	Edward Oliver Thomas Dunkin	For London
22nd June	Master:	Edward Oliver Thomas Dunkin	For London
8th July	Master:	Edward Oliver	For London
5th August	Master:	Edward Oliver	For London
2nd September	Master:	Edward Oliver	For London
28th September	Master:	Edward Oliver	For London
5th December	Master:	Edward Oliver Thomas Dunkin	For London

1693/4

3rd March	Master:	Edward Oliver John Sownflower	For Whitstable
28th April	Master:	Edward Oliver John Sownflower	For Whitstable

1694

7th July	Master:	Edward Oliver Thomas Oliver	For Whitstable
13th October	Master:	Edward Oliver	For London
27th October	Master:	Edward Oliver	For London
3rd November	Master:	Edward Oliver	For London
5th November	Master:	Edward Oliver	For London
1st December	Master:	Edward Oliver Math. Wood	For Whitstable
8th December	Master:	Edward Oliver	For London
20th December	Master:	Edward Oliver Thomas Oliver	For London
22nd December	Master:	Edward Oliver	For London

FRENCH MERCHANT *of Whitstable*

1688

Master: Henry Marlow For London
Daniel Grueber
135 whole barrels and 12 ½ barrels of gunpowder

FRIENDS *of Whitstable*

1688

Master: Henry Marlow For London
John Gillum
25 qtrs wheat
30 qtrs malt
3 small bags 2 cwt. course flocks
– pack of English flax
1 cwt. Canterbury worsted
2 doz. English hatts
1 load of household goods

FRIENDS ADVENTURE *of Whitstable*

1676

19th July Sunderland — Master: Matthew Adrian
42 chaldrons of coal landed at Whitstable

31st July Sunderland — Master: John Watson
36 chaldrons of coal landed at Whitstable

2nd August Sunderland — Master: John Watson
36 chaldrons of coal landed at Whitstable

11th August — 42 chaldrons of coal landed at Whitstable

1677

28th June Sunderland — Master: John Pope
42 chaldrons of coal landed at Whitstable

26th July — Master: John Pope
42 chaldrons of coal landed at Whitstable

FRIENDSHIP *of Whitstable*

1688

16th February	Master: Henry Marlow Adrian Harris 20 qtrs oats 20 qtrs wheat 20 qtrs barley	
7th April	Master: Christopher Castle John Gillum 40 qtrs wheat 40 qtrs malt 5 qtrs beans 12 qtrs oats 2 packs English flax ½ cwt. Canterbury worsted ½ load of household goods	For London
21st April	Master: Christopher Castle Ed. Roger 15 qtrs wheat 10 qtrs malt 2 small weights of linen and woollen drapery ½ cwt. Canterbury worsted 3 loads of household goods and books 1 basket of gingerbread	For London
31st June	Master: Christopher Castle Thomas Dunkin Wheat 60 qtrs of malt Five bags English hops – bags of prest malt 1 load of household goods	For London
17th July	Master: Ed. Piggott Thomas Dunkin 3 baskets of fire boxes 1 parcel of felt casters 1 cwt. paper parcel linen and woollen drapery 2 small caskes, 3 cwt. tobacco 1 runlett brandy 2 caskes syder 1½ ton grocery 1 baskett 2 runlett 1 pott oyle mongers ware 3 parcel tin ware 2 baskets 1 bag of wire Sack of cotton yarn	

1688 continued

17th July	Master: Christopher Castle Wheat 60 qtrs malt 15 qtrs oats – cwt. Canterbury worsted ½ load of household goods		For London
	Master: Henry Marlow Daniel Grueber 120 barrels of gunpowder 20 sacks of charcoal		For London
	Master: Christopher Castle John Hoult 25 qtrs wheat 20 qtrs malt 12 qtrs beans 20 qtrs oats 6 bags of English hops wt. 12 cwt. 6 doz. Canterbury hats 2 bags coney skins ½ cwt. Canterbury worsted ½ load household goods		For London
	Master: Christopher Castle Thomas Dunkin 20 qtrs wheat ½ cwt. Canterbury worsted 50 qtrs malt 15 qtrs oats 1 basket of hattes Household goods 1 load of upholstery		For London

1689

13th July	Master:	Henry Marlow Adrian Harris	For London
17th August	Master:	Henry Marlow Adrian Harris	For London
20th August	Master:	Henry Marlow Phillip Deane	From London
4th September	Master:	Henry Marlow Adrian Harris	For London
27th September	Master:	Henry Marlow Adrian Harris	For London

FRIENDSHIP *of Whitstable (continued)*

1689 continued

11th October	Master: Henry Marlow Adrian Harris		
7th November	Master: Henry Marlow Adrian Harris		
19th November	Master: Henry Marlow Adrian Harris		
29th November	Master: Henry Marlow Adrian Harris		

1691

15th March	Master: Henry Marlow Dan Starke 16 qtrs wheat 20 qtrs malt 29 bags of English hoppes	For London
31st December	Master: Henry Marlowe David Mark 12 bags English hops 40 qtrs malt 7 qtrs wheat ½ ton English fallon 2 cwt. Canterbury worsted One small load of household goods	For London

1692

18th January	Master: Henry Marlow Adrian Harris 20 qtrs wheat 30 qtrs oats 20 qtrs beans 20 qtrs malt 3 packs of English flax 1 cwt. of Canterbury worsted	From London
31st January	Master: Henry Marlow Adrian Harris 30 qtrs wheat 30 qtrs barley 30 qtrs malt 20 qtrs beans	

1693

24th January	Master:	John Hampton Dan Starke	
8th February	Master:	Henry Marlow Dan Starke	For London
22nd February	Master:	Henry Marlow Dan Starke	
22nd July	Master:	Henry Marlow Benjamin Hooper	

1698

15th July	Master:	John Hampton John Sloth
30th July	Master:	John Hampton
26th August	Master:	John Hampton
29th August	Master:	John Hampton Peter Carpenter
10th September	Master:	John Hampton

FURIOUS ADVENTURE *of Whitstable*

1676

29th May	Master: Matthew Adrian 42 chaldrons of coal landed at Whitstable

1677

27th May Sunderland	Master: John Watson 32 chaldrons of coal landed at Whitstable

GOODWILL *of Whitstable*

1680

London

Master: Thomas Oliver
4 runlets strong English spirits
4 drefts of oranges and lemons
3 baskets of gingerbread
5 baskets of earthenware
Cheese half and hogshead
5 tons of iron
6 barrels soap
15 wlt of sheep
Half a load of household goods
6 doz. flagg stones
2 runlets English strong spirits
Landed at Whitstable

1685

12th December

Master: Thomas Oliver
Thomas Harris
For London
80 qtrs malt
30 qtrs oats
10 qtrs wheat
5 qtrs beans
7½ tons copperas
A load household goods

21st December

Master: Thomas Oliver
For London
20 tons copperas
6 qtrs beans

1687

Master: Thomas Oliver
Thomas Dunkin
For London
12 tons copperas
20 qtrs oats
20 qtrs malt
½ load of household goods

1688

28th January

Master: Thomas Oliver
John Ewell
From London
20 cwt. sheep
4 firkins butter
2 of haberdashery
1 basket of pewter
2 barrels of soap
2 ½ bar. of rum
1 box of fruit
1 caske of Syder
12 cwt. of grocery
1 caske of oyle
1 hogshead vinegar
4 barrels of wine
5 boxes of apothecary and confectioners
2 parcels and 8 doz. of bodice and waistcoats
2 parcels upholstery
2 bags feathers
2 trunks apparel
2 cwt. paniers – following woven bundles of pattin rings, frying pans
2 baskets of glass
1 doz. pailes
1 doz. broomes
1 weight linen drapery
1 weight haberdashery
One looking glass

1688 continued

18th February — Master: Thomas Oliver, Thomas Dunkin — For London

50 qtrs malt
6 qtrs wheat
5 qtrs beans
15 qtrs oats
3 loads household goods
6 baggs qt. 12 hund. of English hops
3 baggs qt. 100 woll flocks
2 cwt. Canterbury worsted
2 pieces Canterbury made stuffes
1 baskett of old mettle
5 ton copperas

2nd March — Master: Thomas Oliver, Thomas Dunkin — For London

1 pack English flax
80 qtrs malt
10 qtrs oats
3 loads of household goods
3 basketts of old mettle
3 bags Canterbury worsted
14 woollen drapery returned

15th March — Master: William Phillpott, Thomas Dunkin — For London

12 tons copperas
40 qtrs malt
10 qtrs wheat
½ load household goods
½ cwt. Canterbury worsted

25th March — Master: William Phillpott, Thomas Marshall — For London

23 tons copperas

GOODWILL *of Whitstable (continued)*

1688 continued

12th April

Master: Thomas Oliver — For London
Thomas Dunkin
18 tons copperas
10 qtrs malt
2 bags English hops
1 load household goods
2 small bags of Canterbury worsted

22nd April

Master: Thomas Oliver — For London
Thomas Dunkin
20 tons copperas
30 qtrs malt
50 qtrs wheat
½ load household goods and apparrel
1 barrel Ingas returned
1 bag of Canterbury worsted

Master: Thomas Oliver — For London
Thomas Dunkin
19 tons copperas
10 qtrs beans
10 qtrs wheat
10 qtrs malt
½ load household goods
2 bags of English hops
2 bags of Canterbury worsted

Master: Thomas Oliver — For London
Thomas Dunkin
15 tons copperas
10 qtrs malt
10 qtrs wheat
10 qtrs oats
1 bag Canterbury worsted
½ load household goods

Master: Thomas Oliver — For London
Thomas Dunkin
10 tons copperas
30 qtrs malt
10 qtrs wheat
40 qtrs oats
3 doz. English hattes
2 sacks Canterbury worsted
1 trunk of books
½ load household goods

1688 continued

Master: Thomas Oliver — For London
Thomas Dunkin

20 qtrs wheat
6 qtrs oats
10 ton copperas
½ load of household goods
1 bag of Canterbury worsted

Master: Thomas Oliver — From London

1 bulke tallow
13 barrels of soap
3 cwt. cheese
1 parcel of woollen drapery
5 boxes, 2 bundles, 1 runlet,
apothecary and confection wares
1 cwt. parcel of haberdashery
14 bags, 1 basket of ironmongery wares
1 basket of small things
3 cwt. oranges
14 barrels of linseed
2 ½ barrels of rum
1 cwt. iron
1 barrel of tobacco
1 balle of silk

Master: Ed. Piggott — From London
John Williams

Master: Thomas Oliver — For London
Thomas Dunkin

40 qtrs malt
15 qtrs wheat
10 qtrs beans
10 tons copperas
½ load household goods
16 bags of English hops
(weight 24 cwt. more)
30 qtrs oats
1 bag English hops (30 cwt.)

1689

8th April — Master: William Phillpott — For London
Robert Marshall

13th April — Master: William Phillpott — For London
Thomas Dunkin

GOODWILL *of Whitstable (continued)*

1689 continued

4th May	Master:	William Phillpott Thomas Dunkin	For London
16th May	Master:	William Phillpott Robert Marshall	For London
13th June	Master:	William Phillpott Robert Marshall	For London
29th June	Master:	William Phillpott Robert Marshall	From London
11th July	Master:	William Phillpott John Townesend	For London
13th July	Master:	William Phillpott Thomas Dunkin	From London
27th July	Master:	William Phillpott William Steeres	From London

1692

18th January — Master: William Phillpott — For London

20 qtrs malt — 32 bags 75 cwt. qtrs English hops
20 qtrs oats — 1 bag Canterbury worsted
5 qtrs wheat — 10 tons copperas
12 qtrs beans

28th January — Master: William Phillpott, Robert Marshall — For London

10 tons copperas

HAPPY RETURNS *of Whitstable*

1678

Master: John Jakin — 17th May
42 chaldrons of coal landed at Whitstable

HOPEFUL ADVENTURE *of Whitstable*

1678

Sunderland	Master:	John Watson 32 chaldrons of coal landed at Whitstable	14th May
Sunderland	Master:	John Watson 32 chaldrons of coal landed at Whitstable	30th May
Sunderland	Master:	John Watson 32 chaldrons of coal landed at Whitstable	17th June

HOPEWELL *of Whitstable*

1692

13th August — Master: Richard Hart — 16th August
Matthew Waite

1 fodder lead
21 raw hydes
7 barrels and ½ of 6 firkins soap
One punchon two half casks spirits and strong waters
2 hogshead books
1 load upholstery
5 baskets earthenwares
1 hogshead tobacco
2 barrels 2 rundletts ayle
12 doz. driest hempe
1 weight linen drapery
1 box confectioners wares
1 box window glass
1 box leade
2 cwt. cheese
1½ tons grocery wares

9th September — Master: Richard Hart
Henry Beale

6 pipes canary wine
10 raw hydes
3 weights harup of mercury and haberdashery and linen drapery wares
1 picture
½ barrel soap
250 seales
1 parcell 1 weight raw silks
1 parcell Sadlers wares
½ cwt. hemp
1 parcell wool cards
1 cheese
16 pastebord bones
2 basketts of 5 doz. felt hattes
3 bags dying stuff
2 doz. hatt cases

9th December — Master: Richard Hart — For London
Peter Glaysbrooke

6 tons copperas
24 bags English hopps
1 bag 2½ loads of household goods
10 qtrs malt
9 qtrs wheat
3 cwt. Canterbury worsted

1693 **HOPEWELL** *of Whitstable (continued)*

20th January	Master:	Richard Hart Peter Glaysbrooke
6th February	Master:	Richard Hart Peter Glaysbrooke
3rd March	Master:	Richard Hart Peter Glaysbrooke
1st April	Master:	Richard Hart Peter Glaysbrooke
4th May	Master:	Richard Hart Peter Glaysbrooke
20th May	Master:	Richard Hart Peter Glaysbrooke
8th July	Master:	Richard Hart Peter Glaysbrooke
21st July	Master:	Richard Hart Peter Glaysbrooke

1694

14th July	Master:	Edward Oliver Peter Glaysbrooke
28th July	Master:	Thomas Williams Peter Glaysbrooke
9th August	Master:	Thomas Williams Peter Glaysbrooke
18th August	Master:	Richard Hart Joseph Taylor
30th September	Master:	Richard Hart Peter Glaysbrooke
6th October	Master:	Thomas Williams Peter Glaysbrooke
13th October	Master:	Richard Hart Peter Glaysbrooke
27th October	Master:	Richard Hart Peter Glaysbrooke
24th November	Master:	Richard Hart Peter Glaysbrooke
3rd December	Master:	Richard Hart John Tayler

HOPEWELL *of Whitstable (continued)*

1699

3rd December		John Sherwood. Thomas Oliver. F. Rochester

1700

10th February	Master:	John Sherwood Thomas Oliver
27th March		Leonard Bing. F. Rochester. Tho. Oliver
4th May	Master:	Edward Oliver
1st June	Master:	Edward Oliver
June	Master:	Edward Oliver Thomas Styles
July	Master:	Thomas Oliver
August	Master:	Thomas Oliver
August	Master:	Thomas Oliver Thomas Terry
September	Master:	Thomas Oliver Joseph Taylor
September	Master:	Edward Oliver
October	Master:	Edward Oliver
December	Master:	Thomas Oliver

1701

January	Master:	Richard Hart Edward Oliver
February	Master:	John Browne Edward Oliver
February	Master:	Edward Oliver
March	Master:	Edward Oliver Thomas Skinner
April	Master:	Edward Oliver
May	Master:	Henry Young Edward Oliver. F. Rochester
June	Master:	Edward Oliver
September	Master:	Thomas Oliver

1693 **JAMES** *of Whitstable*

16th February	Master:	Will iam Pysing		21st February
1693/4				
21st June	Master:	William Pysing Roger Hayward	From London	27th June
1694				
13th October	Master:	William Pysing John Cheeseman	From London	16th October
19th October	Master:	Richard Williams William Pysing		23rd October
9th November	Master:	William Pysing		12th November
23rd November	Master:	William Pysing		26th November
24th November	Master:	William Pysing John Cheeseman	From London	28th November
8th December	Master:	William Pysing John Cheeseman		11th December
22nd December	Master:	William Pysing John Cheeseman		29th December

JOHN *of Whitstable*

1662

London 10th January	Master: John Ellenden George Rofe 40 qtrs wheat 8 qtrs oats	17th January
9th February	Master: John Ellenden 30 qtrs wheat 10 qtrs hops 40 qtrs oats	Ret. 20th February
28th May	Master: John Ellenden Nicholas Sympson 20 qtrs wheat	11th June
1663	Master: John Ellenden Nicholas Sympson 8 qtrs fodder lead 3 barres of iron for the copperas works	2nd November
1664	Master: John Ellenden Edward Rofe Wheat Beans Oats	March

JOHN *of Whitstable (continued)*

1664 continued

	Master:	John Ellenden Edward Rofe	April
	Oats Barley	Beans	
1665			
	Master:	John Ellenden Jeremias Rofe	May
	Wheat Oats	Beans	
	Master:	John Ellenden Jarvas Rofe	
	Wheat Oats		
	Master:	John Ellenden Jarvas Rofe	November
	Wheat Barley	Beanes	
1666			
	Master:	John Ellenden Robert Knowles	8th February
	30 qtrs wheat 5 qtrs oats		
	Master:	John Ellenden Robert Knowles	28th April
	20 qtrs wheat 10qtrs barley 10 qtrs oats		
	30 qtrs wheat 10 qtrs oats 5 qtrs beans		5th April
1667	Master:	John Ellenden Robert Knowles	24th May
	30 qtrs oats 10 qtrs wheat		
	30 qtrs oats 40 qtrs wheat		16th January
1676			
Sunderland	Master:	John Watson	5th May
	10 chaldrons of coal landed at Whitstable		

1698	JOHN AND ANN *of Whitstable*			
11th November	Master:	John Hampton Peter Carpenter	For London	17th November
19th November	Master:	John Hampton		23rd November
26th November	Master:	John Hampton Peter Carpenter	For London	29th November
10th December	Master:	John Hampton Peter Carpenter	For London	12th December
22nd December	Master:	John Hampton Peter Carpenter	For London	30th December
1700				
6th January	Master:	John Hampton		8th January
19th January	Master:	John Hampton		22nd January
15h February	Master:	John Hampton		19th February
2nd March	Master:	John Hampton		4th March
15th March	Master:	John Hampton		18th March
27th April	Master:	John Hampton		29th April
10th May	Master:	John Hampton		13th May
June	Master:	John Hampton		
July	Master:	John Hampton		
September	Master:	John Hampton		
October	Master:	John Hampton James Chappleworth		
November	Master:	John Hampton		
December	Master:	John Hampton		
1701				
January	Master:	John Hampton		
January	Master:	James Chappol		
February	Master:	John Hampton		
February	Master:	John Browne John Hampton		
March	Master:	John Browne James Chapperote		

JOHN AND ANN *of Whitstable (continued)*

1700 continued

March	Master: John Browne Stephen Browne	
April	Master: John Browne	
May	Master: John Browne	
May	Master: Richard Willard Thomas Styles	
June	Master: John Browne	
July	Master: John Hampton	
August	Master: John Hampton	
September	Master: John Hampton	

MARY *of Whitstable*

1676	Master: Thomas Baldwin 2 tonnes of iron 5 cwt. Guesory wharves piggs load of fodder 5 cwt. of – 100 coales landed at Whitstable	
Sunderland	Master: John Pope 20 chaldrons of coal landed at Whitstable	8th March

OWNERS ADVENTURE *of Whitstable*

1676	Master: William Barlefrolo 32 chaldrons of coal landed at Whitstable	23rd May
1680		
Sunderland	Master: William Barthelo 32 chaldrons of coal landed at Whitstable	
Sunderland	Master: William Barthelo 32 chaldrons of coal landed at Whitstable	19th July

PROVIDENCE *of Whitstable*

1678	Master: Matthew Adrian 42 chaldrons of coal landed at Whitstable	13th May
Sunderland	Master: Matthew Adrian 42 chaldrons of coal landed at Whitstable	8th June
Sunderland	Master: Matthew Adrian 45 chaldrons of coal landed at Whitstable	2nd July

RICHARD AND MARGARET *of Whitstable*

1662		
2nd March London	Master: Thomas Reynolds Robert Marshall 30 tons copperas	6th March
16th April	Master: Thomas Reynolds Robert Marshall	27th April
28th April London	Master: Thomas Reynolds Nicholas Gads Copperas	9th May
27th November	Master: Thomas Reynolds Robert Marshall 15 tons of copperas	1st December
1664	Master: Thomas Reynolds Robert Marshall Copperas	February
	Master: Thomas Reynolds Robert Marshall Copperas	April
1665	Master: Thomas Reynolds Robert Marshall Copperas	April
	Master: John Ellenden Robert Marshall Copperas Wheat	August
	Master: Thomas Reynolds Robert Marshall Copperas Wheat	October
	Master: Thomas Reynolds Jarvas Rofe 8 tons copperas	November
	Master: Thomas Reynolds John Godfrey Copperas	November
1666	Master: Thomas Reynolds 25 qtrs wheat 30 qtrs oats	23rd February

1666 continued

	30 qtrs wheat 20 qtrs oats 10 qtrs barley	30th April

1667

	Master: Thomas Reynolds 30 qtrs wheat 40 qtrs oats	22nd January

1670

	Master: Thomas Reynolds 20 qtrs wheat 60 qtrs oats	March

SEAWONDER *of Whitstable*

1676

Sunderland	Master: Thomas Watson 29 chaldrons of coal landed at Whitstable	20th March
	Master: Thomas Watson 34 chaldrons of coal landed at Whitstable	23rd May

THOMAS *of Whitstable*

1662

9th February London	Master: Thomas Browne Thomas Sanders 20 qtrs wheat 10 qtrs hops 10 qtrs malt	Ret. 20th February

WILLIAM *of Whitstable*

1698

11th November	Master:	William Phillpott Thomas Back	19th November
2nd December	Master:	William Phillpott Thomas Back	6th December
19th December	Master:	William Phillpott Thomas Back	22nd December

1699

30th December	Master:	William Phillpott	2nd January

1700

10th February	Master:	William Phillpott Thomas Back	20th February
5th April	Master:	William Phillpott Thomas Back	8th April
4th May	Master:	William Phillpott Thomas Back	6th May
18th May	Master:	William Phillpott Thomas Back	23rd May
August	Master:	William Phillpott John Macman	
September	Master:	William Phillpott	
September	Master:	William Phillpott Thomas Back	
December	Master:	William Phillpott	

1701

January	Master:	William Phillpott Ambrose Crowley	
June	Master:	William Phillpott	

WILLIAM AND JOSEPH *of Whitstable*

1677

	Master: Joseph Garson 11 chaldrons of coal landed at Whitstable	10th July
Sunderland	Master: Joseph Garson 11 chaldrons of coal landed at Whitstable	1st August

18th CENTURY SHIPS OF WHITSTABLE

Few records of Whitstable ships during this period appear to have survived even if they had been kept. This may have been due to war, to the unsettled political state of the country, or to the poorly educated mariners engaged in the shipping business. However sufficient evidence may be gleaned from the newspapers of the period to show that Whitstable continued to fulfill its destiny as an active sea-port.

Preserved in the Public Records Office, among the correspondence of the Customs Commissioners, dated 29th January 1702, we have a list and particulars of ships belonging to the ports of Kent, which shows that Whitstable held an important position when compared to the other ports of the county.

SHIPS BELONGING TO THE PORTS OF KENT, 1701

Ramsgate	*45 ships*	*4,100 tonnage*	*388 men*
Margate	*37 ships*	*2,909 tonnage*	*138 men*
Sandwich	*21 ships*	*1,146 tonnage*	*104 men*
Rochester	*22 ships*	*1,054 tonnage*	*70 men*
Faversham	*32 ships*	*888 tonnage*	*47 men*
Milton	*34 ships*	*807 tonnage*	*53 men*
Broadstairs	*17 ships*	*731 tonnage*	*90 men*
Whitstable	*33 ships*	*701 tonnage*	*46 men*
Dover	*7ships*	*415 tonnage*	*44 men*
Deal	*1 ship*	*50 tonnage*	*5 men*

Smuggling was prevalent and most of the Whitstable ships were known to be engaged in the free trade.

Thomas Reynolds, who lived at what is now known as 7–9 Oxford Street is recorded as owning a ship described as a "Shallop", having two masts, was schooner rigged, and was armed with 18 brass 9-pounders, with a crew of 20–40 men.

After his death on 26th August 1744, aged 68 years, the ship continued to be operated by his son-in-law John Pamflett of Shoart, St Nicholas-at-Wade, and then by his grandson Edward Reynolds, with John Rice as master.

As the majority of boys in those days were not taught to read or write a certain man was employed to teach five boys at a time the laws of navigation which they had to master by learning to recite crude verses. While some of the brightest boys learned a poem which enabled them to navigate a ship on what was known as the Great Circle to the Azores and the Mediterranean they all had to learn verses which would enable them to sail a ship from Whitstable to Sunderland. Several corrupt versions survived in the memory of aged mariners until 1918.

"First the Dudgeon,
Then the Spurn,
Flamborough Head is next in turn,
Finley Park you need not fear,
Because Scarborough Castle is drawing near,
Whitby Rocks as we pass by,
Hartlepool Fort is drawing nigh,
Our Captain says if all goes right,
We shall be there tomorrow night."

"First the Dudgeon then the Spurn,
Flamborough Head comes next in turn,
Hudney Foot lies in a bite,
And Whitby Light then shows in sight,
And the Skipper says if all goes right,
We'll be in Sunderland tomorrow night."

"First the Dudgeon then the Spurn,
Two white and one red,
Show the lights of Flamborough Head, etc."

"First the Dudgeon then the Spurn,
Whitby Rocks is next in turn,
Whitby Rocks is drawing nigh,
Scarborough Castle away on high, etc."

"First the Nab, then the Warner,
Block House Fort and Dirty Corner, etc."

Some of the larger vessels owned at Whitstable during this period were:

DRAPER	Built in 1779	MARGARET	Built in 1792
ELIZABETH & SARAH	Built in 1791	RESOLUTION	Built in 1787
ENDEAVOUR	Built in 1790	ROCHFORD	Built in 1787
FRIENDS	Built in 1795	UNITY	built in 1785
INDUSTRIOUS	Built in 1779		

From the Kentish Register we learn that even smaller vessels were classed as brigs.

February 19th 1794. DOVER
The brigs, Friends Goodwill, James Carr, Master, and the Good Intent, Robert Hutchinson, Master, coal laden, from Sunderland to Amsterdam, were a few days ago taken off the Island of Goree by a French brig priviteer, of 18 guns, and re-taken yesterday at the back of the Goodwin Sand by His Majesty's frigate Brilliant, Captain Robinson, and sent in here."

These ships are included in the list of 31 vessels known to have been owned here.

Although there do not seem to be records of the larger Whitstable vessesl during the eighteenth century we have evidence in the various Kentish newspapers of the period of a brisk and regular hoy traffic. In September 1727, we find mention of Henry Hall, hoyman, and in August 1747 of John Martin, whose ship was named the "John and Susannah".

An interesting side-light is thrown upon the relationship that existed between master and man by a tomb-stone in Seasalter churchyard. This was erected by Joseph Talbot hoyman, who thereon pays tribute to his "Faithful servant, Matthew Legay who died October 21st 1752 aged 54 years, and who served his master with the greatest fidelity and justice." In October 1760 the hoymen mentioned in the press are, Stephen Jones, Henry Southouse, Thomas Baynes, and John Sherwood. Then in May 1768 John Martin became bankrupt, and his vessel the "John and Thomas" was advertised to be sold. Later in September 1768 William Philpott, John Chalk, and Lane Cannon, advertised that they were running a regular hoy service between Whitstable and London, and passengers would be taken at the fare of 2/6 each as follows.

FROM WHITSTABLE TO LONDON
September 3rd 1768

The freight of hops from Whitstable to London will be one shilling per pocket, or two shillings per bag, and passengers two shillings and sixpence each.

They gratefully acknowledge the favour of their employers; and as some Principal Ones are convinced of the reasonableness of this small advance, (which is no more than the usual price at other places), they hope the public will favourably aquiesce therewith".

In October 1768 Lane Cannon having died, his vessel, the "Success" was taken over by John Adams. Then in May 1769 William Philpott having died, his vessel, the "John and William", was purchased by Richard Elwyn.

WHITSTABLE SHIPS. 18th CENTURY

ANN SUSANNAH 60 tons Crew of 4 men

DEBORAH Sold in 1793 84 tons Crew of 3 men

DELIGHT 32 tons Crew of 3 men

DRAPER Built in 1779 94 tons
Owners: James J. Goldfinch & Charles Fenn.
Ernest Goldfinch & Fred Goldfinch.
Master: Foster.

DREDGERMAN'S DELIGHT
Master: James Fairbrass

DUKE OF CUMBERLAND
Owners: Messrs Spencer, Shrubsole, and Abbot, 1794

EDWARD & SARAH
Owner: Robert Pizing, 1769.

ELIZABETH & SARAH Built in 1791. 117 tons Crew of 6 men
Owner: James Malborough. Master: Henry Potter

ENDEAVOUR 115 tons Crew of 5 men
Owners: Thomas Eason & John Chalk, 1769.

FAVERSHAM
Owners: Thomas Chapman, Henry Jones, Robert Collier and Edward Jones, 1785.

FRIENDS GOODWILL
Owner: Henry Fairbrass, 1769. Master: James Carr, 1794.

GOOD INTENT (I)
Master: Robert Hutchinson

INDUSTRIOUS Built in 1799. Brig 111 tons
Owners: William Edwards, James E.M. Williams, Philpott Wood, John Deane

JOHN & MARTHA
Owners: John Sales, Henry Minter, 1769

JOHN & SUSANNAH
Owner: John Martin, 1747

JOHN & THOMAS Advertised for sale. 1768
Owner: John Martin

JOHN & WILLIAM
Owners: William Philpott, Edward Elwyn, and John Hunt, 1769

MARGARET Built in 1792 at Irvine, Ayre
Owners: John Graves, George Adams, Robert Brows,
James Hayward, Henry Nicholls.

MARY Built in 1786
Owner: William Elvy.

MATTHEW & JANE
Master: Matthew Smith, 1777

PROVIDENCE
Owner: Stephen Salisbury

ROBERT & ELIZABETH
Owners: Thomas Holmes, William Lepine, 1769

ROCHFORD 1787 — 89 tons — Crew of 4 men
Owner: Thomas Fairbrass

SEASALTER
Owner: John Collard, 1769

SPECULATION — 54 tons — Crew of 4 men
Owner: Thomas Fairbrass

SUCCESS
Owners: Lane Cannon, John Adams, 1768.
Eizabeth Adams & John Adams jun., 1773
William Baldock, 1776.

WHEATSHEAF
Owners: William Amis & John Bailey, 1769.

THOMAS & STEPHEN — 122 tons — Crew of 5 men
Owners: Stephen Salisbury & Thomas Brows, 1790.
Stephen Salisbury & William Nutt, 1791.
Masters: Hockless, 1790. James Randall, Frend.

THREE BROTHERS
Owners: Edward Reynolds & Jarvis Lovel, 1769.

WHITSTABLE
Owners: John Adams, 1769. Elizabeth Adams, widow, &
John Adams son, May 15th 1773. William Adams
Daniel Howard & Joseph Nicholson, 1785.

WILLIAM — Crew of 2 men

19th CENTURY SHIPS OF WHITSTABLE

The same sea waves still beat their tidal rhythm on the mile long shingle sea-front of the north Kent town of Whitstable, the south west wind still sighs its requiem over the extensive sand-flats, the Bay is empty, and the searching eye will look in vain for some slight vestige of the 484 ships that were owned and traded from here. The generations of those who manned those ships, who toiled to plough the seas of empire have long passed into the silence of eternity, and apart from a brief mention in some book of the sea no author has felt persuaded to lift the veil and sing the triumphs of those days. Only an ever-decreasing few can now remember the twenty-eight busy slipways that once adorned our sea-front, or hear the ghostly tap of the caulkers hammers, or the clang clang clang of the anchor smiths, or the squeal of new blocks and tackle.

This record has been compiled that those brave humble mariners who made Whitstable so great shall not pass, to use the words of Sir Walter Scott, "Unwept, unhonoured, and unsung."

Humble in their descent, thrifty in their habits, careful in their business ventures, none of them achieved fame by making a fortune. Most of the vessels were owned by small companies of from four to six ordinary persons. A typical transaction overheard would go something like this, as two men casually met in the street.

"What o' mat, like to shut in with us?"
"What you on for mat,?"
"O Jim's going up to Liverpool to see what's about."
"How many shares are going,?."
"Put me down for four."

No fuss, no writing, only a shake of the hands, and in complete trust another Newfoundland ship would be coming to Whitstable.

Of course, being a soft-wood ship she had to be drawn up on one of the slipways, the trunnels bored out and iron bolts inserted. Then her bottom had to be properly caulked and sheathed in copper in order to conform to the official regulations.

If, as was often usual, she was a brig, the yards had to be taken off her mizzen, for if they remained she would require a crew consisting of a master and seven men, whereas as a brigantine she would only need a master and three hands, and in consequence be much cheaper to run.

It was always a great event when a beflagged ship went down the slipway and plunged into her natural element. A new vessel would probably join the Mediterranean fleet, sail on the Great Circle to the Azores, then westwards to Patras in Greece for currants, call at Alicante for oranges and lemons, south to the north African ports for dates and figs, then back to the Azores for bananas, (real bananas not plantains).

It was always an event when the first fruit ships arrived from the Azores and an expectant crowd would gather outside of Henry Baker's shop. It is true that they smashed his shop window because he was pro-Boer but that did not deter them from patiently waiting for the shop to open that they might sample the first bananas, oranges, or dates.

It was with a keen sense of anticipation that the "Undine" set sail on her regular trips to the West Indies. She was especially built with a large sail area to enable her to make the fast passages necessary for the pineapple trade. Her hold was fitted out with beautifully made mahogany trays.

When at last it was necessary to restrict her trips to the home trade her sail area was reduced, two feet were cut off each end of her yard arms and nine feet was cut off her 72 ft. boom.

Another fast vessel was the "Uncle Ned" which went regularly to the West Indies for sugar and tobacco.

One day she left Kingston Jamaica at the same time as the Royal Mail Steamship, and when that vessel was coming up the channel there was the "Uncle Ned" in front of her.

Little has been written and much has been left to the imagination about the hard life experienced on the colliers as they toiled up the North Sea to Sunderland and the Tyne for coal to feed the ever hungry gas works that were springing up in all directions, besides the demand for domestic purposes.

It is not often appreciated that the early steam engines could not run on coal. Consequently in order to cater for the demand for coke two giant coke ovens were built on the east side of the Harbour and coke was exported to wherever the railways needed it.

In the summer time, when the demand for coal was not so great, the collier ships would have their holds scrubbed out and they would then sail over to the fiords of Norway where they loaded up with ice for the ice-rooms of the butchers shops and the rich mens' houses.

The majority of writers politely gloss over the sordid side of the seaman's life. Stories of hunger, of poor wages, of poverty, of loss of life, apart from the drama of shipwreck, they do not make entertaining reading. It is far more attractive to read about the glamourous voyages to distant parts of the world and the interesting things brought home. Nevertheless there were times of depression when trade was bad and orders did not come in. At such times it was a common sight to see a fleet of idle ships at anchor under what was known as The Ness near the Isle of Sheppey, waiting for orders.

At such times it was not always possible to "Go on the parish", and the Master of the "Conoid" had to come home and take his starving wife and two children on board to share what little food he had.

My Grandfather told the story of how he and his brothers had to go out on bitter dark winter mornings to pick winkles. No winkles, no breakfast!

My father's eldest brother, when a lad of 19, was on the "Flirt", when he strongly complained about the bad food, and as a result he was tied to the mast and flogged. He jumped ship and the next morning at six o'clock my grandfather found him dead in the wood-shed.

The labour of collecting the information for this history has taken over sixty years, and every effort has been made to make every detail correct.

It is hoped that this record will encourage future generations to appreciate a great and glorious epoch in the history of our town and find encouragement in the manner in which the Victorian Natives triumphed over difficulty and disaster.

WHITSTABLE SHIPS

ILLUSTRATIONS

11235 **ABRONA**
Built in 1833 at Yarmouth.
Schooner, 62 registered tons. 60.0 x 14.3 x 8.0.
Owners: John Taylor bought this ship from Yarmouth on the 9th January 1855. She was sold to William Butcher and Stead Laraman on the 16th January 1856, and after several voyages she was sold to Plymouth on the 4th April 1867.
Master: Henry Richard Nicholls, 23rd April 1855.

42160 **ACADIAN**
Built in 1860 at New London, Prince Edward Island, by Bell.
Brig altered to brigantine, then later to schooner.
115 registered tons. 83.0 x 24.2 x 9.4.
Owner: William Burinston, 7th November 1889.
She was engaged in the coal trade, and was broken up at Whitstable in October 1895.

26522 **ACASTUS**
Built in 1840 at Mevagissey.
Brigantine altered to schooner.
140 registered tons. 81.5 x 22.0 x 18.2.
Owners: James Acors, 19th June 1866. Sold to Joshua Downs, Elizabeth Ann Holden, and part owned by James Acors, 4th June 1877.
Masters: Carvell, Edward Maxted.
This vessel was bought from London on the 18th June 1866. On the 24th October 1882 Acastus entered the Thames when bound from Hartlepool to Whitstable loaded with coal. The wind was force 9, when she struck on the Heaps Sand and soon went to pieces. The bodies of Captain Edward Maxted and the crew were never recovered.

5067 **ACTIVE**
Built in 1845 at Guysborough, Nova Scotia.
Brig, 168 registered tons. 87.7 x 22.2 x 11.7.
Owners: Thomas Gann, James Rigden, George Butcher, George Cox, and William Crofts, who formed a company and bought this ship from London on the 1st July 1850.
Masters: James Rigden, 10th July 1850. Thomas Lott, 16th December 1851. Henry Strand, 15th December 1852. George William Bell, 25th April 1854.
She was lost in January 1861.

66314 **ADA**

Built 22nd August 1872 at Prince Edward Island, by D. Egan, Mount Stewart.
Brigantine, 171 registered tons. 102.3 x 24.9 x 12.84.
Owners: G.B. Joiner, Walter Frederick Joiner, William George Joiner, John Joiner, George Edward Joiner, and James George Baker, 10th July 1899. Bought for £520, 31st July 1889.
Masters: J.T. Mortley, 1893-4. George Edward Joiner, James George Baker, J. Jarman, 1901. C.E. Joiner, T. Burrows.

In October 1890 her then captain, T. Burrows, reported that she had stranded on the Cock Edge, and that she had been towed into Harwich by a steamer and was making a lot of water. On the 2nd February 1892 it was reported that she had been in collision with a Dredger on the 28th January at Greys and was sunk. Two tugs towed her on shore while still sunk.

On 25th March 1892 it was reported that the Owners desired to do other repairs in addition to the damage which she had received when in collision with the PERSEVERENCE. The claim was eventually settled for £205.10.0, with costs amounting to £98.15.5, on the 3rd May 1892.

On the 22nd July 1899 ADA was insured for £560 at a value of £700.

On the 27th December 1899 she was in Whitstable Harbour. It was a bitterly cold day, and the galley stove was so banked up that it became red hot and the surrounding woodwork caught fire. For a time her fate seemed uncertain as the tide was out and no water was available. A large crowd gathered and looked on helplessly as the flames took hold. Suddenly somebody had the bright thought of borrowing water from the tanks of the Seasalter & Ham Oyster Fishery Company. Some hundred or more men borrowed buckets from the surrounding houses and formed an endless chain from the tanks to the stricken ship passing the filled buckets with one hand and the empty buckets with the other and eventually managed to conquer the fire. The hull was drawn up on the slipway of the Whitstable Shipping Company and after six months of hard work at a cost of £1,200 she was considered to be fit for sea again. ADA was relaunched on the 10th July 1900 and continued to serve her owners for the next seventeen years. Her connection with this port was severed in 1916 when she was sold to Fowey for £1,100.

She eventually met her end when she was sunk by a German submarine on the 17th February 1917.

81942 **ADIEU**

Built in 1879 at Whitstable.
Ketch, 40 registered tons.
Owner: Henry Summers of Ramsgate.
Master: George Foreman of Whitstable.

Although this vessel was registered as of Ramsgate she traded from Whitstable.

62043 **ADOLPHE & LAURA. EX CHARLES EMMA**

Built in 1867 at Nantes by Ordrannuau.
Brig, 143 registered tons. 87.0 x 21.3 x 11.8. Signal Code L.K.R.C.
Owner: James Collins Hoad.
Masters: T. Wicks, 1882-4. Walter Huson, 1892-4. Sankey, J. Charrington, W. Daniels.

Although this vessel was always classed as a brig she was actually a brigantine. The yards on her mainmast were there solely to enable sailors to train for their master's tickets. She carried square sails on her foremast only.

AGATHA

Built at Lynn in 1859 by W. Skip.
Snow Brig, 186 registered tons.
Owner: Alfred Gann.
Master: Thomas Bell. A collier.

14637 **AGNES**

Built in 1854 at St. Malo, France.
Schooner, 120 registered tons. 95.8 x 20.3 x 9.3. Signal Code L.N.W.R.
Owners: James T. Goldfinch and Thomas Butcher, 9th June 1856.
Ernest Goldfinch, 17th February 1883.
Master: George Lawson, who had shares in her and who insured her in 1873 for £430.

From an old account book it would appear that she never made a profit.

1873,	*October 20th,*	*To Entry Charge,*	*£2. 3.0*
		Policy Duty	*2.6*
		Survey,	*12.6*
	March 10th	*Call*	*£2. 6.9*
	April 1st	*Cash*	*4. 9.4*
	May 21st	*Call*	*4. 2.6*
	July 8th	*Call*	*4. 0.2*
	September 11th	*Call*	*2.17.6*
	December 23rd	*Call*	*2. 2.0*
	1874		
	March 27th	*Call*	*4.14.4*
	June 19th	*Call*	*2. 3.3*

Unfortunately no record has been found which would give information about any voyages she may have made between these dates, unless it may be assumed that she made a profit on those trips. She was reinsured by George Henry Goldfinch in 1875 for £430.

	October 20th,	*To Entry Charge*	*£2. 3.0*
		Policy	*2.6*
		Survey	*13.0*
	January 25th	*Call*	*1.19.4*
	April 13th	*Call*	*3. 0.3*
	June 20th	*Call*	*4. 5.4*
	October 12th	*Call*	*2.16.9*
		Working expenses	*4.3*
	December 7th	*Call*	*2.11.7*
1876	*April 30th*	*Call*	*6.5*

The great gale which took place on the 29th November 1897 was long remembered for the great amount of damage it caused, and the large number of ships that were lost. On that day the AGNES was off the coast of Holland, dismasted and trying to ride the storm out when a passing steamer tried without success to get a tow-line aboard. However she kept afloat until the gale slackened and a fishing boat was able to take her in tow, and get her into more sheltered waters, fortunately her crew were all saved. Eventually she was towed home, pulled up on the slip, thoroughly repaired, and continued to serve her owners until April 1910, when she was converted into a hulk.

52898 **ALARM**

Built in 1866 at Rye by Hessell, and registered at Whitstable 13th July 1866.
Schooner, 158 registered tons. 98.2 x 22.1 x 12.5.
Owners: James Gann sen., William John Gann, Thomas James Gann, Frances Ann Gann, Thomas Gann jun., who bought her 14th February 1866.
Master: T. Rogers.
On the 29th September 1880 she was in collision with the S.S. BOUNTY OF DUMFRIES of Glasgow twelve to fifteen miles S.S.E. of the Lizzard and she became a total loss. At the time she was bound for London loaded with coal from Barry Port. Fortunately the crew were all saved. The wind was E.1.

29062 **ALBERTA**

Built in 1860 at Prince Edward Island by Box.
Brigantine, 1978 registered tons. 106.5 x 23.3 x 12.1.
Signal Code Q.D.C.L.
Owners: William John Collar, James Gann, Edward Parker Read who bought her 3rd November 1860. William John Collar 1874, James Gann in 1884, who sold her to James T. Goldfinch.
Masters: Johnson, Harrison, C.H. Rowden in 1891.
She was originally bought from Plymouth as a nearly new vessel on the 1st November 1860.
For thirty-three years she traded regularly from this port until on the 24th February 1894, when she was on her way from Sunderland heavily laden with coal, she became stranded on the Newcombe Sand off the Suffolk coast. The S.W. by S. wind was blowing at force 8, and after taking a terrific pounding she broke up. Fortunately the crew were all saved.

71405 **ALBERT T. YOUNG**

Built in 1874 at Prince Edward Island, by Young for W. Welsh.
Barque later altered to barquentine, 290 registered tons.
124.9 x 26.9 x 14.7. Signal Code P.B.M.W.
Owners: Henry Pout, George Herbert Gann, James Pout, Frederick Gann, who formed a company and bought her on the 18th October 1882. In 1894 she was sold to the Whitstable Shipping Company, William Henry Prust manager.
Masters: Browning, T. Gibbons 1892-4. S.R. Baker 1901.
Although being only of 290 registered tons this vessel usually carried over 500 tons of coal.
Fortunately on the 18th October 1889 she was insured for £230 because on the 24th November 1889 she was run into by the S.S. KENT and severely damaged. She was brought back to Whitstable, repaired, and served her owners well until in World War I she was taken over by the Government and used as a Q-ship. Having survived her war service she was sold to C. Roe Brevig Norway and renamed HEISTAD.

20267 **ALBION**

Built in 1840 at Sulea, Sweden.
Brig, 187 registered tons. 95.0 x 25.8 x 13.2.
Owners: W.T. Cannon jun., Frederick William Fairbrass, 16th March 1859.
Master: Brand.

She was bought from Hull on the 12th March 1859. From then onward she was employed as a collier, until 21st December 1876 when she was wrecked at Tynemouth.

95655 **ALEXANDRA**

Built in 1891 at Poole by J. Allen & Co.
Ketch, 86 registered tons. 85.0 x 20.2 x 8.3. Signal Code M.C.F.D.
Owner: Frank Nicholls.

This was the last vessel of this type to be owned at Whitstable after 1929. For long periods she was in pathetic loneliness moored out in the Bay, as Mr Nicholls declared that she was moored there in memory of the golden days of Whitstable shipping and he did not care if she had any work or not as the Bay was empty without her.

784 **ALEXANDER ADAM**
Built in 1824 at Syon, Dorset.
Schooner altered to a Ketch 11th August 1882. 103 registered tons.
77.1 x 21.0 x 10.8
Owners: Simon Burton, John Collar, 17th May 1858.
Masters: John Collar, W.G. Joiner, Frend 1864. Bedwell 1870.
In April 1856 she went to Sunderland and back in 5½ days which was considered to be a record.
On the 3rd November 1886 she was seven miles N.N.W. of the Newark Lightship when bound for Newcastle from London, the wind being W. by S. force 5, with a cargo of grease, when she was run down by the barque WILLIAM DAVIE of Swansea. She quickly sank, but all the crew were saved.

ALFRED
Built in 1831 at Rye.
Brig, 170 registered tons. 83.5 x 21.0 x 13.2.
Owners: Edward Adams sen., Edward Adams jun.
Masters: Edward Adams jun., 14th December 1841. George Adams, 6th May 1854.
This ship was bought on the 2nd December 1841 with the intention of trading to the Mediterranean for dried fruit, and her pass was issued on the 11th December 1841. Her figurehead was a man's bust.
She was wrecked on the Lemon Sand on the 6th October 1856.

9522 **ALICE**
Built at Whitstable in 1844.
Dandy, 54 registered tons.
Owner: William Shore Gane.

39012 **ALICE**
Built in 1855 at Prince Edward Island by Joseph Wightman.
Brigantine, 121 registered tons. 89.5 x 20.5 x 10.6.
She was altered to a Schooner on the 28th September 1863.
Bought on the 23rd October 1855.
Owners: George Harris, William Harris, Richard Blaxland, 19th March 1856. Charles Perkins, Thomas Browning, John Gann, 25th September 1863. William Bell 25th October 1870.
This vessel was sold to be broken up in May 1878.

71447 **ALICE H.**
Built in 1874 at St. Peters Bay, Prince Edward Island by McLaine.
Brigantine, 199 registered tons. 103.2 x 24.0 x 12.9. Signal Code L.G.Q.C.
Owner: William Kemp jun., 20th January 1876. She was insured on the 18th October 1889 for £400.
Masters: T. Hopkins, H. Skinner.
In 1875 she suffered severe damage in a storm, but was brought home and repaired. On the 23rd December 1907 she was bound for Llanelly from Southampton with a cargo of iron and was seen sheltering off Lymington. She left shelter on the 24th December and was never seen again.

43762 **ALICE RICHARDSON**
Built in 1862 at Gray, Sunderland.
Brig, 171 registered tons. 89.7 x 23.9 x 12.9. Signal Code T.Q.H.K.
This ship was bought from Sunderland on the 26th August 1864, brought to Whitstable, altered to a Brigantine, and registered 11th October 1864. She was insured with the Whitstable Star Mutual Maritime Assurance Association for £960. She was re-registered as a brigantine in June 1871.
Owners: G. Johnson, John Nicholls, 10th September 1864.
Masters: G. Johnson, Watson.
She was sold away to Portsmouth in October 1885.

67264 **ALICE WATTS**

Built in 1875 at Ipswich by Robertson.
Ketch. 119 registered tons. 100.0 x 24.0 x 8.0. Signal Code N.R.Q.W.
Owner: W. Joiner, 1918-19.
Masters: C. Cooper, W. Joiner 1918-19.

Although she was registered as a ketch she was in fact a flat-bottomed boomie, rigged with topsail braces leading forward to the bowsprit, mizzen topsail and main gaff topsail with short headstock.

It is reputed that ALICE WATTS was the first boomie to be fitted with a steering wheel. She was noted from the fact that she carried a topsail and a top-gallant.

It is said that she originally had a figurehead which represented Alice Watts with long black hair, the daughter of John Watts who had the vessel built, to sail with his fleet from Harwich.

When owned at Whitstable she was often engaged on salvage work and she managed to find cargoes of all descriptions until 1930, but from then onwards she became a pathetic object of neglect moored out in the Bay until she finally broke up leaving her seaweed covered bones and a heap of tin bars as mementoes of better days.

6209 **ALLERTON PACKET**

Built in 1838 at Stockton, Durham.
Snow Brig, 169 registered tons, altered to Brigantine, 144 registered tons after she was brought to Whitstable. 76.2 x 23.1 x 12.9.
Owner: J. Acors, 17th December 1868.
Master: Maxted.

This vessel was already thirty years old when she was bought from Stockton on the 5th November 1868, and after her refit was used as a collier for the next nine years.

On the 9th to the 12th November 1877, when bound from Hartlepool to London with coal, she was caught in S.S.W. gale force 10 and she became stranded on the North Beach at Great Yarmouth, and was written off as a total loss. All the crew were saved.

ALMA

Built in 1855 at Bideford
Schooner, 157 registered tons. Signal Code K.S.C.B.
Owner: John Nicholls jun.
Master: Thomas Harford.

In 1869 she was insured with the Whitstable Star Mutual Maritime Assurance Associaton for £880.

45198 **ALPHA**

Built in 1863 at Perth.
Brigantine, 152 registered tons. 89.8 x 22.8 x 12.1. Signal Code V.C.J.F.
Owners: Seymour Putwain, William Charles Putwain, William Jenkins, Caroline Ann Hopkins, 30th December 1873.
Masters: J. Sutherland, 1874. Hodges, Alfred Reeves.

When bought for Whitstable this vessel was classed as a brigantine, but in 1871 she was badly damaged and when repaired she was re-rigged as a schooner.

On the 4th October 1893, when bound from Sunderland to Whitstable with a cargo of coal, she tried to ride out a gale force 9, but she stranded half a mile N.W. of Cromer and became a total loss. All the crew were saved.

The Whitstable Times on the 20th October 1883 gives a graphic account of the wreck of 45198 ALPHA copied from the Norfolk Times.

On Thursday afternoon, the 4th, the schooner Alpha, of and for Whitstable with coal, was observed to the north-west of Cromer flying a signal with a gale blowing from the north-north-west. At about half-past three o'clock the life-boat was launched in the presence of a large number of spectators, who thronged the jetty and cliffs: but in consequence of the wind and heavy sea she could make no headway.

The ship was now being rapidly driven towards the shore, and great alarm was felt for the safety of the crew. As soon as the vessel was near enough a rocket was sent to her by the Cromer Brigade, who had assembled on the beach in readiness.

It was a splendid shot going over the vessel, Unfortunately however, the line got broken, and was therefore to no avail. Several more rockets were fired, but without success; and soon the Sheringham men arrived with their apparatus. Rockets were now sent out, firstly by one, then by the other, in rapid succession, but all fell wide of the mark. Ultimately the Cromer men got a second shot over the vessel and again the line was broken. It was low water when the vessel struck the beach, and the sea dashing completely over her, was now making water rapidly.

The men who were all together on the bowsprit could be seen distinctly, from the shore. The excitement was intense when it became known that all the rockets were spent, and there seemed no means of rendering assistance to those on board the doomed vessel, which commenced going to pieces.

The beach was strewn with portions of the wreck, amongst it being a piece with name "ALPHA" upon it. Soon both masts fell with a crash, and still the men were not saved. The ship at times was almost hidden by the breakers, which swept over her. Darkness coming on, lights were shown, and the ship being rid of her cargo was driven nearer the Beach. The men were heard calling for a rope, which after a time was taken out by the Cromer Coastguardsman named Davies; and at half past seven one by one of the crew, five in number, were brought to the beach, amid the ringing cheers of the multitude assembled on the shore and cliff. The men were taken to the Hotel de Paris and the Red Lion, where every care was taken with them. The captain's name is Alfred Reeves.

In a subsequent edition of the same paper we find additional particulars of the same incident.

The vessel was of and bound for Whitstable, from Sunderland. At eight o'clock on Thursday morning, of the 4th instant, when about five miles north-east of the Dudgeon, she shipped a heavy sea, which damaged the boat, carried away the skylight, companion way, and other parts of the deck. The main boom which was also carried away struck one of the men on the left eye, wounding him rather severely. Another of the men had his leg hurt by a water cask rolling upon him. The Captain endeavoured to make for the lifeboat, but the ship being full of water was quite unmanageable; in fact she was sinking when she struck. Four lines, it appears, went over the vessel before her masts went.

Two of the lines were secured, but the other two they could not reach. The line thrown over her as she lay close in, could not be made use of, as the deck was gone so that they could not get at it. A couple of the ship's bags were thrown overboard, one of them containing, amongst other things, the ship's papers, in order, (so the captain put it) that those on shore might have the particulars in regard to the vessel in case all hands were drowned, which at one time seemed almost certain.

None of the men have ever been wrecked before. The captain, Alfred Reeves, was owner of one fourth of the vessel, which was only insured one fifth of her value. Four years ago she underwent extensive repairs at Guernsey, when a lot of new work was put into her, costing between £500 and £600.

Such then is the graphic eye-witness account as recorded by the *Norfolk Times* and copied by the *Whitstable Times*, but it does seem strange that no further mention appears to have been made of the heroic act of Coastguardsman Davies who made the rescue possible, however the *Norfolk Times* continues the story.

When the masts fell the captain was thrown into the sea, but was quickly secured by his comrades. Another of the crew fell head foremost, but was hauled back by the leg. The crowd on the Beach was immense, including people from Hunton, Sheringham, Overstrand, Sidestrand, and other parishes. There were besides, numbers of ladies and gentlemen present, the latter making themselves very busy in rendering what assistance they could.

Blankets to wrap the men in as they were landed, were supplied by Mr. S. Hoare, and the Dowager Lady Buxton, and a number of lanterns sent for by Mr. S. Hoare were brought to the scene of the wreck and were found very useful.

Some of the men were able to walk, but the others who had suffered from exposure were conveyed to the town on stretchers after being well wrapped round with blankets. The men spent Friday at the Hotel de Paris, where they were visited by a large number of ladies and gentlemen to make inquiries about them, and to congratulate them on their miraculous escape.

During Friday and Saturday many people visited what had been left of the vessel, which was gone completely to wreck, presenting a most distressing spectacle. The Beach on Friday and Saturday presented a busy scene with people gathering up the coal which was strewn about in every direction. A subscription list has been opened on behalf of the crew. The Captain and crew of the unfortunate schooner, desire through the medium of this publication to express their sincere thanks to the inhabitants of Cromer generally and especially to the Landlady of the Red Lion Inn, for the great kindness shown them from the time of their rescue from a watery grave until their departure on Saturday morning.

As usual in such cases Mr. W.G. Sanford, Honary Agent for the Shipwrecked Fishermen and Mariners Society arranged that whatever board, lodging, and clothing were necessary were furnished to the crew, and railway passes to their respective homes, Sunderland, Boston, and Faversham.

At Cromer and the adjoining parishes the wreck of the Schooner was alluded to on Sunday from the pulpit. The Captain attended service at Cromer Church, and on behalf of himself and the rest of the crew returned thanks for their deliverance from drowning. An earnest and impressive discourse was preached by the Vicar, the Rev. F. Editch, to a large congregation, from Psalm CV11 verses 23 and 24.

With regard to the value of the ship it is of interest to note that she was insured by Charles Putwain in 1875 for £920. To Entry charge £4.6.6, Policy, 4/6, Survey, 5/-, Additional entry, 5/6, Policy, 6d.

52891 **ALPHA**

Built in 1865 at Milton by R.N. Shrubsall.
Schooner, 145 registered tons. 111.3 x 22.4 x 8.4.
Signal Code K.D.F.C. Loading 280 tons.
Owners: Ernest Goldfinch, Thomas Goldfinch, Ann Madams, 1st June 1883. Ernest Goldfinch, 1884.
Masters: A. Camburn, 1892-4. Reeves, J.C. Pout 1894. S.J. Putwain, 1895. H. Sandy.

On the 19th November 1895 she was bound from Newcastle to Courseulles, France, loaded with coal, when she was caught in a north gale, force 11. Stranding near Barfleur Lightship she soon became a total loss, but all the crew were saved.

81922 **ALPHA**

Built in 1879 at Whitstable.
Ketch, 40 registered tons.
Owner: Thomas Goldfinch.
Master: A. Camburn.

She was sold to John Cruickshank of Ramsgate.

28228 **ALPHEUS**
Built in 1860 at Port Glasgow by Fenfew.
Sloop, 52 registered tons. 64.5 x 17.6 x 9.5. 20 H.P. Engine. Signal Code P.W.M.S.
Owner: William Pearson Coleman, 20th May 1881.
This vessel was sunk in the Bay of Baldoga on the 10th November 1881.

53682 **AMANDA**
Built in 1865 at Prince Edward Island by R. Putlin.
Brigantine, 193 registered tons. Signal Code L.H.J.T.
Owners: Gann and Kemp.

19225 **AMORET**
Built in 1857 at Prince Edward Island by J. and C. Pope.
Brigantine, 159 registered tons. 96.0 x 22.4 x 12.9.
Owners: William Gann, 2nd October 1858. Gann and Kemp, Alfred Goldfinch, Miss M. J. Gann, 1874.
Masters: William Gann, Bulger, Clothier.
This vessel was bought from Liverpool on the 11th September 1858. On the 5th March 1881 she stranded at Johnshaven, West Kincardine, and became a total loss. At that time she was bound for Sunderland from Arundal, in ballast. The gale was E.S.E. force 9, and all hands were lost.
This vessel was noted for the different sorts of wood used in her construction, beech, spruce, pine, juniper, cedar, and maple.

ANENOME
Built in 1857 in the north of Scotland by Miller.
Brigantine, 170 registered tons.
Owner: William White Foreman.
This vessel was wrecked in a storm in 1868.

41395 **ANENOME**
Built in 1857 at Intrimaganche, Nova Scotia.
Brigantine, 170 registered tons. 95.3 x 24.1 x 12.0.
Owner: John Goldfinch, 4th November 1862.
This vessel was bought by John Goldfinch from South Shields on the 13th October 1862. She was lost in a gale on the 11th March 1867.

17826 **ANENOME**
Built in 1849 at Sunderland.
Snow Brig, 241 registered tons.
Owners: Charles Hoult, Alfred Hoult, James Reeves.
Masters: Alfred Mann, Sacar Hoult, 12th November 1854.
This vessel was bought from Sunderland, 31st May 1854, and it was sold to South Shields in March 1861.
She was noted for her woman's figurehead.

Aneroid ➧

66423 **ANEROID**

Built in 1874 at Prince Edward Island by Ramsay for John Lefurgey. Brigantine, 212 registered tons. 105.5 x 25.9 x 13.7. Signal Code W.S.Q.G.

Owners: Perkins, Warner, Joiner.

Masters: McArthur, 1874. T.G. Goodwin.

This vessel was always considered to be a "leaky old tub", the crew, consisting of four men and one boy were constantly employed in pumping the water from her hold. In consequence she was a sluggish sailer. Also she was noted for her exceptionally large mainsail which made it still more difficult to control her.

She was sold to the Joiner Bros in 1912.

Although mostly employed in transporting coal from the Tyne to Whitstable, she was also employed in taking scrap iron from London to Swansea, and from Guernsey to London with stone.
In September 1812 she was sold to the Joiner Brothers for £425, and renovated at a cost of £1,100, which enabled her to be sold for £3,000. Alhough not owned at Whitstable at the time it is interesting to note that she survived until 1936, when she was finally broken up at West Appledore.

ANN
Built in 1838 at Prince Edward Island.
Brigantine, 129 registered tons.
Owner: Louisa Alice Gaskin.
A collier.

ANN & SUSANNAH
Built in 1804 at Whitby, Yorkshire.
Sloop, 61 registered tons. 53.0 x 16.1 x 8.6.
On the 15th February 1804 this vessel was sold by William Pysing, (Blacksmith) to Horatio Fedarb, of Whitstable.
Owners: Horatio Fedarb, Thomas Pysing, Thomas Jarrett, 4th August 1827. Thomas Ely, 2nd August 1828. James Prymer, 15th December 1828.
This vessel was lost on the 4th April 1834.

23846 ANNE EX JOHANNES
Brigantine, 119 registered tons. 86.5 x 19.8 x 9.8.
Owners: William White Foreman (Inn Keeper), William Foreman (Butcher), John B. Foreman, John Goldfinch jun., 20th September 1854.
Masters: John Bloomfield Foreman, 20th September 1854. Gaskin, 1873.
This vessel was captured as a prize in the Crimea War in 1854 and was then named JOHANNES. She was bought for local use on the 31st August 1854.

44436 ANNE MITCHELL
Built in 1862 at Aberdeen by Smith.
Brig, 189 registered tons. 101.0 x 23.8 x 13.1.
Owner: Charles Hoult, 25th November 1873.
Masters: W. Wicks, G. Beal.
This vessel was lost in 1874.

26278 ANN & SOPHIA
Built in 1845 at Tredwen, Cardiff.
Barquentine, 195 registered tons. 106.4 x 23.0 x 13.0. Signal Code A.K.L.T.
Owners: George John Drury, 1874. A. Anderson, F.W. Fairbrass, 1884. F.W. Fairbrass, 1885. The Whitstable Shipping Company, 31st December 1892.
Masters: J.R. Daniels, E.W. Walley, S. Clothier, Pout, H.W. Willson, G. Clothier, 1889-1894. D. Charrington, 1904. William Alfred Humphrey.
Although ANN & SOPHIA was built in 1845 and therefore might be considered to be an old ship she showed little evidence of her age. She enjoyed the reputation of being an excellent ship to sail, and she made

frequent and regular voyages to Melbourne, Australia, Tasmania, and the River Plate. On one Tasmanian trip a terrible sickness struck the crew, and the Captain and the Mate died. The only one left who knew anything about navigation and sailing the vessel was James Robert Daniels, a young Whitstable lad of nineteen, who had acted as Second Mate. When the crew got better from the illness he managed to sail the ship home successfully.
In March 1904 she was pulled up on Mr. Fairbrass's slipway, lengthened, and altered to a brigantine.

21577 **ANNE WHYTE**
Built in 1857 at Morell River, Prince Edward Island.
Schooner, 197 registered tons. 104.9 x 22.9 x 13.0.
Owner: Thomas J. Gann, James Amos, Henry William Madams, John Gann, Robert Feakins. These united to buy her from London 1st September 1862.
Master: John Gann.
This vessel was brought to Whitstable on the 13th September 1862. When bought she was classed as a Brig, and described as being built of birch, juniper, oak, and spruce, her bottom covered with felt and yellow metal, and iron bolts. She was broken up in 1881.

54125 **ARABIAN**

Built in 1866 at Prince Edward Island by R. Longworth.
Brigantine, 218 registered tons.
This vessel was one of the well-known Whitstable colliers.

ARAMATHEA

Schooner, flat bottomed.
Master: Robert Laraman, 1853.
This vessel was reputed to be a slow and sluggish sailer and consequently it was always difficult to get a crew for her.

11221 **ARMIN**

Square rig, 35 registered tons. 55.7 x 14.9 x 5.6. Signal Code K.R.S.B.
Owners: George Foreman, 22nd July 1853. George Foreman, Robert Feakins, 1874. T.G. Gann & Co., 1884.
Masters: George Foreman, 22nd July 1853. Edward Spillet, 18th April 1855.
This vessel was bought by George Foreman from Sandwich on the 28th June 1853, and having been brought to Whitstable she was repaired and altered to a schooner.
She was never a success and she was eventually broken up.

28151 **ARNOLDI**

Built in 1860 at St. Mary's, Scilly, by Edwards.
Schooner, 59 registered tons. 73.1 x 16.4 x 7.7. Part oak and mahogany, iron bolts.
Owners: Mark Pearson, Thomas Gann, 13th October 1864.
This vessel was bought from Bridgewater 11th October 1864, and was sold as a wreck at Gorleston in December 1884.

71436 **AUBREY PEAKE**

Built in 1874 at Prince Edward Island by Peake.
Brigantine, 249 registered tons. 115.6 x 26.7 x 12.9.
Owners: George Holden & Bronger, 21st June 1888. The Whitstable Shipping Co. James Robert Daniels.
Master: Harry Johnson.
In *Sea Breezes* in September 1949 the AUBREY PEAKE is described as having been purchased by Jarvis in 1881, from W.A. Mitchell of London, being at that time commanded by Captain A.H. Hall.
In 1887 she was sold to French owners and re-named MARIE-LOUISE. Then on the 21st June 1888 she was bought by George Holden & Bronger of Whitstable.
In August 1888 she was sent to Russia for a load of timber. On her way home from Uleabourg, loaded with deals and battens, on the 7th October 1888 she was struck by a storm, a northerly gale force 7, and stranded on Arneland Island, Holland, and she was reported in December to have broken up. The crew were all saved.

45186 **AVON**
Built in 1863 at Salcombe.
Brig, 183 registered tons. 109.6 x 22.4 x 12.8. Signal Code V.C.H.K.
Owner: George Henry Goldfinch, 8th March 1881.
Master: Alce.
On the 24th October 1882, when bound for Newhaven with coal from Sunderland she was caught in a gale, force 9, from the south-west, and stranded on the Kentish Knock. All the crew were lost.

27517 **AVON**
Built in 1859 at Sunderland by Pace & Son.
Barquentine, 263 registered tons.
Master: Mann.
This was stated to be a Whitstable-owned vessel by Captain Fred Pierce, who was Harbour Master at Faversham.

28151 **AVONOLDA**
Built in 1860 at the Scilly Isles.
Ketch, 59 registered tons.
On the 21st November 1884 she was bound for Hull from Ipswich with a cargo of manure, when a strong E.N.E. gale, force 7, made her unmanageable, and she stranded on the shore at Hopton, Suffolk. The crew were all saved but the vessel was written off as a total loss.

AYLESFORD
Built in 1841 at Aylesford, Nova Scotia, by Thomas Webb.
Boomsail, 91 registered tons. 62.5 x 15.4 x 4.4.
Owner: Charles Tassell.
Masters: R. Laraman, 30th April 1841. Thomas Browning, 10th June 1845. John Greenland, 29th April 1846.
Registered at Whitstable in April 1841.

52094 **AYLESFORD**
Built in 1866 at Aylesford, Nova Scotia.
Brigantine, 143 registered tons.
Owner: Tassell.
Master: R. Laraman.
This vessel was mentioned at the Kent Assizes, on the 11th March 1861, and she was owned by the same person as the previous vessel.

63988 **BALGAY**
Built in 1872 at Dundee by the Tay Ship Building Company.
Schooner, 228 registered tons.
Owners: James Robert Daniels, 1894. The Whitstable Shipping Company.
Masters: Taylor, A. Parsons, 1891. Sidders 1894. F. Packman.
On the 18th October 1889 this vessel was insured for £400. On the 19th October 1891 arrived in Grimsby Harbour with her foremast and

topmast gone as well as all her sails. Three sets of salvers demanded £600, which was refused, and the opposing parties lost no time in going to law. All parties were summoned to appear before the Justices on the Thursday following the 29th October. The salvage claims were then settled by the Justices at £275. The Insurance Claim was settled at £590.0.3.

The *Whitstable Times* gave a very full account of her tragic end when she foundered off the Northumbrian coast with the loss of all hands in 1895. The *Whitstable Parish Magazine* published a graphic account of the finding, and collection of the bodies of the drowned crew, and praised the reverence with which they were taken to the Lifeboat House under the direction of Sergeant George Brown and Chief Coastguardsman Hadley. The body of Captain F. Packman was carried by the sea some miles further north and found at Old Law opposite Holy Island. The names of the crew were, H. Bonner (Mate), H. Apps, B. Fuller, and Geering. The body of Captain F. Packman was buried in Belford Churchyard.

62700 **BELLA**

Built in 1872 at Banff.
Schooner, 88 registered tons. Signal Code L.B.G.Q.
Owner: Seymour Putwain (part owner).
Master: S. Putwain.
Particulars of her stay at Whitstable are not known.

45240 **BELLE**
Built in 1862 at Southtown.
Schooner, 148 registered tons. 91.4 x 20.5 x 12.3.
Owners: Bell, James Reeves, May Bell, John Collar, John Gann, 13th October 1862.
Master: R. Laraman.
This vessel was registered at Whitstable on the 8th October 1862, a quite new vessel.
For nine years she served her owners well, eventually foundering after a collision of Flamborough Head on the 26th November 1871.

104933 **BELMONT**
Built in 1895 at Whitstable by the Whitstable Shipping Company.
Schooner, 139 registered tons. 104.0 x 24.1 x 9.6. Signal Code N.V.J.S.
Owners: The Whitstable Shipping Company, 7th June 1895.
Masters: H. Rowles, Skinner, W. Jessup, 1898. A.E. Jessup, 1905.
BELMONT was built by the Whitstable Shipping Company with money saved by not insuring their other vessels.
She was rigged as a topsail schooner having two masts, setting a square sail, topsail, and topgallant on her foremast. She had no mizzen topmast but carried a jiboom, and she was steered by a wheel.
She was named after the house of Mr. George Holden, one of the directors of the Whitstable Shipping Company.
She was chine built but carried no lee-boards, she had a normal bow and a counter stern, and was flat bottomed to allow her to be unloaded on the hard when the tide was out.
She was written off as a total wreck in October 1920.

19171 **BENACHIE**
Built in 1857 at Aberdeen.
Brig, 156 registered tons. 100.9 x 20.5 x 11.4.
Owner: Charles Hoult, 14th May 1861.
This vessel was bought by Charles Hoult on the 11th May 1861.
She was lost in the Black Sea on the 21st October 1861.

28363 **BENLEDI**
Built in 1859 at Grangemouth by Adamson.
Barque, 229 registered tons. 103.4 x 23.1 x 14.3, later altered to barquentine.
Owner: Stephen Rigden, 3rd November 1863.
This vessel was bought from London by Stephen Rigden on the 2nd November 1863. She was lost off Nassau on the 15th May 1864.

BERENDINA
Schooner, 170 registered tons.
Owner: W. Lawson.
Masters: Camburn, T. Page.
A well known Whitstable vessel.

Sunday Morning on the Brenda. (Mission to Seamen).

28111 **BETHESDA**

Built in 1859 at Prince Edward Island by Cox.
Brigantine, 157 registered tons. 97.5 x 22.3 x 11.5, iron bolts.
Owner: George Baker, 15th September 1860.
Masters: Madams, Charles Fowel.
This vessel was bought from Plymouth on the 14th September 1860.

60246 **BLONDE**

Built in 1874 at Newhaven by Tolman.
Schooner, re-rigged as a barquentine, 208 registered tons.
115.4 x 25.1 x 13.1. Signal Code N.J.F.W.
Owners: George Henry Goldfinch, 24th August 1874. W. Foreman & Co.
Masters: T.W. Minter, 1884. C. Kemp, 1885-1889.
E.J. Hall, 1899-1904.
This vessel was bought by George Henry Goldfinch on the 24th August 1874. W. Foreman & Co. The Whitstable Shipping Company.
An interesting letter regarding this vessel has survived. It was written by Mr. T.J. Reeves, the Secretary of the Whitstable Star Mutual Maritime Assurance Association to Mr. J.T. Handly the Registrar of Shipping, Faversham, on October 27th 1887, as follows:

Dear Sir *BLONDE*

Some of the Owners of the above Ship have been to me with reference to making an application to have another of the Owners Mr Foreman have recorded as the O and also that you had informed them the late Philip Warner's part had not been transmitted to his Executrix. I beg to enclose form of transmission and the application shall be sent in a few days signed by the others.

Yours obediently,

J.T. Reeves

It would appear to have been taking a rather optimistic risk when on the 18th October 1889 she was insured for £100.
However she would seem to have led a charmed life until 29th November 1897 when she was dismasted in a great storm and towed into Lowestoft. After being repaired she continued to give good service for some years until on the 28th February 1906, when bound from London to Barrowstroness with a cargo of scrap iron she again encountered a great storm, the wind being force 7, and she foundered when about thirty miles E. by S. of Whitby. All the crew were saved.

28764 **BLUE JACKET**

Built in 1860 at Aberystwith by Jones.
Schooner, 181 registered tons. Signal Code Q.B.T.M.
Owner: Walter W. Hills, 1893.
Master: J. Parker.
This vessel was employed in the Mediterranean fruit trade, going to Patras in Greece for currants, to Alicante for oranges, and to the Canaries for bananas.

Blonde

52151 **BOXER**

Built in 1865 at Port Elgin, New Brunswick.

Brigantine, 172 registered tons. 108.0 x 23.4 x 12.8. Signal Code M.S.P.Q.

Owners: George Holden, Thomas Gann jun., Henry Pout, William John Bronger, 19th November 1872.

Masters: C. Luckie, 1874. Matthew John Allen, H. Wilson, M.J. Allen, 1891-1895. J. Fairbrass, 1895. W. Joiner, 1901.

During her early years in Whitstable ownership this vessel was mainly engaged in trading between London and the Mediterranean ports, but in later years her activities were restricted to east coast ports.

On the 18th October 1889 she was insured for £450, but as time passed she appeared to increase in value. So we find that on the 13th May 1892 she was valued at £1,250 and insured for £500.

On the 14th November 1901 she was caught in a great E.N.E. gale, force 10, when bound from Gravesend to Hartlepool with a cargo of chalk. In consequence she stranded about half a mile south of Scarborough Harbour and became a total wreck. The crew of eight were all saved.

The *Scarborough Post* published a graphic account of this incident as follows:

Chief excitement in Scarborough centred this morning in the terrible predicament of a schooner. This afterwards proved to be the "Boxer", from London to Hartlepool, in ballast. She was first seen at Burniston about seven o'clock, and it was very evident she was almost beyond control, drifting south before the gale. The crew had the utmost difficulty in keeping her off the north side where, had she been driven in, it was felt she must have foundered. The schooner happily was kept off, and she rode round the Castle Hill dipping and tossing in a most alarming fashion, sometimes up as though the merest plaything.

There were those who entertained grave doubts whether she could get safely round. A crowd of excited people watched the rolling of the "Boxer" as she sometimes came in view round Castle Hill, and straining eyes watched her every movement, while everyone's sympathy and pity went out to the poor crew drifting then between life and death. Happily she had a cool and courageous captain, who performed wonders with his storm-tossed craft. Gradually with her canvas she neared the pier, and it then became a question whether she would be driven across on the rocks, or find a sandy bottom opposite the Fore-shore Road. Her movements at this critical juncture were watched with the greatest excitement, but she gradually, getting more under control as she felt the shelter of the pier, headed into the north of the Spa, passing over a bed of rock without striking, and finally stranding on the sands opposite the Grand Hotel. Meanwhile the life-boat which had been out since before seven, owing to a report of the foundering of a ketch, now struck out from under the shelter of the Lighthouse Pier, where she was riding, and made for the stranded schooner. Coxswain Owston, with rare judgement, directed the boat alongside the shore, and passing under the bow of the "Boxer", got to the sheltered side of the schooner.

Now the major portion of the crew, who had been up in the rigging clinging for very life, were seen to scramble down the rope ladders, and in a very few minutes all the eight members of the crew, including the captain, were safe in the lifeboat. The schooner had gone ashore at ten o'clock when the tide was nearly out and there was a very short distance for the lifeboat to traverse. Nearing the shore a rope was thrown out, and scores of men, up to the knees and deeper in the water, seized hold of the rope, and the lifeboat was hauled out of the water. The rescued sailors were also cheered as they were being led away for much-needed food and shelter. They represented a sorrowful spectacle, dripping with wet, shivering from exposure, and half dead with fright and exhaustion, as they dragged themselves across the sands to the shelter and refreshment awaiting them.

It should be mentioned that prior to the lifeboat taking off the crew the Coastguard under Chief-Officer Winter, brought the rocket apparatus into operation, but did not effect communication. It was then seen to be needless to throw another, as the lifeboat could manifestly now cope with the situation. At the Coastguard Station, to which the captain (William George Joiner) and three of the crew were first taken, Captain Joiner said to our reporter that they had a dreadful night in the schooner. They met the gale on Tuesday, but continued their voyage towards Hartlepool and passed Scarborough going north on that day. About four o'clock this (Wednesday) morning, however, the storm was terrific. Then, said Captain Joiner, "we turned round and came south again," adding with a grim smile, "because we had to do so."

They were thus driven before the wind until daylight, when they found themselves off Scarborough. The rest we have related above. There were eight of them on the schooner said Captain Joiner, seven Englishmen and one Russian. He could not tell their names, but the Englishmen belong to Whitstable, the same place as the schooner.

The damage done to the craft, he added, consisted of the breakage of wheels, stays, jibs, etc, whilst the canvas had all been blown to ribbons. All agree that Captain Joiner, who is a slightly built man, handled the schooner splendidly under the circumstances and probably the fact that he saved the crew, and the vessel, is due in some measure to the fact that he possesses an intimate knowledge of the coast. It is thought that the schooner will become a wreck. She belongs to Whitstable and is a brigantine of 172 tons register.

This long descriptive eye-witness account imparts life and reality to the often recorded one word such as "lost" or "foundered" used to describe the end of a Whitstable ship. The tragic end and loss of well-known local men, and the humble craft that they sailed in was an all-too-frequent event and accepted risk to the Whitstable natives of past generations one hundred years ago, but can only be appreciated by modern generations in reading an eye-witness account as preserved in the columns of the old *Scarborough Post.*

52156 **BOYER**
This vessel was registered at Whitstable 29th October 1872.
Owner: Thomas Gann jun.

77928 **BRENDA**
Built in 1879 at Mount Stewart, Charlotte Town, Prince Edward Island, by Peake.
Brigantine, 249 registered tons. 116.4 x 26.6 x 12.9.
Signal Code W.M.K.P.
Owners: George Holden, Thomas Gann, 18th April 1882. George Holden, 1884. Alfred W. Daniels. The Whitstable Shipping Company, 19th May 1914.
Masters: W. Sampson, 1882-1894. W.A. Dodd, H.J. Witnall, 1896-1904.

BRENDA was reputed to have graceful lines, and she carried a Royal. Her stem and stern posts were of birch. While she was employed in the coal trade she was considered to hold the Blue Ribband of the east coast. During this period of her life she was employed in carrying chalk to Newcastle to be made into cement and returning with coal.
On the 18th October 1889 she was insured for £600.
On the 9th October 1891 she was damaged in a storm, and drawn up on the slipway at Pelaw Main. The repairs cost £94.17.1.
On the 7th January 1917 when off Dungeness she was sunk by a German submarine.

28429 **BREEZE**
Built in 1859 at Sunderland by Short.
Snow Brig, 216 registered tons. Signal Code P.W.K.F.
Owner: George Peters.

10088 **BRITAINS PRIDE**
Built in 1856 at Kingston-by-Sea, Shoreham, by May.
Brig, 166 registered tons. 104.5 x 23.9 x 12.6. Built of oak and pitch pine.
Owners: George Gaskin, William Harnett, John Edward Pierce, Edward Gaskin, 26th March 1874.
This vessel was mostly engaged in the Mediterranean trade. On the 12th October 1878 she was off Cape St. Mary, Portugal, bound for London laden with ore, the wind being force 7. When she was twenty-three miles off the coast she foundered, but all six of the crew were saved.

15353 **BRITISH ENSIGN**
Built in 1857 at Dumbarton.
Brig, 190 registered tons. 101.4 x 22.1 x 13.1. Felt and yellow metal.
Owners: W. Kemp jun., William Gann, 24th November 1871.
Master: S. Flick.
During most of her life at Whitstable she was employed as a collier. On the 28th October 1880 when bound for Shields in ballast from Ramsgate, when two miles north of Seaham Harbour, the wind being N.E. force 9, she stranded and became a total loss. Of the crew of seven one was lost.

BRITISH FAIR
Owners: William Camburn. The Whitstable Shipping Company.

65494 **BRITONS PRIDE**
Built in 1871 at Brixham.
Cutter, 38 registered tons.
Master: Gaskin.
This vessel traded regularly to the Channel ports and Islands.

65657 **BROCKLESBY**

Built in 1872 at Lowestoft by Westaway.
Brigantine, 182 registered tons. 98.8 x 24.3 x 12.1.
Signal Code K.T.W.F.
Owners: James Pout, 12th February 1891. A. Parsons, 1895. J.G. Gann, 1903. J.T. Reeves, 1904. Pout Brothers.
Masters: Allen, 1892. James Pout, 1893-4. L. Pout, G. Clarke, 1904.
On the 6th January 1891 she was valued at £840, and insured for £670. On the 6th February 1892 she arrived at Sunderland and reported that she had been in collision with and sunk the Brigantine ASTREA of Newcastle, and had saved the crew. The collision had occurred at 5.15 a.m. on the 5th February when she was 18 miles off Hartlepool. The claim for the ASTREA was settled at £375, being the amount for which she was insured being £310 and two thirds value of her cargo, being £95. Then on the 11th October 1892 £167.3.1 was paid on account of the counter claim for damage, and the final balance of the claim amounting to £210.16.9 was paid to Mr. Pout on the 11th January 1893. This ship was written off as missing since leaving Swansea on the 17th November 1916.

5265 **BROTHERS**

Built in 1801 at Thorpe near Norwich.
Brig, 95 registered tons. 65.0 x 20.1 x 9.7.
Owners: E. West, 30th December 1852. William James Gann, Edward West, 30th December 1855. Robert Frend, 5th October 1858.
Masters: William Gann, 19th October 1833 and 7th June 1836. E. West, 30th December 1852, when he bought the ship from William Gann.
In March 1835, when owned by the Gann family she was turned into a schooner. Then on the 7th June 1836 she passed into the sole ownership of William Gann. It is recorded that when owned by Edward West she regularly made fourteen voyages each year to the north for coal.
On the 18th October 1856 the *Kentish Independant* reported a tragic incident in connection with this ship, as follows:

Brigantine "BROTHERS" under the command of the 1st Mate Friend, (acting captain) whilst passing between Yarmouth and Cromer Light in the early part of last week, saw a man in the water 20 miles off shore, supported by a cork life jacket and two spars, and although he spoke and asked for assistance Friend could not stop to pick him up.

No reason is given for this apparently hard action, but those were hard days.
BROTHERS was briefly reported lost on the 21st December 1852.

22054 **CABERFEIGH**

Built in 1859 at Garmouth, Moray, by Duncan.
Brig, 151 registered tons. 89.1 x 22.6 x 12.1. Felt and yellow metal.
Owner: James Rigden, bought from Inverness 26th August 1861, and registered at Whitstable 29th August 1861.
Master: Nicholls.
This vessel was reported lost on the Ouris on the 18th March 1867.

11279 **CALEDONIA**

Built in 1835 at Peterhead.
Brigantine, 96 registered tons. 63.9 x 19.8 x 11.7.
Owners: Joshua Downs, Cyrus Jutson, J. Acors, bought from Wokington 6th May 1849. Registered at Whitstable, 3rd November 1849. W. Allen, R.B. Newing, W. Rigden, 11th January 1861. R. Newing, 1869. W. Allen, 1874.
Masters: James Acors, 24th March 1849, and 11th October 1850. W. Allen.
This ship was valued at £350, and is recorded as being broken up, on the 23rd September 1875.

47211 **CALEDONIA**

Built in 1864 at Garmouth, Elgin, by Geddie.
Schooner, 171 registered tons. 104.1 x 23.9 x 13.0. Signal Code V.M.Q.H.
Owners: Charles Putwain, 14th August 1875. Henry Pearson Coleman, 1894-1904. E. J. Nicholls, 1884. Sarah Ann Coleman, R. Newing.
Masters: A. Reeve, 1895. H.R. Coleman, W. Allen, J.E. Kemp, 1902-05. N.H. Wilmot, 1905.

She was insured for £1,000 in 1873 by Charles Putwain. On the 13th April 1907, when bound for Whitstable from Seaham with coal she stranded on the Newcome Sand. The wind was described as "wrong" at the time, but there was a strong sea running and she started to break up. Two of the crew of five were lost in getting away from her, and she became a total loss.

The *Whitstable Times and Herne Bay Herald* of Saturday April 20th 1907 gave the following graphic description of the incident

WHITSTABLE VESSEL LOST

A terrific gale raged off the East Coast on Friday night, and continued on Saturday morning with but little moderation. While the storm was at its height about half past four in the morning, a Schooner, which turned out to be the CALEDONIA, of Whitstable, was seen to strike the dangerous Newcome Sand almost opposite Lowestoft South Pier. The life-boat was manned and towed by a tug through the rolling sea. Meanwhile the Schooner had gone over almost on to her beam ends and in the faint light it was seen that men were clining to the masts, over which the waves repeatedly dashed volumes of spray.

Just as the life-boat got alongside the Caledonia's topmast it fell right over on to her, and two men who had been gripping the rigging were swept away. Encumbered with the wreckage, the lifeboatmen were powerless to succour the poor fellows, who shouted for help as they drowned. Three other men were left on the wreck which by this time was nearly submerged, and were speedily rescued.

One, the captain, H.P. Coleman, who is also owner of the ill-fated schooner, and is seventy five years of age, was in a state of collapse, and it was first feared that he was dead. The two others, young men, were almost unconscious, but rallied slightly on the lifeboat as she made for the Harbour. On arrival they were carried to the Sailors Home.

One of the drowned men was George Nicholls, of Stockton-on-Tees, mate of the vessel, the other victim being a Danish seaman whose name is unknown. John Greenhow, a survivor, in an interview, said "I was the last to leave. I swung on a chain with the sea dashing over me and knocking me against the side of the ship. I had given up all hope. I was half dead with cold, and in a few more seconds I must have let go."

The rescued men are – Henry P. Coleman, of Whitstable, captain and owner of the schooner; Ernest Metz, a German, and John Greenhow, a seaman of Keswick, Cumberland.

Coxswain Mence says the rescue was the most perilous he had undertaken during fifteen years.

451 **CANTON**

Built in 1823 at Deptford.
Ketch, 53 registered tons. 54.5 x 18.2 x 8.9.
Owners: John Marshall, William Tassel.
Masters: John Greenland, 13th March 1846. Thomas Greenland, 13th June 1859.
This vessel was sunk two miles off the Port of Arundel, in August 1859.

73939 **CARMENTA**

Built in 1875 at Prince Edward Island by Angus McMillan, Summerside, Egmont Bay, launched 16th October 1875.
Brigantine, (Carvel built) 199 registered tons. 103.0 x 24.3 x 12.75.
Owners: William Kemp, 14th January 1881. William Kemp jun. 1884. Bought by G.B. Joiner for £826 in 1894. Joiner Bros.
Masters: S. Flick, 1891. W.F. Joiner, Rowden, J.G. Baker, 1892-4, 1902-4. J. Gibbons, 1907. Walter Joiner, 1915.
On the 18th October 1889 she was insured for £600.
On the 9th March 1891, her then Master, Samuel Flick, reported that in a dense fog, while in the Downs on the 3rd March he had run into a French smack, breaking his jiboom and damaging the smack.
During the hard winter she was frozen up in Whitstable Harbour and when ice began to break up she was carried out of the Harbour and about four miles to the westward.
During a great storm on the 23rd February 1916 she ran ashore at Thorpeness and was wrecked, but the crew were all saved by the Breeches Apparatus.

The wreck of the Carmenta

39195 **CAROLINE**

Built in 1857 at Mount Stewart, Prince Edward Island.
Brig, 173 registered tons. 93.2 x 23.3 x 12.8. Signal Code S.N.G.W.
Owners: Charles Hoult, 14th February 1865. Ward, J.H. Nicholls, C. Hoult, 24th August 1889.
Masters: R. Clinking, H.J. Nicholls, Ward, Thomas Clark, 1868.

This vessel was bought from Bristol on the 10th February 1865, and was insured with the Whitstable Star Mutual Maritime Association for £400. On the 29th March 1869 she sank in Whitstable Bay, but at low tide she was salvaged and drawn up on the slipway for repairs.

In June 1879 she was altered to a brigantine.

On the 18th October 1889 she was re-insured for £520. Altered by Charles Hoult to £800.

On the 11th December 1891 she stranded off the coast of Holland when the crew were not aboard, and on the 31st December 1891 she was confirmed as a total loss. It is curious that her insurance money was paid by instalments as follows,

9th August 1892	on account of total loss,				£100.
11th October 1892,	,,	,,	,,		£300.
9th November 1892,	,,	,,	,,		£220.

45554 **CASSANDRA**
Built in 1863 at Rye.
Brigantine, 176 registered tons. 101.0 x 23.6 x 12.9.
Owners: Charles Hoult, Isaac Terry, James Kemp jun., Alfred Hoult, 18th February 1863.
Masters: Hoult, 1864. J. Allen.
On 28th October 1880 she was off Ambul, Northumberland, in ballast, bound for Shields from Gravesend. The E.N.E. gale, force 10, drove her ashore, and she became a total loss. The crew of seven were all saved.

20751 **CATHERINE JANE**
Built in 1858 at Pembroke Dock.
Brigantine, 166 registered tons. 94.6 x 24.3 x 12.9. Zinc to light water mark.
Owners: Stephen Houlden, Philip Newman, James Acors, Charles Jutson, James Rigden, Edwin Rigden, Alfred Rigden, Daniel Rigden, 19th February 1872. This was a case of members of a family and relations having a few shares each.
Masters: Wraight, Forster, 1869.
This vessel was bought from Milford on the 2nd December 1862 and sold back to Milford again in January 1876.

17323 **CAUTIOUS**

Built in 1854 at Rye by Hoad Brothers.
Schooner, 138 registered tons. 86.0 x 23.3 x 12.6.
Owners: William White Foreman, William Kitchingham Foreman, John Goldfinch, 13th July 1859.
Masters: Cooper, C. Merritt, Parker.

This vessel was bought from Rye on the 12th July 1859, and insured for £450. Mainly used in the coal trade, on the 12th July 1893 she was in Ramsgate Harbour when her cargo was found to be on fire. The crew fought the fire with great heroism, one of them losing his life. Great damage was suffered, but the hulk was saved, towed to Whitstable, drawn up on the slipway and she was practically rebuilt. She went back to the coal trade for another ten years and then on the 1st August 1903, when she was six miles E. of N. near Sandhead, Kent, with coal from Sunderland for Ramsgate she sprang a leak, but with careful sailing she made port, where she was unloaded and was condemned. However in April 1904 she was converted into a hulk.

5748 **CESAR**

Built in 1853 at Prince Edward Island.
Brigantine, 144 registered tons. 87.7 x 22.2 x 12.1.
Owners: Thomas Richard Culver, William Waters, David Thomas Waters.

This vessel was bought from Guernsey on the 27th November 1860, and she was sold to Malden on the 12th November 1861.

5056 **CHANCE**

Built in 1842 at Sunderland.
Square rig, 134 registered tons. 68.4 x 19.8 x 12.0.
Owners: George Foreman, Goldfinch, William Foreman, Hannah Foreman, Edward Kemp.
Masters: Richard Foreman, 13th December 1845. Henry Coleman, 6th January 1849. John Foreman, 21st July 1852. G. Foreman, 27th October 1854.

This vessel was originally a brig but was altered to square rig when she was bought from Chatham on the 20th November 1845. She was lost off Hartlepool on the 2nd January 1857. Her figurehead was salvaged and for many years adorned the gable of a wooden building in Horsebridge Road until it was blown up by a German Bomb. This figurehead was again salvaged and it may now be seen in the Whitstable Museum. The curious building is made reference to by Charles Dickins in "All the year Round", No. 31, 25th November 1859, where he describes a Whistable Native. *As he grows older he sees nothing to wonder at if a wooden staircase comes down from the top rooms of his father's house at the exterior of the side wall; and he thinks an old figurehead of Minerva, swept ashore, perhaps from the wreck of some collier, an ornament for a parapet superior to any statue that was ever hewn out of stone.*

It is of interest to know that it was customary for the Foreman of the Oyster Company to stand on that stairway to issue his orders to the dredgermen as they stood in the street below. It was also the place from which the traitor William Joyce, (Lord Haw Haw) would frequently address his black shirts.

42934 **CHARLES**

Built in 1862 at Ornell, Prince Edward Island by L.C. Owen and J. MacDougal.

Brigantine, 178 registered tons. 96.0 x 23.4 x 12.8. Signal Code T.L.V.F.

Owners: George Peters, 18th November 1862. Richard Wheeler, William Holden.

Masters: Camburn, J. Strand.

This vessel was bought on the 13th October 1862, and was insured with the Whitstable Star Mutual Maritime Assurance Association for £400. She was re-insured for £900 by William Holden, on the 20th October 1875. She was broken up in October 1904.

71420 **CHARLES P. KNIGHT**

Built in 1874 at Prince Edward Island, by James C. Pope.
Brigantine, 189 registered tons. Signal Code P.B.Q.K.
Owner: William J. Lawson.
Master: Baldock.
She was a well known collier.

19925 **CHARLOTTE**

Built in 1837 at Bayonne, France.
Brigantine, 140 registered tons. 91.3 x 23.4 x 11.2
Owners: Josiah Reeves, William Charles Gibbons, George Butcher, 23rd October 1863. Josiah Reeves, George Butcher, John Collar, 22nd January 1874.
Master: Moyes.
This vessel was bought from Ramsgate on the 21st October 1863. On the 18th January 1881 she was in Hartlepool Bay being bound for Shields from Gravesend with chalk. A gale, E.N.E. force 9, caused her to drag her anchor and she was driven ashore where she became a wreck, but all the crew were saved. In April 1881 her hull was found to be in good condition and she was converted into a hulk.

39178 **CHEBUCTO**

Built in 1857 at Pinnette, Prince Edward Island.
Brig, 216 registered tons. 101.8 x 24.3 x 13.6.
She was built with black birch, spruce, pine, maple, felt and zinc.
Owner: Edward Kemp, 7th November 1863.
She was bought from Liverpool on the 5th November 1863, and was sold to Falmouth on the 7th May 1866.

56646 **CHRISTABEL**

Built in 1867 by Hessell at Rye.
Schooner altered to Barquentine, 175 registered tons.
98.8 x 23.1 x 12.9. Signal Code J.R.W.M.
Owners: Thomas James Gann, Thomas Gann, James Gann, 5th June 1867. The Whitstable Shipping Company, 17th March 1916.
Masters: R. Claringbold, Chadwick, Goldfinch, G.W. Johnson.
This vessel was bought from Rye and registered at Whitstable, 4th June 1867. An interesting letter concerning damage sustained in a storm has survived.

This Certifies that the undersigned Surveyor at the request of George Baker Esq., did survey the Christabel to ascertain what damage she sustained by stranding at St. Brieue.

I find both the metal dove tail plates broken and the after end of the main keel dropped about ¾ of an inch each way. And in my opinion when the vessel is afloat the keel is a ¼ of an inch down. The keel seam and keel above has been caulked and payed since her stranding. The thick plates under both bilges are grubbed a bit but will dress off smooth.

Captain states he believes this was got at Exeter or the previous voyage. The caulking is somewhat disturbed from the bends downwards especially on the Port side under the quarter.

The vessel requires the after keel to be set up and bolted and the after garboards additionally bolted, the bilge planks cleaved off and treenail heads caulked, and also caulking from the Bends to keel fore and aft.

Whitstable April 30th 1888

J. R. Daniels

Evidently these repairs were carried out and she continued to serve the Gann family until 1902 when negotiations were started to sell her to the Whitstable Shipping Company. She was then valued at £200. During this period she broke adrift in a storm and was washed up against the Company's slipway where she sustained damage. However she was repaired, and continued to give good service until she had the misfortune to run on the Gunfleet Sand when racing for home in an effort to beat the tide. Although she was written off as a total loss she did not break up, and after a time was salved, repaired, and turned once more into a barquentine.

Her eventful life ended when she was sunk by a German submarine in January 1917.

CHRISTABELLA

Master: Hickman.

As this vessel was recorded by Capt. Fred Pierce, the Harbour Master at Faversham as belonging to Whitstable it would seem to be right to include it.

41139 CHRISTIAN

Built in 1856 at New Glasgow, Nova Scotia.
Brigantine, 197 registered tons. 105.4 x 25.5 x 12.6. Signal Code T.C.K.N.
Owners: William Kemp, James Goldfinch, David Waters, 3rd May 1862.
Master: J. Phillips.

This vessel was bought from London 29th January 1862, and insured with the Whitstable Star Mutual Assurance Association for £600. Originally a brig, she was altered to a brigantine on the 30th June 1865. On the 4th December 1878 she was in collision off Southampton, damage £120. She was condemned 30th May 1883.

42894 CHRISTINA

Built in 1861 at Orwell, Prince Edward Island.
Brigantine, 165 registered tons. 92.0 x 23.0 x 12.4
Owners: C.H. Rowden, James Jutson, registered at Whitstable 7th March 1864.
Masters: Jutson, H. Rose.

This vessel was bought from Shoreham on the 20th December 1865 and insured with the Whitstable Star Mutual Maritime Assurance Association for £800.

58190 CHRYSOLITE

Built in 1869 at Whitehaven by Shepherd.
Schooner, 161 registerd tons. 95.6 x 21.6 x 12.00. Signal Code J.D.C.M.
Owners: C.J. Perkins, Perkins and Joiner.
Master: J. Gibbons.

This vessel was bought at Penzance in February 1914 for £250.

65752 CLYDE

Built in 1871 at Teignmouth by Mansfield.
Brig, altered to Brigantine. 204 registered tons. 107.9 x 24.1 x 12.9. Signal Code K.E.P.W.
Owners: T.G. Goodwin, George Henry Goldfinch, George Holden, Henry Gann, 22nd December 1883. The Whitstable Shipping Company.
Masters: G. Hasland, Friend, William Alfred Humphrey.

This vessel was altered to a brigantine in November 1904. She was blown up by a German submarine in April 1916.

63913 **COCK O' THE WALK**
Built in 1876 by Surridge at Mill Wall, London.
Ketch, 111 registered tons. Signal Code P.R.N.L.
Owner: Fred Frend.
Master: F. Frend.
This vessel was a boomie and she had a clipper bow.

65058 **COILA**
Built in 1871 at Brucehaven, Fife.
Jackass, Brig, 173 registered tons. 97.8 x 22.4 x 12.9. Signal Code K.H.L.F.
Owners: George Henry Goldfinch, Eliza Camburn, James Camburn, John Christian Brown, Frederick Browning, 21st January 1884.
Master: A. Court.
Originally classed as a jackass she was altered to a brigantine in November 1891. She was sunk by collision in the Bristol Channel on the 14th May 1895.

29065 **COLLINA**

Built in 1860 at Prince Edward Island, by Coffin for J. Peake.
Brigantine, 167 registered tons. 100.3 x 22.4 x 11.5. Signal Code Q.D.C.P.
Owners: Henry Holden jun., and James Anderson, 28th December 1860. Henry Holden, George Holden jun., William Holden, Henry Nicholls, Osborne Nicholls, Alfred Nicholls, George Nicholls, George Peters, 25th December 1871.
Masters: William Jacobs, 1879. Fittal, 1891. George Nicholls.
This vessel was bought at Plymouth on the 26th December 1860, after her maiden voyage across the Atlantic.
On the 20th October 1875 she was insured by Henry Holden for £850 and then re-insured on the 18th October 1889 for £680.
On the 27th April 1891 Captain Fitall reported to the Owners that she had on the 26th April struck rock at St Sampsons, that her stem carried away, and that her keel and planks were damaged.
During the great tidal surge on the 29th November 1897 she was washed off Hollaway's slip.
Finally on the 21st July 1898 she was sold for breaking up.

50402 **CONOID**

Built in 1865 at Peterhead by Carnegie and Matthews.
Brigantine altered to Schooner. 165 registered tons.
100.0 x 23.7 x 11.7. Signal Code W.J.B.D.
Owners: H. Holden jun., George Herbert Gann, 2nd May 1884. The Whitstable Shipping Company.
Masters: G. Nicholls, F. Larcombe, W. Joiner, 1897-98. Frederick Maxted for thirty six years.
In August 1897 she was fitted with new decks.
She was sold to Fowey in January 1917.

71454 **CONSUS**
Built in 1874 at Prince Edward Island, by William Welsh and J. Johnson.
Brigantine, 193 registered tons. 107.0 x 24.8 x 12.7. Signal Code P.K.D.C.
Owners: George Holden, Thomas Gann jun., William John Bronger, Henry Pout, 22nd January 1876.
This vessel was insured by George Holden on the 18th September 1875 for £800.
Masters: G.B. Joiner, W. Sampson.
On the 19th May 1882 this vessel, when moored at Queenborough Pier, caught fire, and despite all attempts to save her she burned out.

39257 **CONTEST**
Built in 1857 at Mount Stewart, Prince Edward Island.
Brig, 228 registered tons. 115.0 x 26.2 x 13.1.
Owners: Camburn and George Baker, 21st December 1863.
Master: G. Madams.
This vessel was lost off Milford on the 18th March 1867.

36413 **CORA**
Built in 1859 at Grand River, Prince Edward Island, by McDougal.
Brigantine, 146 registered tons. 93.7 x 21.7 x 11.7.
Owners: William Kemp, David Waters, James Goldfinch, Herbert T. Sankey, 10th December 1959.
Master: Strand.
This vessel was bought after her maiden voyage from Prince Edward Island on the 31st August 1859.
She was lost off Shields on the 6th January 1867.

62258 **CORDELIA**
Schooner, 151 registered tons.
Owners: The Whitstable Shipping Company, 1886-1900.

52502 **CORNUCOPIA**
Built in 1865 at Findhorn, Elgin.
Barquentine altered to Schooner, 202 registered tons.
107.1 x 24.5 x 12.7. Signal Code H.C.T.J.
Owners: William Holden, Richard J. Wheeler, Thomas Cane, Mary Ann Wheeler, 29th October 1894.
Masters: Richard Wheeler, Horace Wheeler.
The newspapers of the period record that when she was moored in Whitstable Harbour, a paraffin oil lamp exploded in the cabin setting her on fire. Many willing hands under the direction of Captain Horace Wheeler performed deeds of heroism in getting the flames under control. The damage to the cabin, skylight, and deck, was estimated to cost £100.
This vessel was broken up in August 1909.

51149 **COURTNEY**
Built at Topsham, Devon.
Brig, 185 registered tons. Signal Code H.V.Q.W. Insured 20th October 1875 for £1,000.
Owners: Thomas Goldfinch, E. Nicholls.
Masters: Newing, R. Court.
A well-known collier.

63044 **COUNTESS**
Built at Newhaven in 1863.
Ketch, 40 registered tons. Signal Code P.Q.F.H.
Owner: Thomas Gann.
Master: Gough.
Registered at Whitstable on the 9th November 1863.

COUNTESS OF LIVERPOOL
Built in 1823 at Dover.
Cutter, 44 registered tons. 51.0 x 15.7 x 8.5.
Owner: Thomas Gann, 23rd September 1835.
Masters: Thomas Gann, 23rd September 1835. Ebenezer Cotton, 23rd June 1836. Sacar Hoult, 25th March 1840. T. Bedwell, 24th October 1840. W. Charosin, 14th October 1842. E. Goldfinch, 23rd October 1843. William Kemp, 3rd February 1844. E. Adams, 11th August 1845. W. Carr, 10th October 1846. H. Coleman, 17th March 1847. William Camburn, 4th October 1848.
She was lost in 1848.

71408 **CRAIGH ALVAH, formerly J.T.FRASER**
Built in 1874 at Prince Edward Island.
Brigantine, 210 registered tons. Signal Code P.C.S.Q.
Owners: The Whitstable Shipping Company.
Master: S. Baker
She was lost at the mouth of the Tees.

73388 **CUBA**
Built in 1875 at Dysart by Watt.
Barquentine, 271 registered tons. 120.3 x 25.7 x 12.8. Signal Code: P.B.L.N.
Owners: Anderson and Rigden.
Master: S. Baker.
This vessel was lost off the Humber.

Cornucopia, see previous page

70467 **CUMBERLAND LASSIE**
Built in 1874 at Amlwch by William Thomas.
Barquentine, 208 registered tons. 114.6 x 24.0 x 13.0. Signal Code M.W.Q.N.
Owner: G. Nicholls.
Masters: W. Hogg, D. Court, H. Tilley.

22067 **CYRUS**
Built in 1858 at Prince Edward Island of birch, juniper, spruce, red pine.
Brigantine, 149 registered tons. 92.2 x 22.0 x 11.4.
Owners: George Baker, 2nd February 1859. J. Baker.
Masters: H. Nicholls, J.A. Beal.
This vessel was bought at Plymouth after her maiden voyage, 21st January 1859. She was insured with the Whitstable Star Mutual Maritime Assurance Association for £775 on the 20th October 1875, by George Baker. On the 29th November 1875 she lost her anchor, and on the 8th February 1876 her owner was paid £5.13.5 in compensation.
Previously on the 4th December 1870 a strong wind drove her on the Spaniard Sand and all attempts to get her off failed and she was written off as a total loss. However with the spring tide she was refloated and brought back to Whitstable where she was repaired.
She was eventually sold as a hulk in June 1883.

53461 **DAGMAR**

Built in 1866 at Hartlepool by Blumer.
Brig, altered to a brigantine, 206 registered tons.
101.9 x 23.7 x 13.0. Signal Code T.V.B.G.
Owners: Henry Wooton Gann, Absolom Anderson, 16th May 1880. Henry L. Daly, Thomas Gann, A. Nicholls. The Whitstable Shipping Company.
Masters: Walter Wallace Gann, Ernest Gann, Carlton, Payne, Franklin.

On the 18th October 1889 she was insured for £640, and again on the 7th January 1890 she was insured for £700 at a value of £1,250.

She was altered to a jackass brigantine, that is having square sail yards on the main mast, in order that her master, Walter Gann, could qualify as a Pilot. After the death of Ernest Gann at the early age of twenty-five DAGMAR was converted into a normal brigantine.

She was lost when she stranded near Dieppe in January 1914.

11260 **DAPHNE**

Schooner, 195 registered tons. 103.0 x 25.0 x 10.0
Owner: Charles Fenn, 24th December 1873.
Master: Harris.

On the 30th April 1871 when bound from Whitstable to Hartlepool she was in collision with a brig eight miles off Whitby, whereby she sustained loss of bulwarks, rigging etc.
In March 1875 she was lost when off Robin Hoods Bay.

33940 **DARING**

Built in 1851 at Tatamagouchi, Nova Scotia.
Brigantine, 110 registered tons. 78.8 x 20.8 x 11.3.
Owners: Philip Newman, Stephen Rigden, William Gilbert, 13th December 1861.
Masters: Ashby, Keen, 1864. Alce, 1870.

This vessel was bought at Liverpool on the 10th June 1861, and she was insured with the Whitstable Star Mutual Maritime Association for £450. She was sold foreign on the 31st July 1874.

6066 **DAZZLER**

Built in 1850 at Ipswich.
Brigantine altered to Schooner, 162 registered tons.
101.0 x 21.6 x 12.8. Signal Code J.M.G.K.
Owner: William Waters, 19th October 1861.
Masters: Burton, A. Fryer, who was her master for 20 years.

This vessel was bought from London on the 19th October 1861. She was insured with the Whitstable Star Mutual Marine Assurance Association for £700. She was insured again on the 20th October 1875 for £800.
She was noted from the fact that she was steered by an exceptionally long tiller.
This vessel had an evil reputation because for a time she was engaged in the Slave Trade, but for the most part she traded to the Baltic, and the coasting trade.
She had the same fourteen man crew for twenty-five years, and every year Mrs Fryer knitted each man a seaman's jersey.
She was sold as a wreck at Grimsby on the 23rd August 1883, and turned into a Powder Hulk.

47883 **DEVONIA**

Built in 1865 at Ipswich, by Read.
Schooner, 162 registered tons. 98.1 x 24.0 x 12.3 Signal Code V.Q.L.D.
Owners: Anderson & Rigden.
Master: J. Phillips.

26353 **DIANA**

Built in 1853 at Prince Edward Island.
Brig, 177 registered tons. 106.6 x 24.5 x 12.8. Spruce and birch, felt and zinc.
Owners: W.C. Gibbons, G. Pilcher, J.S. Sharp, G. Butcher, 29th July 1861. Josiah Reeves, 25th November 1871. C. Gillan.
Master: W. Amos

This vessel was bought from Newcastle on the 26th July 1861.
She was altered to a brigantine in October 1869, and was sold foreign in March 1874.

62900 **DOLLY VARDEN**

Built in 1871 at Bideford by Cox.
Brig, altered to Brigantine. 200 registered tons.
115.9 x 23.4 x 12.1. Signal Code W.Q.V.K.
Classed as a three masted schooner in 1915, 185 registered tons.
Owners: William Allen, 1877. W.G. Lawson, 1890. Thomas Rigden, 1914. Anderson, 1916.
Masters: G. Gisby, Allen, C. Cooper, H.W. Beasley, 1909. J. Phillips, 1917.

Her first owner was J. Wyatt of Bideford who sold her to F. Perquer and Sons of Havre in 1873, and she was then renamed Sainte Rose. In 1877 she was bought by William Allen of Whitstable and her name was changed back to Dolly Varden, and she was then changed into a brigantine. In 1914 she was bought by Thomas Rigden of Whitstable, who in 1915 had her changed into a three-masted schooner.
Her final owner was Abie Anderson of Whitstable who bought her in 1916. On the 14th November 1917, having delivered a load of coal to Dieppe she was on her way back to Newcastle in ballast, and when 25 miles north west of Treport she was sunk by a German submarine. The crew were all saved.

5202 **DOLPHIN**

Built in 1853 at Tidries, Nova Scotia, by Reinold Chappele and John Read.
Brig, 154 registered tons. 90.0 x 23.4 x 11.5.
Owners: George Cox, James Goodwin, William Henry Randall, 18th September 1853.
Masters: Henry Randall, 21st September 1853. Joiner, 1870.
This vessel was bought from Charles F. Allison, of Sackville, New Brunswick, on the 16th September 1853 after her maiden voyage. She was written off as a total wreck in 1881.

DOUBTFUL

Built in 1835 at Middlesboro.
Square Rig, 204 registered tons. 81.7 x 22.2 x 13.2.
Owner: Thomas Fairbrass.
Masters: Abraham Fright, 8th May 1844. A.P. Gardner, 23rd May 1846. William Allen, 25th November 1849.
This vessel was lost on the 2nd December 1849.

5127 **DOVE**

Built in 1851 at Truro, Nova Scotia.
Brig, 183 registered tons, altered to Brigantine. 81.4 x 22.8 x 13.0.
Owners: George Holden, William Blackman, Thomas Gann jun.
Masters: Thomas Lott, 30th August 1854. Silk, 1864. Curling 1870.
This vessel was bought from Belfast on the 21st July 1854, she was then brought to Whitstable and altered to a brigantine. She was sold foreign in March 1876.

11857 **DRAPER**

Built in 1779 at Woodbridge, Suffolk.
Schooner, 94 registered tons. 83.5 x 19.1 x 9.1. Signal Code K.V.J.L.
Owners: James J. Goldfinch, Charles Fenn, 14th August 1875. E. Goldfinch, Fred Goldfinch.
Master: Foster.
This vessel was first insured by Charles Fenn, 15th September 1875 for £500 after he had bought her from Bailey of Ipswich on the 8th May 1875. She was sunk in Margate Harbour on the 30th January 1877 but was raised and repaired.
Her first voyage when in Whitstable ownership was on the 30th June 1875, and her last voyage was on the 11th November 1893 when she foundered in the North Sea on voyage No 210. An interesting mention in a newspaper of the period gives the following information.

There is now in West Hartlepool coal dock a right-little, tight-little-looking craft called the "DRAPER" whose registers date back exactly a century having started her career in 1779. Possibly she is something like the old woman's stocking, which got a new top one year and a new foot and ankle the other; and there may not be much of the original "DRAPER" left.

10113 **DRIVING MIST**
Built in 1854 at Sunderland.
Brigantine, 156 registerd tons. 98.8 x 23.5 x 11.9. Yellow metal. Signal Code K.M.D.F.
Owners: Edward Joiner, John Joiner, George Joiner, James Baker, 13th July 1877.
Masters: Edward Joiner, William Joiner, 1879-1886.
She was insured on the 18th October 1889 for £440.
This vessel was sold to Sunderland on the 4th November 1890.

98406 **DRUIDE**
Built in 1875 at Reden, in France.
Brigantine, 131 registered tons. 84.1 x 23.1 x 11.6. Signal Code M.B.S.R.
Owners: Collar Bros, Harry Collar, 22nd February 1894.
Master: James Elgar Goldsack.
This vessel was altered to a schooner in May 1894.

37747 **DUCHESS**
Built in 1855 at Picton, Prince Edward Island.
Brig, 211 registered tons. 113.2 x 24.5 x 13.0. Ash, birch, spruce, yellow pine.
Owner: Henry Richard Nicholls, 28th October 1864.
This vessel was bought from Hartlepool on the 26th October 1864 and was lost on the 2nd November 1867.

71445 **EAGLE**
Built in 1874 at Murray Harbour, Prince Edward Island, by D. Davies.
Barquentine, 226 registered tons. Altered to brig. 110.0 x 24.6 x 13.3. Signal Code J.T.D.L.
Owners: Alfred Pout, Joshua Caleb Pout, John Pout, James Pout, John James Coppleston Pout, 31st July 1894. Gann & Co.
Masters: L. Pout, J.C. Pout, Boughton.
A newspaper account, published just before Christmas 1899 informs us,

At present time Captain J.R. Daniels has on hand three collision cases for the Whitstable Star Mutual Maritime Insurance Association. The EAGLE belonging to Messrs. G. Gann was early in the present month run into and damaged by the Norwegian vessel "LIVIG". The owners of the latter disclaim liability, and steps are being taken to enforce payment. The Eagle had four planks cut and damaged by the Livig's chain, and the claim amounts to just under £50.

On the 1st October 1905 this vessel was anchored near the Mouse Light Vessel in the Thames Estuary, waiting for the tide to turn to enable her to enter Whitstable Harbour with her cargo of coal from Hartlepool. The wind was N.W. force 4, when suddenly without any warning she was run into by the steamship "TEMPO" of Newcastle, and in a very short time she went down, but the crew were all saved.

23201 **EAGLE (ex HOPPETT)**
Built in Finland.
Barque, 279 registered tons. 97.0 x 24.2 x 16.8.
Owners: George Holden, William Blackman, Thomas Gann jun.
Master: Henry Coleman, 10th September 1853.

4496 **EAGLE WING**
Built in 1845 at Bideford, Devon.
Schooner, 159 registered tons. 96.5 x 21.3 x 11.6. Yellow metal. Signal Code J.C.R.Q. Registered at Whitstable in 1862.
Owners: Charlotte Faith Woodcraft, George Henry Foreman, 29th May 1874. George Foreman, John Goldfinch, Benjamin Knell, Joseph Day, 22nd April 1867.
Master: A. Brett.
This vessel was bought from London on the 20th June 1862. Two very interesting letters have survived which tell the story of her end.
20th December 1886. Supt of Customs, Faversham, to Mr. F. Laggett, Whitstable.

Please call on John Goldfinch and get the particulars relative to the loss of the Eagle Wing of Faversham and let me know as early as possible.

J.T. Handley.
Registrar.

The reply is as follows.

The Eagle Wing on Dec 8th at about 8.0 A.M. in attempting to enter Ramsgate Harbour for shelter during a S.W. gale struck the East Pier and afterwards drove ashore on the East side of the pier and became a total wreck.

The Captain has the register which shall be forwarded tomorrow for cancellation. Crew all saved but Captain injured his knee.

F.L. & Co.

A newspaper account informs us that at the time Eagle Wing was bound from Sunderland to Portsmouth with a cargo of coal, and that the crew of seven were saved.

2532 **ECONOMY**
Brig, 144 registered tons. 74.2 x 21.0 x 12.8.
Owners: W. Kemp, George Holden, Dr J.E.M. Williams, O. Kemp, 11th January 1850.
Masters: Edward Jarrett, 11th January 1850. G. Taylor, 8th January 1853. John Flick.
This vessel was bought from foreign very early in 1850.
1859, John Flick, master of the Whitstable ship ECONOMY was charged at the St Augustines Petty Sessions with refusing to pay Robert Slater the balance of his wages amounting to £1.13.4. He was directed to pay.
ECONOMY was lost off the Scilly Isles on the 7th October 1869.

42893 **EDITH**
Built in 1861 at Cardigan, Prince Edward Island.
Brigantine, 142 registered tons. 90.5 x 23.0 x 11.3.
Owner: Thomas Gann sen., 24th October 1862.
This vessel was bought 22nd January 1862, and she was lost off Yarmouth by collision on the 20th February 1877.

20555 **EDITH**
Built in 1858 at Prince Edward Island, by Ball.
Brigantine, 166 registered tons. 92.6 x 21.5 x 12.8. Felt and zinc.
Owners: W. Rowden, George Goldfinch, 24th June 1865. Insured for £600.
Masters: Gibbons, G. Camburn.
This vessel was bought from Falmouth on the 22nd June 1865. She was sold away to be broken up on the 29th July 1879.

27837 **EDWARD FAIRBRASS (ex SARAH)**
Built in 1839 at Stettin, Prussia.
Brig, 246 registered tons. 95.4 x 25.5 x 15.0.
Owner: Edward Fairbrass, 19th April 1860.
This vessel was sold to Rochdale on the 28th July 1862, but in 1875 she returned to local ownership, was pulled up on the slipway of W. Fairbrass, was cut in halves and a new section was built into her. Then on the 16th January 1875 she was launched by Master T. Cannon and renamed GRATITUDE.

10992 **EFFORT**
Built in 1858 at Rye.
Schooner, 166 registered tons. 91.6 x 23.1 x 12.9.
Owners: Edward Adams sen., Edwin Adams, Edward Adams jun., George Bennett, 12th February 1856.
Master: Edward Adams, 1860
Originally she was altered to a brigantine on the 18th March 1863. She was lost off Guernsey on the 1st January 1869.

9785 **ELEANOR (ex GORGO EPICTOR)**
Brig, 237 registered tons. 89.2 x 26.8 x 14.0.
Owners: Thomas Fairbrass, Thomas William Fairbrass, 28th November 1855.
This vessel was lost in the Swin, Thames Estuary.

28715 **ELEANOR**
Built in 1860 at Yarmouth by Beeching.
Brig, altered to Brigantine, 176 registered tons. Yellow metal.
Owner: Josiah Reeves.
Masters: Adams, Sayer, 1871.
On the 10th May 1871 news was received that she was driven ashore by the ice near St Petersburg.

969 **ELIZA**

Built in 1850 at Three Rivers, Prince Edward Island.
Brigantine, 165 registered tons. 92.6 x 21.6 x 12.7.
Owners: John Lawson, Edward Kemp, Thomas Edward Gaskin, 21st May 1859.
Masters: Gann, C. Gaskin.
This vessel was bought from Liverpool on the 16th May 1859. She was lost near the Girdler Light-ship on the 6th December 1865.

37162 **ELIZA B.**

Built in 1861 at St Martins, New Brunswick.
Brig, 178 registered tons. 101.7 x 25.2 x 11.1.
Owners: J.T. Reeves, George Butcher, William Charles Gibbons, George Pilcher, John Stephen Sharp, 4th July 1862.
Master: H. Goldfinch.
This vessel was bought on the 3rd July 1861.
On the 27th April 1879 she was four miles off Southwold, bound for the Tyne in ballast from Folkestone. The wind was N.N.E. force 5, when she was run into by the steamship "James Hog" of Middlesborough, and became a total wreck. The crew of seven were all saved.

47865 **ELIZA BLAXLAND**

Built in 1863 at Rye.
Schooner, 174 registered tons. 98.0 x 23.7 x 12.4. Signal Code V.Q.J.W.
Owners: Alfred Nicholls, George Blaxland sen., William Thomas Blaxland, 7th December 1863.
Masters: Cotton, H. Browning, Henry Nicholls.
This vessel was originally a brigantine. On the 18th October 1889 she was insured for £600. In April 1910 she was converted into a hulk, was sold by auction, and moored in the Thames, where she served as a small-pox hospital.

ELIZABETH

Built in 1839 at East River, Prince Edward Island.
Schooner, 149 registered tons. 78.2 x 19.1 x 12.3.
Owners: William Amos, who sold the "Elizabeth" to Hiram London, on the 15th April 1847.
Masters: Hiram T. London, 22nd December 1846. George Barnes, 22nd November 1850.
This vessel was sold to London in February 1853.

6824 **ELIZABETH**
Built in 1839 at Aberdeen.
Brig, 148 registered tons. 81.5 x 21.4 x 12.7.
Owner: Richard Blaxland, 12th May 1866.
This vessel was bought from Aberdeen on the 10th May 1866, and she was lost off Flamborough Head on the 30th September 1866.

811 **ELIZABETH**
Built in 1851 at Peterhead.
Schooner, 84 registered tons. Signal Code H.F.L.B.
Owner: Alfred James Anderson, 22nd May 1889.
On the 11th April 1890 she was insured for £280 at a valuation of £350. On the 3rd October 1891, when near Gravesend, off the Lobster, she was in collision with the steam-ship "Historian". The case was tried in the Queen's Bench Division on the 12th May 1892, and resulted in a verdict in favour of the pilot, Mr Hookham. The jury finding was that the ELIZABETH was guilty of negligence in going about where she did.

ACCOUNT for the damages for the collision between Elizabeth and Historian.

Damage, towage and expenses	*£98.17.1*
Pilot and solicitors expenses	*125.18.0*
Water men	*10.14.0*
Lowless & Co.	*131. 4.3*
Owners expenses at trial	*6.10.0*
	373. 3.4
Survey by Mr Charles Hoult	*3. 0.0*

ELIZABETH
Built in 1853 at Rye by Hoad Bros.
Brig, 148 registered tons. 84.0 x 19.7 x 12.6.
Owners: Joshua Downs, William Charosin, John Jutson.
Master: William Charosin, 18th November 1853.
This vessel was bought when new, and she was wrecked at Mogadon on the 7th January 1856.

23951 **ELIZABETH**
Built in 1854 at Wheatley Prince Edward Island.
Brig, 189 registered tons. 104.0 x 22.9 x 13.2.
Owner: William Wraight, 26th February 1862.
This vessel was bought from Liverpool on the 12th February 1862, and she was sold to Rochester on the 2nd May 1867.

10997 **ELIZABETH**
Built in 1856 at Garmouth.
Brig, altered to Brigantine, 172 registered tons. 100.0 x 22.2 x 12.5.
Signal Code K.Q.T.C.
Owners: Alfred Nicholls, George Blaxland, John Cooper, Thomas Terry, John Jutson, 4th March 1867.
Masters: J. Cooper, Woodcock.
This vessel was bought new, then on the 10th December 1867, when bound from Seaham to Portsmouth with coal, she stranded on Saltsear Rocks, Redcar, Yorkshire, and became a total loss. The wind at the time was N.N.W. force 5, and the crew of seven were all saved.

44563 **ELIZABETH**
Built in 1863 at Montrose.
Schooner, 91 registered tons.
Owner: R. Secker.
Master: W. Secker.
This vessel was registered at Whitstable on the 15th October 1866, and she was insured with the Whitstable Star Mutual Maritime Insurance Association for £440.

ELIZABETH & SARAH
Built in 1791 at Sandwich.
Brig, 118 registered tons. 71.0 x 20.4 x 11.0.
Owner: James Malborough.
Master: Henry Potter, 31st December 1825.
This vessel was a collier with a crew of six.

ELIZABETH ANN
Master: Jacobs.
We have to rely on a brief newspaper report for information regarding this vessel. She was a well-known collier. On the 22nd November 1882, in a N.N.E. gale she was compelled to moor in the Bay to await her turn to come into the Harbour, when she dragged her anchor and was driven on shore.

21888 **ELIZA GANN**
Built in 1858 at Morell, Prince Edward Island, by Cox.
Brigantine, 172 registered tons. 103.1 x 23.0 x 11.5.
Owners: James Gann, Thomas James Gann, William John Gann, 19th July 1859.
Master: A. Mann, 1860.
This vessel was wrecked on the Barrow Sands on the 20th February 1865.

7082 **ELLEN**
Built in 1849 at Rye.
Brig, 169 registered tons. 82.2 x 22.7 x 13.6.
Owners: Stephen Richards, William Bronger, Edward Thomas Jarrett, 20th July 1863.
This vessel was bought from London on the 9th July 1863, and it was lost off Shields on the 25th January 1868.

54853 **ELLEN**
Built in 1866 at South Hylton, Durham.
Snow, altered to Brigantine, 191 registered tons. 95.5 x 24.9 x 13.7.
Owners: Holden & Gann, Thomas Gann jun., Henry Pout, George Holden, William John Bronger, 13th February 1871.
Master: James Baker.
This vessel was altered to a brigantine in April 1875.
On the 28th October 1880 ELLEN was off the coast of Yorkshire being bound for Newcastle in ballast from Ramsgate, when she stranded at Clowton, and became a total loss. Five of the crew were saved, but one lost his life.

28453 **ELLEN JANE**
Built in 1860 at Sandwich by Hoad.
Schooner, 140 registered tons. 90.5 x 21.9 x 12.3.
Owners: James Acors, Charles Jutson, Joshua Downs, 14th January 1861.
Masters: F. Acors, James Acors, 1861. Pool.
On the 7th March 1878 this vessel was off the Northumberland coast bound for Grangemouth with a cargo of scrap iron from London when she was caught in a gale, force 10, and she stranded outside the Fairway Islands and became a total loss. The crew of five were all saved.

67044 **ELLEN SMEED**
Built in 1872 at Sittingbourne, Kent.
Schooner, 134 registered tons.
Owner: C.W. Marshall.
Master: A. Austin.
Although Mr Marshall was a Faversham man the ELLEN SMEED operated from Whitstable and her crew were all Whitstable men.

19469 **EMERALD**

Built in 1857 at Sunderland.
Snow, altered to Brigantine, 184 registered tons. 92.2 x 23.7 x 13.5.
Yellow metal.
Owners: J. Reeves, John Collar, 14th August 1863.
Masters: Ernest Hoult, 1870. J. Strong, 1860. A. Smith.

On the 19th November 1879 EMERALD was at the entrance to the River Tyne, with a cargo of chalk from Gravesend, when she was run into by the steam-ship "Blue Cross" of Newcastle, and sunk near the South Pilot Buoy. Three of the crew of seven lost their lives. The Captain, Ernest Hoult, was only 22 years old.

1879
THE CANTERBURY PRESS & COUNTY NEWS
WHITSTABLE SUPPLEMENT
Saturday, November 29th

The Late Collision between The BLUE CROSS and EMERALD.
Inquest on the Captain's body

An inquest was held at the Police Station, Tynemouth, before the Deputy Coroner, (Mr. R.Y. Green), on the body of Captain Ernest Hoult, of the Schooner EMERALD of Whitstable, belonging to Messrs Josiah Reeves and Co., which was sunk off the Tyne on Wednesday evening, the 19th inst., owing to a collision with the screw steamer Blue Cross.

Mr W.M. Roche, solicitor to the British Ship-Masters Protection Society, watched the enquiry on behalf of Capt Scarth and the owners of the Blue Cross. Mr Daniels of Whitstable, appeared for the underwriters and the friends of the deceased. There were also present Mr Supt., Anderson, Mr Weisencraft, Messrs T. & W. Smith, (North Shields) and other gentlemen. The enquiry lasted upwards of three and a half hours.

During the earlier portion of the enquiry, Mr Roche suggested that he should be allowed to examine the witnesses and put several questions.

Mr Daniels objected, and said everybody belonging to the schooner lived in the south, and the fact of the inquest being held that day was only made known on Friday. As the steamer's party were represented by a solicitor, he (Mr Daniels) thought the owners of the schooner would like to have someone.

Mr Roche: if this gentleman is going to make a speech–

The Coroner: I will take care that everyone is represented fairly. It was not an Admiralty Court, but they had met simply to hold a preliminary enquiry, and point out the cause of the man's death.

The first witness called was Fred W. Wilson, first mate of the schooner Emerald, who identified the body as that of the Captain, Ernest Hoult, aged 22 years. About half-past seven on Wednesday night, they were coming into the Tyne. The Emerald had about 150 tons of chalk on board. All lights were up, and it was high water, the wind being east. James Heselton, an able seaman, was at the wheel. He, witness was forward, and he never saw the steamer until it was a ship's length from them.

By Mr Roche: He meant their own ship's light. When he saw the steamer he had its port light open. The steamer struck the vessel on the starboard bow about one hundred yards on the north-east side of the south Pier. She sank about fifty yards from the buoy at the south Pier, going down instantly. There were seven hands on board – the Captain, mate, two able seamen, two ordinary seamen, and a boy. The last he saw of the Captain, was when he was walking the deck a minute or two before the occurrence. The steamer put out two boats. The weather was sometimes a drizzling rain, but at the time of the accident it was pretty clear, and they could see lights a long way. The name of the steamer was the Blue Cross. He saw the steamer's masthead light also. He – witness – was busy at the time, and that prevented him from seeing the vessel. The quarter deck was about two feet higher than the main deck, and the captain was on the look out. There was no other man forward on the look-out. He scrambled up the steamer's side by a line flung to him.

By a juror: When he saw the steamer, he thought it was going at the rate of about five knots. The captain sang out to him at the same time, "look out here comes a steamboat." Could not say what the captain did at the time. If the captain had either fronted or starboarded his helm, it would not have avoided the collision, the time being too short. Could not give any idea as to what course the vessel's head pointed, as he had not been forward to look at the charts, but they had the leading lights a little open to the southward. That was the proper course to steer by in coming into the harbour. He believed the Blue Cross struck them about the cat-head, and went into the centre of the vessel. Then they rebounded away from it, and it hit them again, a little further aft. The foreyard of the schooner fell, he – witness, was hanging on to the steamer. The yards were square at the time. Could not say whether the yard hit the captain in its fall, for he did not know where the captain was. Did not hear anyone cry out. Could not see the lights plainly on the shore before the accident. He – witness – and the captain generally kept the look-out from the quarterdeck. The vessel was going from three to four knots.

By another Juryman: It was not a usual thing to keep a look-out from the quarter-deck on vessels. The fore-sail was set. Could not say whether the captain was killed by a blow or drowned.

Jno, Willoughby, living at Lower Lights, North Shields, said he was a striker, and found the body on Friday morning in Swaddle's Hole. The body was in the water. It was afterwards conveyed to the dead house in the Haven.

John Newman, a Swede, A.B. of the Emerald said he was forward in the vessel in the Emerald. Saw a steamer coming about one ship's length off. Shouted out that a steamer was coming in to us. A square foresail, lower topsail, upper topsail, and top-gallant sails set. The distance between the foot of the foresail to the deck was a good height. There was a red light on board the steamer. Reckoned she was coming about six knots, and they were going about three or four. The captain was abaft, but when the steamer struck he ran forward. The captain was on the starboard side.

By a juryman: The captain could see very well forward. He had been in the vessel two years. The captain told him he could swim very well. The lights were all right.

By the Foreman: The captain had time to get down the stairs after the accident. It was customary for him to carry his money in his pocket, and he had a watch and chain.

James Paysden, ordinary seaman of the schooner Emerald, was forward on Wednesday night, and he had just got the port anchor in, and was hooking the tackle, when he saw the steamboat about a ships length off. Saw a red light on board the steamer, which was coming at about six knots an hour, they were going at about three or four. He was on the starboard side of the vessel. I jumped on the steamer, when she struck the second time. Did not know how long it was between the first and second blows.

By a Juryman: I did not see the harbour leading lights as I was busy.

James Scarth, Captain of the Blue Cross, said his vessel left Tyne Dock, at about 6.45 p.m., and the pilot left abreast of the Fish Quay about 7.15 p.m. They were going about half speed, or five or six knots, and they had a look-out forward. Two steamers passed the Blue Cross exactly abreast of the gearing and the South Pier end. I saw the schooner Emerald following the steamers, saw a red light on board the Emerald. When he first saw her she was about three-quarters of a mile or a mile off. Could not alter his course on account of the two steamers on the port side. The collision occurred close outside of the buoy and the pier end. We struck the schooner once. We did not blow any signals. It was very clear at the time.

He was keeping his course as close as it was possible for them to keep. The course was in accordance with the bye-laws of the harbour. Ordered hard-a-port as soon as he was abreast of the buoy. He was in the highbridge of the steamer. Saw no other light on board of the schooner but the red light. Did not see the green light until the mate reported it, which he did immediately after I had ported the helm to get clear of her. The mate was in the forecastle. He ordered the engineer to, "Stop and full astern". These orders were attended to. I saw none of the crew of the steamer. He ordered two boats out.

By a Juryman: The first steamer passed him, abreast of the gearing of the South Pier. He saw the sailing vessel at the time, but did not anticipate a collision. His vessel's full speed was about 9½ knots. He considered 5 or 6 a safe speed to go on with. He thought there was no tide at the time.

By the Coroner: If they went at less speed than five or six knots they would not be able to steer properly, and he increased the speed that she might steer better. We had a crew of 21 all told. Had been in charge of the Blue Cross four years, and had gone in and out the Tyne 3½ years.

The minute he gave the order to the engineer, that minute the mate spoke. It was owing to the Emerald changing her course that I saw the green light.

By a Juryman: The boats were out in two or three mintues, and they were about 60 yards off the vessel.

James Martin, Chief Mate of the Blue Cross said he was on the forecastle head on Wednesday night and he just saw the schooner's red light, when they were drawing towards the woodwork of the South Pier. Shortly afterwards saw the green light, and had gone perhaps half a mile. Reported the green light to the captain.

By the Coroner: Had you any fear of a collision? Witness, (after considerable consideration) He could see the ships could not very well get clear of each other. At the time they were about 440 feet off the South Pier. The buoy was perhaps half the length of the vessel on the starboard side.

By a Juryman: When he saw the green light, they were perhaps a length and a half of their vessel from the schooner. (Their steamer was 220 feet long). The helm was hard aport. It was so both before and after the green light.

By aother Juryman: The schooner was following in the wake of the two steamers. Charles McKenzie, second Mate of the Blue Cross, said he was at the wheel, and when towards the work of the South Pier the rudder was about at steady. Proceeding on a straight course. As soon as the Captain saw the red light of the schooner he gave orders to port, and immediately afterwards, hard-a-port. Saw red light of the schooner on the port bow. They would be about five or six hundred yards off. When she struck the helm was hard-a-port.

By Juryman: Before we passed the Pier and buoys our helm was hard-a-port. Saw no other light on board the schooner after the Mate sung out. Saw the green light.

Thomas Skyles, chief engineer of the Blue Cross, went down the river at rather better than half-speed. The telegraph stood at full speed behind but he had not sufficient steam. The engine was stopped as he was reversing it just at the moment of collision.

Edward Foster, captain of the steam-tug Wizard, said they were alongside the Emerald on Wednesday night when they were sailing in for the harbour lights. They were outside the buoy. Saw the collision. It occurred about 100 to 150 yards to the north side of the buoy. It was a little to the east of the buoy. The Blue Cross was coming down the north side of the schooner and the lights were blue and green. The Blue Cross changed her course after that. The Emerald never changed her course and he never changed his course but kept alongside. As soon as he saw they were going to collide he got out of the way. If the Blue Cross had stuck to her original course she would have got clear.

By a Juryman: The Blue Cross came to the Emerald.

By the Coroner: The Blue Cross in his judgement was too much to the north side, so far as the bye-laws were concerned. The Emerald was coming in at the south side because the Blue Cross was showing the green light, and so was the Emerald. He had the lights fair on.

The Coroner: If she was coming in on the south side she was clearly wrong according to Rule 17.

Witness: She was outside the buoy.

By a Juryman: The Blue Cross could never be near the Pier.

The Coroner briefly summed up, the Jury after a few minutes deliberation, returned a verdict to the effect that the deceased lost his life in a collision on Wednesday, 19th inst., but whether he was drowned or killed by a blow they were not agreed. The body of the unfortunate captain – who was only twenty-two years old – was brought to Whitstable on Monday night, via the London, Chatham, and Dover Railway, and interred in the Cemetery on Wednesday. A procession of a number of Captains, companions, and relations followed the remains. The service was conducted by the Rev. F.H. Smith, Wesleyan.

A youth of about 16, son of Mr Edwin Coleman also perished. His body has not been picked up. This was his first voyage.

1976 **EMILY**

Built in 1850 at South Shields.
Barquentine, altered to Brigantine, 214 registered tons.
112.0 x 23.6 x 14.0. Signal Code H.M.F.R. Felt and yellow metal.
Owners: George Butcher, 30th January 1861. George Butcher, George Barnes, George Pilcher, Frances Bundock, 22nd April 1872. Frederick William Fairbrass, 25th September 1884. Josiah Reeves.
Master: H. Lawson.

This vessel was bought from Liverpool on the 26th January 1861. By the 26th February 1861 she had been altered to a brigantine. Soon after coming to Whitstable she had the misfortune to sit on her anchor, but at low tide she was patched up and was got in nearer to the shore. Here her troubles were not over for she came to rest partly on a bank of hard clay. Consequently when the tide further receded she went over on to her side. However she was got up on to the slipway and repaired. She then continued to give her owners satisfactory service until on the 23rd January 1903 when she was involved in a collision with the 132 ton ketch, "Lord Dufferin" of London. This incident took place fifteen miles S.E. of Flamborough Head, the EMILY being bound for Newcastle with burnt ore from Queenborough. She quickly sank, and two of the crew of seven were drowned.

EMILY
Brigantine, 380 registered tons.
Owner: F.W. Fairbrass.
Master: Baker.
This vessel was bought by Mr Fairbrass when she was a nameless hulk, pulled up on his slipway, practically rebuilt and given a name. She was manned by Whitstable men.

36245 **EMILY STEWART (ex GRAF ADOF)**
Built in 1855 in Holland.
Schooner, 113 registered tons. Signal Code R.V.B.H.
Owners: Hilton, Anderson & Co, The Whitstable Shipping Company.
Masters: Fredericks, G. Smeed.
This vessel was insured with the Whitstable Star Mutual Maritime Assurance Association for £700.

11258 **EMMA**
Built in 1852 at Rye by Hassell Bros.
Schooner, 145 registered tons. 93.2 x 21.7 x 12.7. Signal Code K.R.V.L.
Owners: Alfred Nicholls, George Barnes, Edward Baker, 3rd November 1857. George Blaxland, Osborne Nicholls.
Masters: Osborne Nicholls, George Barnes, 3rd January 1853.
This vessel came into Whitstable ownership the year after she was built. On the 18th October 1889 she was insured for £480.
On the 9th March 1891 Captain Osborne Nicholls reported to the owners that she been towed into Scarborough Harbour making water. Her foremast, jibboom, main top-mast, and every sail that had been attached were all gone. The Scarborough Harbour Authorities were paid £75.2.0. for the towage. On the 5th May 1891 the Insurance Association paid £264.7.11 as a final claim for the damage sustained. On the 29th October 1897 she was dismasted and sold as a hulk.

17848 **EMMA**
Built in 1857 at Conway, Carnarvon.
Schooner, 68 registered tons. 68.7 x 18.7 x 7.9.
Owners: Alfred James Anderson, 16th April 1889. James Rogers.
Masters: H. Lawson, G. Kean.
This vessel was engaged in the glass bottle trade from Sunderland. In October 1903 she was converted into a lighter.

70555 **EMMA ERNEST**

Built in 1876 at Hakin, Milford, by Jones.
Brig, altertеd to a Brigantine altered to Schooner. 198 registered tons.
109.2 x 23.7 x 12.5. Signal Code P.N.V.F.
Owners: Abie Anderson, 20th February 1900. Anderson & Co.
Masters: H. Lawson, F. Wilson, Clarke.

This vessel was finally altered to a schooner in October 1919. She was the last of the Whitstable vessels to be a collier, and she brought the last cargo into the Harbour in 1923. Another claim to fame is that she was the last vessel to have her cargo "jumped" out. In February 1934 she was converted into a hulk and sold.

Although her subsequent history does not concern Whitstable it is of interest to know that she was reconditioned and moored in the Thames near to Charing Cross Bridge, where having been renamed "Friendship" she served as a club house. Later she was renamed the "Seven Seas" by another club. During the second World War a bomb fell near to her and blew her over to the other side of the river. In 1946 vandals proceeded to break her up, but her original name-plate was acquired by Captain Long John Silver of Gravesend.

88706 **EMPRESS**
Built in 1885 at Connah's Quay, Flintshire.
Schooner, 131 registered tons. 94.5 x 23.2 x 10.4. Signal Code K.G.L.M.
Owners: The Whitstable Shipping Company, 12th February 1886.
On the 7th August 1910 she was leaving the Thames bound for Llanelly with a cargo of scrap-iron from London, when she was half a mile north of No. 1 Fairway Buoy Sea-reach she was run into by the steam-ship "Marina" of London, and she quickly sank, three of her crew being saved and one lost.

107761 **EMPRESS**
Built in 1901 at Montague, Prince Edward Island, by George Wightman.
Schooner, 360 registered tons. 118.0 x 30.8 x 12.6.
Owners: C. Anderson, George Henry Goldfinch.
Master: Goldfinch.
This vessel was owned here about 1912 and in 1915 she was badly damaged by fire.

19032 **ENERGY**
Built in 1854 at Sandwich.
Brigantine, 171 registered tons. 93.4 x 22.7 x 12.7. Signal Code M.Q.G.S.
Owners: J. Lawson, Edward Kemp, Amanda Mary Ann Gaskin, Thomas Edward Gaskin.
Masters: Fisher, R. Gaskin.
This vessel was bought from Ramsgate on the 17th June 1862, and insured with the Whitstable Star Mutual Maritime Association for £800. She was run down in Barking Reach in March 1877.

ENDEAVOUR
Built in 1790 at Strood.
Sloop, 116 registered tons. 61.3 x 22.0 x 8.7.
Owners: J. Randall, Hoult, John Headdy.
Masters: J. Bing, Robert Laraman, 23rd September 1825.
This vessel traded between London and the west country ports.
She was broken up in 1834.

ENDEAVOUR
Built in 1815 at Southtown, Yarmouth.
Brig, 115 registered tons. 67.9 x 19.11 x 11.2.
Owners: William Blackman, James Randall, Thomas Barnes, William Knight, Henry Hunt.
Masters: Thomas Barnes, 25th August 1826. James Randall, 8th January 1827. William Rose, 29th June 1828. George Smither, 27th September 1827. Henry Frank, 26th September 1828. James Randall, 12th November 1838.
This vessel was wrecked off Shields 28th February 1844.

50457 **ENIGMA**
Built in 1865 at Burnham.
Schooner, 29 registered tons. 54.8 x 14.9 x 7.9
Owners: Frederick Kemp, bought on the 16th October 1876.
Master: W.G. Joiner, 1893.
This vessel was chiefly employed in the potato trade from Barfleur and other channel ports to London and Newhaven.
She was sunk in Whitstable Bay in April 1898.

Estafette

2704 **EQUIVALENT**

Built in 1847 at Whitstable by James Daniels.

Schooner, 187 registered tons. 84.4 x 23.2 x 10.5. Signal Code H.Q.G.F.

Owners: Henry Holden sen., Edwin Adams, James E.M. Williams, John Broadbridge, Henry Holden jun., James Robert Daniels, 12th January 1858.

Masters: Edwin Adams, 7th September 1847. W. Court, E.A. Court, 1870.

This vessel was insured with the Whitstable Star Mutual Maritime Assurance Association for £800. She was noted for the bust of a female as her figurehead. On the 28th October 1882 she was off the coast of Suffolk bound for Rye with a cargo of coal from Sunderland, the wind was W.S.W. force 1, when by an error of judgement she stranded on the Newcombe Sand and became a total loss. The crew of five were all saved.

28460 **EROS**

Built in 1861 at Hillsborough, Prince Edward Island.
Brigantine, later altered to a Schooner, 189 registered tons.
Owners: George Holden, Thomas Gann jun., William Blackman jun., 21st September 1861. George Holden, Thomas Gann jun., 9th August 1871.
Master: J.H. Taylor.
On the 10th July 1880 this vessel was seven miles N.E. of the North Foreland being bound for Ramsgate with coal from Newcastle. The wind was W.S.W. force 3. As she tacked to get into a position to enter Ramsgate Harbour she was run into by the Dutch steam-ship "Whymoder" and she quickly sank. The crew of eight were all saved.

80516 **ESTAFETTE**

Built in Italy.
Brigantine, 276 registered tons. 127.2 x 25.9 x 14.1. Signal Code K.R.V.Q.
Owners: Frederick William Fairbrass, 18th March 1881. The Whitstable Shipping Company, 1st December 1892.
Masters: G. Adams, R. Care, C. Cooper.
ESTAFETTE was considered to be one of the most beautiful vessels ever owned here. She was employed to bring to Whitstable the stone used in the construction of the platforms of the present railway station. Finally she was sold to London on the 14th March 1916.

42907 **ETHEL**

Built in 1862 at Summerside, Prince Edward Island, by James C. Pope.
Brigantine, 138 registered tons. 93.5 x 21.8 x 11.1
Owners: Thomas Gann jun., J.R. Daniels, Thomas Gann, Herbert Stroud, 16th October 1862.
Masters: E. Kemp, J. Kemp, Earle, 1878.
This vessel was bought after her maiden voyage on the 14th August 1862. On the 8th February 1889 she was making her way up channel bound for South Shields in ballast from Newhaven, the wind being N.N.W. force 8. When off Deal she ran on the Goodwin Sands, and was a total loss. The crew of six were all saved.
A letter has survived written on the 20th February 1889, from the Whitstable Shipping Company to Mr. J. Stammers, The Custom House, Whitstable.

Dear Sir,

The "Ethel" having been wrecked on the Goodwin Sands recently, we desire you to cancel the Registry of the said vessel.

We settled wages of the crew immediately after the wreck so that they could at once get about their work again.

The Certificate of Registry was lost with her.

Yours truly,
M. Daniels.

11285 **EUGENIE**
Built in Swiremunde, Prussia.
Schooner, 100 registered tons. 98.9 x 21.5 x 10.6.
Owners: Matthew Browning sen., Matthew Browning jun., George Richards, 8th September 1855.
This vessel was lost in the Boston Deeps on the 3rd January 1859.

11327 **EUREKA (ex ALEXANDRA)**
Built in Borgo Finland.
Schooner, 191 registered tons. 100.6 x 25.3 x 11.3. Signal Code K.S.F.C.
Owners: Frederick William Fairbrass, William Cannon, 18th June 1857. The Whitstable Shipping Company, 1887.
Masters: Gray, H. Sandy, Bushell, 1870.
This vessel was bought in 1856, drawn up on the slipway, thoroughly re-conditioned and launched again on the 26th May 1857.
She was known as a soft wood vessel.
On the 8th October 1898 she left Ramsgate Harbour in ballast for Sunderland stranding off Broadstairs she was a total wreck. The crew of seven were all saved.

58530 **EUROPA**
Built in Sittingbourne 1871.
Ketch, 98 registered tons. Signal Code K.G.N.L.
Masters: Sweetman 1891. Austin.

EUROPE
Built in 1804 at Sunderland.
Barque, 217 registered tons. 88.9 x 20.7 x 14.0.
Owners: William Blackman, Thomas Fairbrass.
Masters: John Scrimgour, 2nd February 1844. William Charosin, 15th August 1845. John Belsey, 25th June 1847. James Mayhow, 11th February 1846. James Camburn, 13th November 1850. Pout.
This vessel was a well known collier, and she was lost in December 1850.

573 **EVA**
Built in 1853 at Rustico, Prince Edward Island.
Schooner, 134 registered tons. 85.6 x 21.9 x 12.1.
Owners: George Butcher, Thomas Ougham, Nathaniel Smeed Ougham, Ozias Ougham, 4th August 1857.
This vessel a well-known collier was lost on the 12th February 1869, her master was then Captain Walker.

11262 **EXCELSIOR**
A Russian prize ship. (ex BOG MOJA MODESCHDA)
Schooner, 116 registered tons. 71.9 x 19.6 x 12.1.
Owners: Frederick William Fairbrass, 16th February 1855.
F.W. Fairbrass, William Cannon, 4th December 1858.
Masters: William Maxted, 16th February 1855. Chilson, Skinner, Earl, 1864. Hodges, 1873.
This vessel was re-registered here on the 17th January 1871.

EXCHANGE
Built in 1821 at Sunderland.
Brig, 161 registered tons. 73.3 x 21.2 x 13.3.
Owners: James Reeves, Thomas Reeves, bought from North Shields, 10th April 1848.
Master: Thomas Hoult, 5th May 1848.
This vessel was lost 1848.

EXPERIMENT
Built in 1825 at Wapping, Middlesex.
Schooner, 136 registered tons. 82.0 x 19.4 x 10.6.
Owners: William Blackman, who sold her to Thomas Fairbrass, 6th February 1835.
This vessel was lost on the 9th January 1838.

46873 **EXPERT**
Built in 1864 at Pisquid, Prince Edward Island by John MacDonald.
Brigantine, 160 registered tons. 92.0 x 22.9 x 12.3. Signal Code V.L.G.S.
Owners: G.H. Gann, John Collar, 13th December 1864. Josiah Reeves, 1876.
Masters: Reeves, A. Parsons.
On the 4th September 1884, when bound from Shields, the wind being E.N.E. she ran on the Swin Middle Sand and was lost. The crew of six were all saved.

22997 **FAIRY**
Built in 1854 at Rustico, Prince Edward Island.
Brigantine, 162 registered tons. 88.9 x 21.8 x 12.3.
Owners: Robert Frend, Henry Larkin, Edward West, 26th May 1862.
This vessel was bought from Newport on the 23rd May 1862, and she was lost in November 1863.

13735 **FAITH**
Built in 1856 at Rye.
Brig, 168 registerd tons. 93.5 x 23.4 x 12.3. Yellow metal.
Owners: W.H. Hoult, N.S. Ougham, C.C. Jutson, C. Humphrey, C. Waters, W. Andrews, J.F. Jutson, 9th June 1865.
Master: J. Pettman.
This vessel was bought from London on the 8th June 1865, and was insured with the Whitstable Star Mutual Maritime Assurance Association for £870. She was lost off the Welsh coast in the Bristol Channel in June 1871. Joseph Pettman, her master, was drowned.

58879 **FAITHLIE**
Built in 1868 at Fraserburgh by Webster.
Schooner, 226 registered tons. Originally a Barquentine.
116.0 x 24.6 x 13.5. Signal Code H.N.F.V.
Owners: George H. Gann, Henry Gann, 3rd October 1885. The Whitstable Shipping Company.
Masters: W.H. Willson, Setterfield.
This vessel was altered back to a barquentine in January 1913. On the 29th March 1916 she stranded on the Margate Sand and was written off as a total loss, but she was got off and sold away.

28601 **FANNY**
Built in 1859 at Prince Edward Island by Joseph Wightman.
Brigantine, 151 registered tons. 104.0 x 22.6 x 11.1.
Owners: W. Charosin, William Harry Randall, Ann Goldfinch, 17th October 1864.
Master: Eastland.
This vessel was bought from Limerick on the 13th October 1864. She was insured with the Whitstable Star Mutual Maritime Assurance Association for £785. She was sold foreign in May 1884.

41738 **FANNY FORESTER**
Built in 1858 at Trout River, Prince Edward Island.
Brigantine, 113 registered tons. 81.0 x 21.5 x 10.6. Black birch, maple, spruce and pine.
Owner: Henry Cornelius, 8th October 1858.
Master: Cornelius.
This vessel was bought on 12th July 1858, and was condemned to be broken up on the 11th December 1876.

FANNY GANN
Built in 1850 at Whitstable by Thomas Gann.
Schooner, 97 registered tons. 77.0 x 18.7 x 11.1.
Owner: Thomas Gann sen.
Masters: William John Priest, 13th January 1851. George Griffiths Page, 27th April 1855.

A catastrophe from which she survived is best described in the words of the newspaper which reported the event.

COLLISION AT SEA

On the morning of the 15th instant, the schooner "Fanny Gann", the property of Mr Gann, ship-builder, Whitstable, and which had sailed from this port the day before, bound to St Michael's, was run into off Folkestone, by a Breman brig, with such force that her masts fell instantaneously overboard, carrying with them, we are sorry to add, a young lad named Greenland, who was up aloft reefing at the time, and was drowned. The Captain and crew jumped on board the brig, and the "Fanny Gann" was towed into Ramsgate Harbour in the disabled state here described. We understand that the parents of the unfortunate lad have offered a reward of £2 for the discovery of the body.

There is much of interest that could be written of the subsequent events, but the newspapers of the day have left it to our imagination.
The FANNY GANN was lost between St Michaels and the Azores on the 9th January 1861.

44098 **FLASH (ex THOR)**
Built in 1855 at Oscarshamm, Sweden.
Schooner, 123 registered tons. 92.4 x 22.8 x 10.1.
Owners: William Blackman, George Holden, Thomas Gann jun., 10th July 1862.
Master: Porter.
In August 1873 she was sold to Penzance.

45238 **FLIRT**
Built in 1862 at Rye.
Schooner, 151 registered tons. 91.6 x 23.6 x 11.5. Signal Code V.C.L.S.
Owners: J.R. Daniels, W. Blackman, George Holden, Thomas Gann jun., 26th October 1862.
Masters: G. Mills, G. Shilson, Chadwick.
On the 18th October 1889 she was insured for £300.
On the 23rd November 1898 she was off Barton, Bradstock, near Bridport, Dorset, bound for Topsham, Exeter, with a cargo of copper ore from London when she was caught in a S.S.W. gale, force 10. In a desperate attempt to save themselves the master, Captain Chadwick, the mate Mark Rigden, and the Apprentice, jumped overboard. An able seaman, named Neat followed their example, but he was the only one to reach the shore, the other three were drowned. Two other members of the crew, named Sharp and Knight, who could not swim, remained on board and were saved.
This vessel was noted for her tiller steering.

59757 **FLIRT**

Built in 1869 at St Peters Bay, Prince Edward Island, by J.A. Maclain.
Brigantine, 187 registered tons. 104.3 x 24.1 x 12.7. Signal Code L.W.B.H.
Owners: G.B. Joiner, J.G. Joiner, J. Joiner, W.G. Joiner, E. Joiner, W.F. Joiner, 17th February 1894.
Masters: Pout, John Joiner, 1907.
On the 18th October 1889 she was insured for £620.
The writer's uncle, Charles Albert Harvey, born on the 28th October 1878 was a member of the crew of this vessel. On the 9th April 1898 he complained about the bad food, and in consequence he was tied to the mast and flogged. Early the next morning his father found him in the garden shed dead. It was often said that in those days it was not unusual that you had to tap the weevils out of the sea biscuits before you could eat them.
On Monday 16th August 1909 this vessel was condemned and taken on to what was known locally as the Grass Bank. Then in October 1909 she was registered as a hulk. Then in that same month she was sold to Brock's Fireworks Company. However on the 29th October 1909 she was driven ashore and it is not known if Brock's had any further interest in her.

42960 **FLORA**
Built in 1862 at Egmont Bay, Prince Edward Island, by Angus MacMillan.
Brig, altered to Brigantine, 196 registered tons. 100.0 x 23.7 x 12.8. Signal Code T.L.V.W.
Owners: H.W. Nicholls, 21st March 1865, with J. Reeves 1883. James Henry Taylor, Josiah Reeves, William Buddle London, William Carlton, Alfred Woolcock, Henry Barden, 27th March 1884.
Masters: G. Gaskin, H. Barden.
This vessel was bought from Liverpool on the 18th March 1865. She was insured with the Whitstable Star Mutual Maritime Assurance Association for £1,000. On the 7th December 1885 she was bound for Weymouth with coal and iron from Hartlepool, but owing to an E.N.E. wind force 6, she could not make the harbour, and ran ashore at Ringsted near Weymouth, where she became a total loss. The crew of eight were all saved.

76/20
39130 **FLORA**
Built in 1856 at Pinnette, Prince Edward Island.
Brig, 179 registered tons. 96.0 x 23.3 x 12.5.
Owners: Carlton, Henry Larkin, Nathaniel Smeed Ougham, Joseph Pettman, Charles Humphrey, 21st June 1861.
Masters: Humphrey, Hammond.
This vessel was bought from Liverpool on the 19th June 1861.
She was lost off the Sunk Light-ship on the 4th May 1869.

53344 **FLORENCE**
Built in 1866 at Sunderland.
Brigantine, 196 registered tons. Signal Code J.F.N.B.
Owners: Henry Holden, Henry L. Daly.
Master: W. Williams.

52894 **FLYING SCUD**
Built in 1865 at Rye.
Schooner, 186 registered tons. 101.5 x 24.1 x 12.5.
Owner: William Bragg Allen, 29th August 1865.
Master: Allen.
In October 1867 this vessel was altered to a brigantine.
On the 13th August 1876, when off St Albans Head, she was run down by the "Voorlichte" and lost.

56628 **FRANK EMMETT**
Built in 1867 at Brixham.
Brigantine, 129 registered tons. Signal Code H.P.R.G.
Owners: The Whitstable Shipping Company.
Masters: Humphrey, and R. Skinner, 1901.
In a great storm on 12th November 1901 she was lost with all hands on the Cockett Sands.

23672 **FREDERICK**

Ketch, 78 registered tons. 67.7 x 14.9 x 7.9.
Owner: George Butcher.
Master: Edwin Griffiths, 19th March 1855.
This vessel was stranded on the North Sand off Whitstable on the 25th November 1854. She was then known as the "Friso" described as a Dutch galliot, her Master being Deok Hindrich Duintyer. However, she was bought by George Butcher, got off the Sand, drawn up on the slipway and thoroughly repaired. Under her new name she traded from this port until she was wrecked off Folkestone on the 21st September 1857.

FRIENDS

Brig.

The Kentish Gazette. Tuesday January 13th 1795.

Run away from the brig. "Friends" of Whitstable, Henry Hunt, master, on the 16th September last, Owen Hughes, mariner, about sixteen years old, five feet three inches high, dark complexion, and dark hair. Had on a blue Jacket and breeches. Whoever harbours him or employs him, after this notice, will be prosecuted as the law directs.

FRIENDS

Sloop.
Master: Thomas Ely, the elder. 1819.

FRIENDS

Built in 1829 at Sunderland.
Schooner, 40 registered tons. 55.2 x 13.5 x 6.5.
Owners: William Woodward, Robert Young.
Master: William Woodward.
This vessel was bought from North Shields on the 15th January 1849. An interesting document dated 8th March 1850 describes her end.

I Robert Young of the Parish of Whitstable in the said County of Kent do solemnly and sincerely declare, That the schooner FRIENDS of the burden of forty tons or thereabouts belonging to the Port of Faversham whereof William Woodward and Robert Young were owners and the said William Woodward was master, was totally lost near Bridlington Bay on the seventh day of October 1849, and that the Register and Licence was lost in her at the same time.

And I make this solemn Declaration, conscientiously believing the same to be true, and by virtue of the Provisions of an Act made and passed in the 5th and 6th year of the Reign of His late Majesty King William the 4th intituled "An Act to repeal an Act of the present Sessions of Parliament intituled "An Act for the more effectual Abolition of Oaths and Affirmations taken and made in various Departments of the State, and to substitute Declarations in lieu thereof, and for the more entire Suppression of voluntary and extra-judicial Oaths and

Affidavits; and to make other provisions for the Abolition of unnecessary Oaths.
Robert Young

Taken and received before me, one of Her Majesty's Justices of the Peace for the said County of Kent at Whitstable in the said County, this eight day of March 1850.
W. Hyder

124361 **FYN**
Built at Thuro, Svendborg, Denmark.
Schooner, 194 registered tons. 111.0 x 25.9 x 11.7.
Owners: Abbie Anderson, Stanley Anderson, Thomas Rigden, 29th November 1912.
Masters: E.A. Court, E. Court.
This vessel was sold to Portugal, in April 1914.

36411 **GANNYMEDE**
Built in 1859 at Hillsborough, Prince Edward Island, by Longworth.
Brigantine, 149 registered tons. 97.0 x 21.5 x 12.0
Owners: Thomas Knowles, John Cooper, John Edenden, Edward Edenden, 29th December 1859.
Master: John Cooper, 1860.
This vessel was bought on the 2nd August 1859.
From the Kentish Express of 1869 we learn the following information.

The owners of the Gannymede, Messrs Blaxland & Co, of Whitstable, have received intelligence from the captain of that vessel, which was on her passage from Jersey to Runcorn, loaded with china clay, that whilst proceeding up the Mersey in charge of a pilot, the vessel ran ashore on Crosby Sand, near Waterloo and sank, but that she now dries.

The Underwriters, The Whitstable Star Mutual Maritime Assurance Association, have sent Mr John Collar from Whitstable to superintend efforts for her removal, and if the weather holds fine there is every probability of her coming off.

She was insured in the above Club for £750.

However, the optimism regarding her salvage was not justified and it is recorded in the Register that she was written off as Lost at Liverpool on the 13th November 1869.

26565 **GEM**
Built in 1857 at Bideford, Dorset.
Schooner, 161 registered tons. 83.7 x 22.4 x 13.8.
Owners: George Pitcher, James Amos, G.W. Bell, Thomas Bundock, 21st August 1858.
Master: G.W. Bell.
This vessel was bought from Falmouth on the 17th August 1858.
She was lost 1st December 1862.

GEORGE
Built in 1804 at Wells, Norfolk.
Square, 112 registered tons. 75.6 x 18.1 x 10.7.
Owners: William Amos, Hiram Tilbe London, Thomas Richards, Henry William Madams, George Castle, George Wate, 31st December 1846.

GEORGE ANSON
Built in 1830 at Yarmouth.
Schooner, 168 registered tons. 97.7 x 21.4 x 13.5.
Owners: William Cannon, Frederick William Fairbrass, 11th October 1858.
Master: Frend.
This vessel was bought from Yarmouth on the 9th October 1858.

67274 **GERALDINE**
Built in 1873 at Salcombe by Vivian.
Barquentine, 244 registered tons. Signal Code M.N.C.T.
Owner: F. Friend.
Masters: F. Friend, W.A. Wood.

60644 **GILPIN**
Built in 1869 at Bideford, Prince Edward Island.
Brig in 1885, altered to Brigantine. 108.4 x 25.5 x 12.4. Signal Code K.J.L.G.
Owners: G.H. Gann, H. Gann, G.H. Goldfinch, J. Pout, Alfred Pout, John Thomas Reeves, George Henry Pout, 16th September 1882.
Masters: Carden, Pout.
This vessel was altered to a brigantine in October 1889. She was insured on the 18th October 1889. On the 10th June 1912 when she was bound for Newcastle from London with a cargo of burnt ore when she stranded on the Velvet Red Rocks off the coast of Durham and became a total loss. The crew of eight were all saved.

58378 **GIRL OF THE PERIOD**
Built in 1870 at Hayle, Cornwall, by W. Harvey.
Brigantine, 226 registered tons. 117.8 x 24.9 x 13.8. Signal Code J.P.Q.S.
Owners: G. Holden, W.J. Brongar, T. Gann, Henry Pout, Fairbrass, 19th October 1881.
Masters: S. Goldfinch, G.S. Nicholls, J. Hubbard, J. Pout, 1881. Fred Maxted.
This vessel was unique in having an iron frame, the rest being of wood. She was noted for her full-length figure-head, and was insured for £600. She was sold to Manchester on the 15th August 1917.

Gilpin

Girl of the Period

21769 **GLENMORE**

Built in 1858 at Garmouth, Moray.
Barquentine, 254 registered tons. 105.8 x 24.6 x 14.2. Built of fir, larch, and red pine. Felt and yellow metal.
Owners: G. Lawson, William John Lawson, 30th December 1873.
Master: T. Stone.

On the 29th September 1880, when she was nine miles off Excro Island, bound for London with a cargo of timber from Ormskirk, in a S.W. by W. gale force 6, she stranded, and became a total loss. Her crew of eight were all saved.

53258 **GOLDEN SHEAF**

Built in 1866 at Aberdeen.
Brig, 225 registered tons. 113.1 x 24.3 x 14.0. Signal Code H.M.L.P.
Owners: C. Hoult, A. Hoult, 16th May 1881. Thomas Goldfinch, E. Nicholls.
Masters: Hoult, T. Rigden, C. Wellard.

On the 24th June 1875 this vessel was insured for £950.
She was altered to a brigantine in November 1884.
On the 28th November 1885 she was driven by a S.W. gale, force 8, on to the Swan Shoal off Dunkirk, being bound for Dunkirk from Beckton in Essex with a cargo of pitch and became a total loss. The crew of eight and one passenger were saved.

49965 **GOWRIE**

Built in 1865 at Perth.
Schooner, 83 registered tons.
Owner: John Camburn.
Master: Thomas Camburn.

This vessel was bought in 1871 for £400.
An interesting account which has survived shows that the GOWRIE did not make a fortune for her owners.

1871 July 8th. Rec'd from Ship,	*£2.16.0.*	*March 1st paid for 1/40 part,*	*£11.18.0*		
1872 Mar 25th	*„ „ „*	*2. 0.0.*			
Jun 17th	*„ „ „*	*1.12.0.*			
1873 Sep	*„ „ „*	*2. 8.0.*	*Mar 10 Pd on Acc for repairs*	*3.4.0*	
Nov	*„ „ „*	*2. 0.0.*	*Apr 12th „ „ „ „ „*	*4.0.0*	
1874					
1875 Jul 9th	*„ „ „*	*2. 0.0.*			
1877 Mar 1st received from sale		*17. 0.0.*			
Total receivings		*32.12.0*			

This vessel was condemned in 1875.

67094 **GRATITUDE**
Built in 1875 at Whitstable by Dyason.
Barquentine, 298 registered tons. 128 x 29 x 18. Signal Code N.Q.J.S.
Owners: W. Fairbrass, The Whitstable Shipping Company.
Masters: Gardner, G. Goodwin, S. Flick.
Originally known as the "Edward Fairbrass", she was drawn up on the slipway, cut in halves, an entirely new section was built into her, she was given the fore lower rigging and bell of the "Northfleet", launched and renamed the GRATITUDE in 1875, by Master T. Cannon on Saturday 1st January.
On Wednesday 30th November 1910 she was moored near the Mouse Light-ship. At 2 a.m. she was run down by the s.s "Lord Stewart", and foundered. Six of her crew of eight were drowned and two, who were brothers, were saved.

8454 **GREEK SLAVE**
Brig, 126 registered tons. 71.6 x 23.5 x 13.3. Signal Code K.C.G.P.
Owners: John Stephen Sharp, George Pilcher, William Charles Gibbens, Frances Bundock, 14th January 1862.
This vessel was bought from London on the 9th January 1862.
She was then named the "Arieta".
She was sold to Southgate on the 6th February 1863.

12719 **GREENWICH**

Built in 1850 at Rye.

Brigantine, 214 registered tons. 97.6 x 24.5 x 13.6. Signal Code L.C.W.T. Yellow metal and felt.

Owners: F. Bundock, John Foat Cozens, Thomas Foat Cozens, John Brown Dyason, 14th March 1867. George Albert Cox, William White Foreman, 7th August 1901.

Masters: Hall, J. Dyason, A. Dadd.

This vessel was bought from London on the 13th March 1867.

She was insured by George Cox on the 14th October 1875 for £400.

She had the strange habit of suddenly leaking badly, when it was all hands to the pump. Then she would go for a long time without leaking at all. In a gale, on the 29th November 1897 she stranded on the Gunfleet Sand and was given up as lost. After a time her hulk floated off and she was towed into Lowestoft. Repaired and re-fitted, she continued in the coal trade, until the 17th March 1907. At that time she was twenty-two miles N.E. of Flamborough Head bound from Newcastle to Exeter with a cargo of coal, pig iron, and lead, when she foundered in a W.S.W. gale, force 9. The crew of seven were all saved.

59779 **GUIDE**

Built in 1870 at Bideford, Lot 12, Prince Edward Island, by Ellis.
Brig, 180 registered tons. 101.0 x 24.8 x 12.5. Signal Code K.T.S.J.
Owners: Matthew Browning, 22nd March 1871. David Waters 1883.
William Harnett, J. Milner, 1916.
Masters: Groombridge, A. Dadd, J. Gaffry.

This vessel was bought after her first voyage.

During the time that Arthur Dadd was her master he had the reputation of never running her at a loss.

On the 24th March 1903 she was a quarter of a mile N.W. of the Burness Light at Haddington, bound from London to Barrowstromness with a cargo of scrap iron. In a S.W. wind, force 4, she stranded and soon began to break up. The crew of seven were all saved.

11259 **HANNAH**

Built in 1841 at Whitstable by William Blackman.
Schooner, 113 registered tons. 77.9 x 20.9 x 11.1. Signal Code K.R.V.M.
Owners: William Blackman, 31st July 1841. William Blackman jun., Thomas Gann jun., James Randall, 6th January 1859. F.W. Gann, George Herbert Gann, 1884.
Masters: James Randall, 31st July 1841. Henry Clothier, 10th January 1850. George Richards, 5th November 1850. Joseph Day, 5th August 1853. J. Adams, Shelson.

This vessel was built especially for the Mediterranean trade, for which her pass was issued on the 31st July 1841. When owned by the Gann family she regularly made fourteen voyages to the north each year. On the 4th July 1884 she was off Souter Point, Durham, bound for Blyth in ballast from Whitstable and was in collision with the s.s. "Kepier" of Sunderland, and was a total loss. A letter which has survived gives the following information.

G. Herbert Gann, shipowner, The Elms, Whitstable, July 24th 1884, to Mr J. Handley, Custom House, Faversham.

Dear Sir,
In reply to yours of the 21st inst., addressed to Mr Frank W. Gann, The register and all documents belonging to the Hannah were lost with the ship in collision on July 4th between Souter and Sunderland.
Yours truely,
J. Herbert Gann.
The crew of five with one passenger from Folkestone were all saved.

5296 **HAPPY FAMILY**

Built in 1837 at Sunderland.
Brig, 209 registered tons. 82.0 x 22.0 x 14.1.
Owners: Henry Madams, John Graves, George Hayward, George Butcher, John Spencely, 21st November 1849. George Foreman.
Masters: George Foreman, David Charosin, 21st November 1849. William Randall, 23rd January 1854. William Allen, 15th February 1854. Richard Gaskin.

This vessel was bought from Southend on the 19th November 1849. She was broken up at Lowestoft on the 16th February 1865.

1981 **HARRY CLEM**

Built in 1854 at Cape Cansa, Nova Scotia.
Brigantine, 154 registered tons. 99.0 x 23.3 x 11.7. Felt and doubled, birch and spruce. Yellow metal.
Owners: W. Gann, W. Kemp, 30th August 1862. George Herbert Gann.
Masters: Wellard, Dawkins, 1870.

This vessel was bought from Liverpool on the 21st July 1862.
On the 28th October 1880 she was off South Shields bound for Seaham from Whitstable in ballast, when she foundered in an E.S.E. gale force 10. Two of the crew of six lost their lives.

HAVALOCK (ex SARAH LYON)

Brigantine, 154 registered tons. 95.4 x 22.8 x 11.4.
Owners: T. Gann jun., T. Gann sen., J. Gann, 19th June 1858.
Master: Hoult.
This vessel was an Admiralty prize, and she was bought on the 2nd June 1858. She was lost off Southwold on the 15th January 1869.

25684 HAWK

Built in 1853 in Finland.
Brig, 172 registered tons. 92.4 x 24.4 x 12.3.
Owners: William Blackman, Thomas Gann jun., George Holden.
Masters: Rowden, William Henry Sharp, 23rd November 1854. Thomas Clark, 1873 and 1878.
This vessel was a Russian prize named "Dido". She was bought on the 11th October 1854, and she was changed to a brigantine in October 1860. She was broken up in July 1880.

23765 HELEN

Built in 1839 at Stettin, Prussia.
Brig, 200 registered tons. 83.0 x 21.4 x 13.6.
Owner: Thomas Fairbrass.
Masters: William Allen, 29th July 1850. Edward Vincer, 4th August 1851. John Jones, 11th December 1851, Hiram Tilbe London, 16th April 1852. James Jarrett Warner, 6th August 1852.
This vessel was originally the "Leonidas" of St Petersburgh.
She was wrecked on the 21st August 1856, near Walton-on-Naze.

The Crew of the Herbert c1894

39207 **HELEN**

Built in 1857 at Prince Edward Island, by James C. Pope.
Brig, altered to Brigantine, 194 registered tons. 104.0 x 22.4 x 12.9.
Owners: George Baker, 16th November 1863. Thomas Carr Camburn, 6th May 1873. Henry Baker.
Masters: Harris, Henry Barden.

This vessel was altered to a brigantine on the 27th July 1866, and she was insured with the Whitstable Star Mutual Maritime Assurance Association for £800.

On the 6th March 1881 she was bound for Newcastle in ballast from Northfleet when she stranded on the Menie Sands, near Newburgh, County Aberdeen, and was wrecked. The wind was S.E. force 10. The crew of seven were all saved.

2954 **HELENA**

Built in 1847 at Bras D'or, Cape Breton, Nova Scotia.
Brig, 154 registered tons. 78.5 x 21.5 x 12.7.
Owners: George Holden, George Butcher, Henry Clothier.
Master: Henry Clothier, 6th December 1850.

This vessel was bought on the 19th November 1850, and she was sold to Rochester in January 1861.

66288 **HENRY**

Built in 1872 at Summerside, Prince Edward Island, by Angus MacMillan.
Brigantine, 173.13 registered tons. 106.9 x 24.7 x 12.8. Signal Code M.W.G.S.
Owner: George B. Joiner, 10th February 1894.
Masters: G.E. Joiner, Holsen, Arthur Cornhill, 1909.

On the 5th March 1909, she was twelve miles N.W. by N. of the Newarp Light Vessel off the Norfolk coast, bound for Whitstable with coal from Seaham, when she was run into by the s.s. "G. Player" of Teignmouth, and sunk. The crew of seven were all saved.

5211 **HENRY**

Built in 1825 at Gainsborough.
Snow, 105 registered tons.
Owners: Camburn & Lawson. Sold to Samuel Hills of Seasalter, 30th April 1852.
Masters: Stone, Samuel Hills, 30th April 1852. Joseph Beal, 3rd May 1855.

This vessel was altered to a Schooner in September 1856. On the 20th November 1861 she was lost on the Shivering Sands, two of the crew being drowned. In April 1862 the hull was recovered, drawn up on the Slipway and repaired. She was eventually lost on the Redcar Rocks on the 17th February 1863.

89851 HEINRICH

Built in 1868 in Germany.
Schooner, 95 registered tons. Signal Code: J.N.M.Q.
Owner: W.J. Murton.

She was insured with the Whitstable Star Mutual Maritime Assurance Association at a value of £300, on the 6th February 1890 for £200.

16th October 1890, she was re-insured for		£200.
20th „	„ „ „ „ „	£280.
23rd „	„ „ „ „ „	£300.
26th „	1891 Loss of anchor „	£ 5.13.0.
5th Sept	„ „ „	£ 9.11.0.
14th October re-insured		£300.
16th January 1892 Loss of anchor		£ 8.7.1.
11th October „	„ „	£ 6.18.1.

A curious record!

89861 HERBERT

Built in Norway.
Barquentine, 272 registered tons. 128.0 x 28.3 x 12.2.
Signal Code L.B.V.P.
Owners: The Whitstable Shipping Company 9th March 1889.
Master: C. Cooper.

This vessel was originally named "Granen".

She was involved in a collision near Dover, and was bought by The Whitstable Shipping Company as a wreck, in 1889. For some years she was employed in the coal trade in winter, and in transporting ice from Norway in the summer. In the early days of the film industry she was employed to make a pirate film. In January 1908 she was sold to Mr Thomas Rigden and used in his diving enterprises. In 1913 she was bought by the Whitstable Hoy and Trading Company, broken up and her timbers used to contstruct their loading wharf. This wharf was demolished in August 1956.

6316 **HERO**

Built in 1854 at Rye by Hassell & Holmes.
Brig, 195 registered tons. 95.4 x 20.7 x 13.3.
Owners: William Croft, James Rigden, Richard Saffary, 31st August 1858.
Masters: William Ranson, 1st July 1854. J. Harvey, 1860.
She foundered after a collision off Caen on the 9th March 1872. An excellent model of her has been lent to the Science Museum by Mr S.E. Appleton, (Inv, 1932-447). This shows her clipper bow and figure-head, at that time unusual in small coasters.

42165 **HERO**

Built in 1860, at Seal River, Prince Edward Island.
Brigantine, 186 registered tons. 105.0 x 24.2 x 12.4.
Owners: Thomas Gann, John Gann, 15th May 1862. Thomas Gann, Thomas Gann jun., John Gann, Frances Ann Gann, James Hoult, Thomas James Gann, William Amos, Edward Sandy, Henry Bartlett, 15th June 1872.
Masters: Goodwin, Foster, Kean 1870.
This vessel was bought from Liverpool on the 7th May 1861.
She was run down and lost off Folkestone on the 22nd February 1876.

81405 **HILDA**

Built in 1879 at Appledore, Devon, by Pickard.
Barquentine, 223 registered tons. 116.5 x 24.9 x 12.9. Signal Code S.R.P.Q.
Owners: The Whitstable Shipping Company. T.R. Dadd, E. Foreman, T. Dadd sen., William White Foreman, W. Foreman, D. Horlock, F.C. Ashby, W.E. Sampson, 15th February 1898.
Masters: T.S. Sweetman, J. Sinclair, Thundow.
This vessel was sunk in collision off Nova Scotia, on the 9th December 1930.

77667 **HILDRED**

Built in 1878 at Mount Stewart, Charlotte Town, Prince Edward Island, by Peake.
Brigantine, 243 registered tons. 115.2 x 26.6 x 12.9. Signal Code W.J.C.K.
Owners: Bronger, George Holden, Thomas Gann, 18th April 1882. The Whitstable Shipping Company 6th May 1905. She was insured for £600 on the 18th October 1889.
Masters: H.G. Clothier, Thomas Allen 1885, Merritt, H. Wilson 1911.
When employed as a collier her loading capacity was, Main Hatch 110 tons, Galley Hatch 110 tons, Fore hatch 75 tons, After hatch 75 tons. This vessel stranded at Troon and was a total loss in July 1916.

Hilda

Hildred

Hilda, see previous page

4867 **HOPE**

Built in 1842 at Salcoates, Kingston-on-Hull.
Schooner, 54 registered tons. 57.8 x 17.3 x 8.1.
Owners: John Holman, Edwin Griffiths, 30th October 1858.
Masters: Whidditt 1864. Fullager.

This vessel was bought from London on the 28th October 1858, and she was wrecked off Burnham, Norfolk, in March 1872.

8451 **HUMILITY**

Built in 1839 at Portmadoc.
Schooner, 85 registered tons. 62.6 x 20.8 x 10.3. Signal Code K.C.G.L.
Owners: G. Daniels, 1869-1870. James Robert Daniels, 6th January 1871.
Masters: Hoult, R. Gowing.

This vessel was built especially for the slate trade. She was insured for £350. The end of this schooner came about in a curious manner. In 1868, loaded with slates she was waiting her turn to enter Whitstable Harbour, when the changing tide from east to west caused her to roll. The slates in her hold were stacked on edge, and as she rolled the layers of the slates were made to open out and allow the upper layers to fall in between, thus creating an ever increasing pressure. This pressure caused her seams to open and she sank. Fortunately she was in shallow water and between the 5th and 12th May 1868 the "Sydney" was able to salvage her cargo. It was then found possible to float her into a spot near the Battery at Seasalter known as the "Lily Banks". In the hope of making her seaworthy again she was purchased by Mr G. Daniels and later by Mr James Daniels, but their hopes were never realised and she became a feature of the landscape, which inspired Daniel Sherrin, the famous artist to paint a picture of her.

26348 **HUNTLEY**
Built in 1860 at Rye.
Brigantine, 171 registered tons. 87.8 x 23.4 x 19.1.
Owners: F.W. Fairbrass, E. Fairbrass, T.W. Fairbrass, 11th April 1860.
Masters: Harvey, W. Gray, Woolley.
This vessel was altered to a brigantine on the 9th July 1860. On the 28th October 1880 she was bound for the Tyne with a cargo of chalk from Gravesend. When near the entrance to the river Weir she was struck by an E.N.E. gale, force 10, and sank. The crew of six were all saved.

49789 **HUNTLEYS**
Built in 1865 at Pallion, Sunderland, by J. Robinson.
Brig, Snow, Brigantine, 185 registered tons. 92.4 x 24.1 x 13.4. Signal Code W.F.L.G.
Owners: George H. Gann, H. Gann, 6th October 1885.
Masters: Melson, C. Allen, Howlett.
This vessel was sunk by a German submarine on the 25th March 1917.

IANTHE
Built in 1831 at Trinity Bay, Newfoundland.
Square, 117 registered tons. 69.0 x 19.4 x 11.3.
Owners: Stephen Rigden, Ebenezer Cotton, 13th April 1840.
This vessel was mainly used in the coal trade and was broken up 22nd June 1844.

41797 **IANTHE**
Built in 1856 at Pugwash, Nova Scotia.
Brigantine, 173 registered tons. 93.3 x 23.4 x 12.0.
Owners: T. Blakely, T. Rigden, W.C. Tilley, 9th October 1861. W.J. Lawson, W. Turner, 1876.
Masters: G. Sayer, W.L. Tilley.
This vessel was bought form Liverpool on the 5th October 1861. She was altered to brigantine on the 30th October 1869, and was insured for £800. On the 28th October 1880 when bound for Shields in ballast from London, the wind being E.N.E. force 10, she ran ashore at Boulby, Yorkshire, where she became a total loss. Of the crew of seven one was lost.

80512 **IBEX**

Built in 1879 at Whitstable.
Ketch, 52 registered tons. 77.1 x 17.6 x 5.2.
Owners: Henry Gann, George Herbert Gann, 18th October 1879.
Master: G. Goodwin.

On the 14th February 1880 she was bound from Seaham to Whitstable with a cargo of coal. When about six miles south of Flamborough Head Light she was run into by the steam-ship "Kenley" of London, and she rapidly sank. The wind at the time was S. by W., force 3, and two of the crew of four were drowned.

73934 **IBIS**

Built in 1875 at Murray Harbour, Prince Edward Island by Daniel Davies.
Brigantine altered to Barquentine in November 1911. 217 registered tons. 110.2 x 24.4 x 12.9. Signal Code P.L.R.N.
Owners: T. Gann, W.J. Bronger, 9th December 1880. George Holden and Gann
Masters: R. Groombridge, F. Baker, Knight, E. Adams.

On the 18th October 1889 she was insured for £450. On the 29th March 1919 she was pulled up on the slipway at Harvey's Yard at Littlehampton and dubbed. She was broken up in April 1927.

Ibis, see previous page

47869 **IDA**

Built in 1864 at Rye.
Schooner, 179 registered tons. 101.1 x 23.5 x 12.7.
Owners: George Holden, Thomas Gann jun., Charles Brannen, 29th June 1864.
This vessel was lost near Cape Orlando, Sicily, on the 10th February 1870.

81989 **IDA**

Built in 1881 at Ipswich by W. Bayley & Sons.
Ketch, 128 registered tons. Signal Code V.J.S.F.
Owners: Henry Pearson Coleman, George Baker.
Master: Court.
On the 3rd April 1890 she was insured for £400 at a value of £1250. On the 18th October 1890 it was reported that the IDA belonging to Mr George Baker of Whitstable was on shore near Calais, and that she was broken and part of her cargo was washed out. On the 22nd October 1890 it was reported that when about four miles from Calais the captain had mistaken the lights, that the vessel's sides were level with the sand, that she was much up on her port side, and the tide flowed in and out of her. She was considered to be a constructive loss.
However it was decided to send a vessel and crew with an anchor and steel hawser to try to get her off, after the cargo was got out of her. This operation was successfully accomplished on the 29th October 1890, and she was then put in dry dock at Calais. After examination it was reported on the 1st November 1890 that she was "making water all over", and had sustained very considerable damage. As Mr Baker very much wished to have her brought home two shipwrights and two men were sent in an effort to make her light enough to be towed home, and Messrs Watkins were engaged to make the attempt for £20.
On the 9th December 1890 it was decided to allow the claim for assistance amounting to £179.18.0. On the 5th May 1891 the final bills amounting to £950.14.2 were passed less £39.0.3.
On the 5th January 1892 it was reported that the IDA had carried away her mast-head, foreyard, and gaff.
The claim for assistance was £10, and for towage into Margate £40. 3rd May 1892, the claim settled for £56.4.5.

19009 **IMPETUOUS**

Built in 1854 at Rye by Hoad.
Snow in 1855, Brig in 1860, Brigantine 1864, 163 registered tons. 89.1 x 20.3 x 13.2.
Owners: Thomas Wood Minter, William White Foreman.
Master: T.W. Minter.
Registered at Whitstable. Insured for £920. Sold to Guernsey.

INDUSTRIOUS

Built in 1799 at Swansea.
Brig, 111 registered tons. 62.3 x 17.6 x 11.6.
Owners: William Edwards, James E.M. Williams, Philpott Wood, John Deane.
Masters: William Watts, 30th March 1840. Thomas Richards, 31st May 1842. William Thomas Blaxland, 28th October 1844. Abraham Fright, 12th May 1846. Edwin Adams, 5th September 1846. George Hoult, 1847.
For some reason this vessel had a remarkable succession of well-known captains. On the 6th January 1848 she was lost at the entrance of the river Tay.

INDUSTRY

Built in 1816 at Horne, Yorkshire.
Sloop, 52 registered tons. 55.11 x 14.1 x 6.8.
Owner: William Tassel.
Masters: Isaac Terry, 31st January 1823. James Greenland, 17th February 1826. John Greenland, 29th August 1826.
This vessel was lost on April 14th 1837.

5221 INDUSTRY

Built in 1840 at St Peters, Prince Edward Island.
Brigantine, 165 registered tons. 79.7 x 19.8 x 12.7.
Owners: George Holden, William Blackman, Thomas Gann jun., 3rd October 1857.
Masters: Henry Coleman, 10th July 1852. Thomas Lott, 7th September 1853. Henry Cornelius, 22nd July 1854.
For some unexplained reason the owners were not registered until they had owned the vessel for five years, but she was certainly bought at Cork on the 2nd July 1852. She was lost near Whitburn on the 16th November 1865.

INO

Built in 1835 at Sunderland.
Schooner, 140 registered tons. 69.1 x 20.4 x 12.9.
Owners: Thomas Gann jun., George Cox, Baker, William Robertson, William Kemp.
Master: William Robertson, 21st June 1849.
This vessel was bought from New Shoreham on the 8th June 1849. She was wrecked on the Island of Scheermonick, Friesland, on the 9th February 1850.

45058 INTERNATIONAL

Built in 1862 at Prince Edward Island.
Brigantine, 192 registered tons. Signal Code V.B.G.S.
Owner: William Goldfinch.
Master: W. Court.
This vessel was lost off Guernsey on the 23rd January 1908.

47863 **INVICTA**
Built in 1863 at Murston.
Ketch, 93 registered tons. Signal Code V.Q.J.S.
Owners: Thomas Rigden, Frend, Baker.
Masters: Coleman, C. Allen, Bains, 1901.
On the 29th November 1897 she was off Lowestoft laden with coal when a gale caused her to lose both her anchors and she was driven on to the Newcome Sand. Then when the gale abated she was towed off and taken into Lowestoft Harbour. After a year had passed arrangements were made to have her brought back to Whitstable, and in 1899 she was drawn up on Collar's slipway where she was fitted with new bulwarks and was considerably strengthened aft. She was launched again on the 11th July 1899. She sank off Scarborough on the 12th November 1901.

52892 **INVICTA**
Built in 1865 at Rye.
Schooner, 178 registered tons. 98.8 x 23.7 x 12.8. Signal Code H.S.Q.R. Registered at Whitstable 6th June 1865.
Owners: Edward Adams, Edward Adams jun., Walter Adams, John Lawson, George Kennett Baker, 7th June 1865. Edward Adams sen., 1876. The Whitstable Shipping Company.
Masters: E. Adams, G. Allen, Tupper, W.S. Ruff, T. Rigden.
This vessel was bought when she was quite new and, for years, under the direction of Capt. E. Adams sen., she was engaged in the Mediterranean trade, going regularly to Patras in Greece and calling at Italian, Spanish and north African ports. Under Capt. Thomas Rigden she established an all-time record for the voyage to the West Coast of Africa. She took ninety days on the outward trip, and sixty days on the homeward. Her crew on that momentous voyage were Edward Dunn, W. Peachy, George Dunn and T. Philpot. On the 28th May 1906, when in the East Swin Channel, she was run down by the Norwegian steam-ship "Hein" and was a total loss. All the crew of six were saved.

IRIS

Built in 1819 at Grangemouth, Sterling.
Brigantine, 103 registered tons. 62.6 x 19.8 x 11.6.
Owner: William Edwards, 6th December 1833.
Master: William Edwards, 6th December 1833.
This vessel was sold to Richard Fox, ropemaker of Dartmouth, on the 2nd February 1835.

35177 IRIS

Built in 1857 at Tidnish, Nova Scotia.
Brig, 199 registered tons. Birch, spruce, hackmatack.
Owners: C. Lawson, 10th April 1866. W.J. Lawson, W. Jordan.
Masters: C. Lawson, J. Camburn.
This vessel was bought from Belfast on the 6th April 1866. She was insured with the Whitstable Star Mutual Maritime Association for £900. She foundered in the Black Deeps on the 9th November 1878.

18720 ISABEL

Built in 1848 at Three Rivers, Prince Edward Island.
Schooner, 101 registered tons. 71.4 x 19.4 x 10.7
Owners: David Moyes, Isaac Mitchell, 1st August 1866.
This vessel was bought from Exeter on the 30th July 1866. She was sold to Maldon on the 28th November 1867.

22463 ISABELLA

Built in 1844 at Port Hill, Prince Edward Island.
Schooner, 89 registered tons. 65.0 x 17.4 x 10.7.
Owners: George Richards, Matthew Browning sen., Matthew Browning jun., 12th September 1853.
Masters: George Richards, 12th September 1853. Hills.
This vessel was bought from Appledore, Devon, on the 9th August 1853. She was noted for her beautiful figurehead, a woman's bust which was removed in September 1855. She was sold to Liverpool on the 14th August 1858.

2452 ISABELLAS

Built in 1856 at Blythe.
Snow, altered to Brigantine, 133 registered tons.
Owner: Charles J. Perkins.
Masters: George Mills, Hills.
She was insured with the Whitstable Star Mutual Maritime Assurance Association. The Whitstable Times of the 5th January 1885 reported that the ISABELLAS had gone ashore at Covenithe Ness and had gone to pieces but the stores had been saved. The hull was sold for £65.

24791 **ISIS**
Built in 1843 at Sunderland.
Brigantine, 126 registered tons. 74.6 x 22.3 x 12.0.
Owner: William White Foreman, 12th September 1872.
This vessel was wrecked off Havre on the 31st August 1876.

26327 **ITHIEL**
Built in 1851 at Sunderland.
Snow, altered to Brigantine, 165 registered tons. 84.6 x 23.8 x 12.5.
Owner: C. Hoult.
Masters: Thomas Ougham, 7th November 1865. G.F. Boucher, W.H. Philpott.
This vessel was bought from Lynn on the 4th November 1865. She was insured for £600. On the 15th November 1878 she was bound for London with granite from Guernsey, when off the Isle of Wight she became stranded on the Brook Ledge. The wind was N.N.W. force 4. The crew of six were all saved.

JACK A LANTERN
Built in 1824 at Hastings.
Schooner, 102 registered tons. 72.9 x 19.6 x 10.1.
Owners: George Holden, Robert Feakins.
Masters: Thomas Bedwell, 29th August 1845. Edward Bell, 20th November 1846.
This vessel was bought from London on the 13th August 1845. She was lost in 1848.

42999 **JAMES**
Built in 1863 at Orwell, Prince Edward Island.
Brigantine, 183 registered tons. 99.4 x 23.6 x 13.0.
Owner: William Madams, 5th February 1864.
Masters: S. Holden, E. Alce, J. Reeves.
This vessel was bought on the 19th September 1863 after her first voyage, and she foundered off Beach Head on the 20th February 1877.

4408 **JAMES HARMER (sometimes spelt ARMER)**
Built in 1842 at Jersey.
Schooner, 56 registered tons. 81.0 x 20.2 x 7.5.
Owner: C. Lawson, 20th April 1872.
Master: Charles Lawson.
This vessel was sold to Jersey on the 2nd January 1874.

9791 **JANE**
Built in 1844 at Whitstable.
Boomsail, 47 registered tons. 63.3 x 15.3.
Owners: Thomas Fairbrass, Acors.
Masters: George Pawley, 7th June 1844. George Berry, 23rd September 1844. Edward Spillet, 13th October 1845. Janus Saffery, 16th January 1846. John Lott, 7th November 1846. Richard Edwards, 7th May 1850. John Laraman, 15th January 1852. Gardner.
On the 30th April 1866 she was run into by the "Venus" and sank.

53029 **JANE**
Built in 1865 at Kingstone, Shoreham.
Schooner, 183 registered tons. 108.6 x 22.3 x 12.2. Signal Code K.T.V.J.
Owners: James Thomas Goldfinch, Robinson, William John Lawson, 17th July 1874.
Master: John Camburn.
This vessel was burnt at Exeter in December 1882.

22445 **JANE**
Built in 1842 at Rye, by James Hoad.
Schooner, 131 registered tons. 75.2 x 19.0 x 11.4.
Owners: William Kemp, William Griffiths Lawson, John Camburn, William Robertson.
Master: William Robertson, 21st December 1850.
This vessel was bought from James Hoad of Rye on the 28th November 1850. She was lost near the Outer Downs Light Vessel on the 25th October 1865.

2514 **JANE**
Built in 1850 at Rye by Hoad Brothers.
Schooner, 141 registered tons. 79.0 x 19.4 x 12.1.
Owners: James Acors, Charles Jutson, James Downs, 25th September 1850.
Master: James Acors, 25th September 1850.
This vessel was bought from Hoad Brothers on the 25th September 1850. She foundered off Hasborough on the 12th April 1875.

3470 **JANE**
Built in 1829 at St Martin's, New Brunswick.
Schooner, 77 registered tons. 62.2 x 14.9 x 10.1.
Owner: David Moyes, 21st November 1863.
Master: Clothier.
This vessel was bought from Colchester on the 19th November 1863. She was sold to Ramsgate on the 27th October 1865.

27834 **JANE GARDNER**
Built in 1859 at Sandwich by Hoad.
Schooner, 135 registered tons. 88.8 x 22.1 x 11.8.
Owners: Stephen Rigden, 20th January 1860. J. Rigden.
This vessel was lost in mid Atlantic on the 11th January 1868.

11281 **JEAN**
Built in 1803 at Barrowstroness, Linlithgo.
Brigantine, 163 registered tons. 79.0 x 22.0 x 12.0.
Owners: Frederick W. Webster, Robert Anderson, George Southwell, 24th November 1846. Robert Anderson, Frederick W. Webster, 13th July 1865.
Masters: James Camburn, 24th November 1846. J. Harman, 1860. Anderson, 1870.

18299 **JESSIE**
Built in 1857 at Pallion, Durham.
Brigantine, 163 registered tons. 89.4 x 23.6 x 13.1.
Owner: Edward West, 30th June 1864.
This vessel was lost on the 22nd December 1868 when going from Trouville to Guernsey in ballast.

38989 **JOHN DOWSE (sometimes spelt DOUSE)**
Built in 1855 at Orwell, Prince Edward Island.
Brig 199 registered tons. 101.3 x 23.2 x 13.0. Black birch, pine, spruce, felt and zinc.
Owners: George Butcher, Thomas Ougham, Ozias Ougham, George Taylor, 13th February 1860.
Master: George Taylor.
This vessel was bought from Newcastle on the 11th February 1860. She was sold to Falmouth on the 30th June 1870.

2911 **JOHN & EDWIN**

Built in 1850 at Chipman, New Brunswick.
Brigantine , 153 registered tons. 92.5 x 23.0 x 11.5.
Owners: Frederick William Fairbrass, William Cannon, 23rd August 1869.
Masters: Hudson, G. Dunn.

It is not certain when this vessel was first owned at Whitstable, but she was altered here from a brig to a brigantine in October 1860.

On the 10th May 1885 she was bound for Whitstable with coal from South Shields when she stranded on the Redcar Rocks, Yorkshire, and was a total loss. The wind was W.N.W. force 5. The crew of six were all saved. Both the ship and cargo were uninsured.

2946 **JOHN ELLIOTSON**

Built in 1845 at Durham by Southwick.
Brig, 195 registered tons. 87.9 x 25.5 x 14.3.
Owners: Thomas Fairbrass, 22nd June 1858. Edward Fairbrass, T.W. Fairbrass, 25th July 1859. George Cox.
Master: Alexander Paul Gardner, 27th November 1848.

This vessel was sold to Rochester on the 5th October 1867.

50884 **JOHN PITCAIRN**

Built in 1864 at Prince Edward Island.
Brig, 257 registered tons. Signal Code W.L.B.G.
Owners: F. Fairbrass, The Whitstable Shipping Company.
Masters: T. Barden, Brand.

10985 **JOHN WHITE**

Built in 1855 at Rye.
Brigantine, 188 registered tons. 96.4 x 23.2 x 13.6.
Owners: W.H. Hoult, C.C. Jutson, T. Ougham, L. Frend, J. White, Jane White, Cephas Foad, 20th December 1855. N. Ougham, 1876. H. Pout, 1889. The Whitstable Shipping Company.
Masters: C.E. Jutson, A. Shilling.

On the 18th October 1889 she was insured with the Whitstable Star Mutual Maritime Assurance Association for £350. On the 10th December 1889 she was insured for £600, her value being £750. In 1894 she was insured for £900.

This vessel came to Whitstable when she was quite new in 1855. On the 17th February 1894 she was in the Thames Estuary with a cargo of cement from Rochester bound for Sunderland, when an E.S.E. wind, force 7, drove her on to the Gun Fleet Sand, where she became a total loss, The crew of seven were all saved.

77945 **JOSEPH**

Built in 1879 at Mount Stewart, Prince Edward Island, by William Welsh and D. Eagen.
Brigantine, 285 registered tons. 103.3 x 24.8 x 12.9. Stem and stern post of birch. Signal Code M.C.T.P.
Owners: George Herbert Gann, 12th April 1884. Frank Nicholls, The Whitstable Shipping Company, Nathaniel S. Ougham.
Masters: Hubbard, E. Bruce, C. Cooper, A.W. Ericson, G. Gisby.

Having loaded coal at Howden Dock, River Tyne, she left on the 20th April 1917 bound for Caen. She went to Southend then round the coast to St Helens Roads, Isle of Wight, in convoy, at the rear of six others. During the night the wind dropped and at daylight she was all alone, the other part of the convoy having sailed out of sight. This was evidently seen by a German submarine lurking near at hand. It took 21 rounds from the U-boat's gun to make the Joseph heave-to. The German officer ordered the crew of the JOSEPH to take to the boat. They then sent a boarding party to look for provisions as they were starving, and they also looked for any piece of brass. Having robbed the ship, and heavily loaded their own boat the Germans proceeded to fix a bomb to her side. At this point the U-boat commander saw danger approaching and blew his whistle. The Germans were in such a hurry to escape that they did not wait to unload their boat. The bomb exploded a few moments later, and so the JOSEPH sank at 7 a.m. on the 7th May 1917. The crew of seven were all picked up shortly after.

Joseph, see previous page

46868 **JUNO**

Built in 1863 at St Andrews Point, Prince Edward Island.
Brigantine, 178 registered tons. 99.0 x 23.7 x 12.7.
Owners: G. Goldfinch, George Peters, 1st February 1865.
Masters: Goldfinch, Harris.
This vessel was bought on the 4th October 1864, and insured with the Whitstable Star Mutual Maritime Assurance Association for £500.
She was sunk by collision near the Mouse Light Ship, on the 7th December 1875.

39165 **KATHLEEN**

Built in 1856 at Bedegabl, Prince Edward Island, by J & C Pope.
Brigantine, 154 registered tons. 95.0 x 22.2 x 12.2. Signal Code S.N.D.W.
Owner: C. Hoult, 21st July 1859.
Masters: J.W. Miller, Austin, C. Hoult, Richard John Foreman, Stephen Rigden 1891. Richard Payton, 1890.
This vessel was bought from Liverpool on the 19th July 1859. She was insured for £350. In August 1888 she fell over on her side while discharging coal at Northfleet and was damaged.
On the 18th October 1889 she was insured for £440.
On the 9th November 1891 it was reported that she had sailed from Sunderland on the 25th October, and that she was seen off Whitby on the 26th October by the Master of the "Vivid" and that she had not been heard of since. On the 31st October it was reported that her boat had been picked up off Clacton. Later it was reported that, "A man, name unknown, had been found drowned on Filiestone beach on December 4th 1891. From the Filiestone parish records we learn.

Assented February 1892 by the widow of husband John Foreman of Whitstable, Kent, to be the body of her husband who was Master of the Brigantine "Kathleen" of Whitstable, lost with all hands off Walton-on-the-Naze October 17th 1891. The deceased was 41 years of age.

From an official report we learn that on entering the Thames Estuary she had the misfortune to run on the Gun Fleet Sand, and although she got off she sank in the East Swin with the loss of all hands.
The Insurance Company paid the Owner on "Account of her total Loss", £150, and on the 5th April 1892, £175.

144 **KENT**

Built at the Crown Quay, Sittingbourne, Kent.
Schooner, 134 registered tons. 77.4 x 18.1 10.5.
Owner: Thomas Gann, 22nd April 1837.
Masters: Thomas Walker, 30th December 1837. John Collar, 25th September 1844. Thomas Hoult, 12th November 1846 and 1st December 1851.
This vessel was bought by Thomas Gann on the 22nd April 1837 and she was lost in 1852.

39035 **KINBURN**
Built in 1855 at Rustico, Prince Edward Island.
Brig altered to Brigantine, 171 registered tons. 90.0 x 22.0 x 12.1.
Black birch, spruce, yellow pine.
Owner: George Baker, 9th October 1863.
Master: Tunbridge.
This vessel was bought from Stornaway on the 3rd October 1863. She was sold to Dover on the 29th June 1869.

5242 **LADY FLORA HASTINGS**
Built in 1839 at Dundee.
Brig altered to Brigantine, 155 registered tons. 102.9 x 20.5 x 12.1.
Signal Code J.G.T.L.
Owners: Thomas Gann jun., W. Blackman, 24th September 1857. The Whitstable Shipping Company and Thomas Gann jun., 25th October 1873.
Masters: G. Joiner, John Collar, 14th December 1846. William Charosin, 4th March 1847. George Sharp, 22nd October 1852. Field, H. Skinner, J. Joiner, 1907.
This vessel was altered from a brig to a brigantine September 1856. On the 6th July 1908 she was in the Tyne with a cargo of loam from London. When anchored off White Hill Point she was run down by the German steam-ship "Emma Sauber" and she was a total loss. All the crew of six were saved.

5692 **LADY MANSELL**
Built in 1840 at Guernsey.
Schooner, 94 registered tons. Yellow metal.
Owner: J.B. Dyason.
Master: Dyason.
This vessel mostly traded to the Channel ports and Mediterranean.

57018 **LADY ROWENA (ex ROWINA)**
Built in 1867 at Mount Stewart, Prince Edward Island.
Brig, 187 registered tons. 103.2 x 23.4 x 12.6.
Owner: George Holden, 16th May 1878.
Masters: Pout, A. MacDonald.
On the 19th August 1881 she was entering the Thames Estuary with a cargo of ice from Drobalk, Norway, for London. When she was near the West Maplin Buoy she was run into by the steam-ship "Meredith" of London and quickly sank. The wind was W.S.W. force 4. The crew of eight were all saved.

20202 **LAMPLIGHTER**
Built in 1855 at Rye by Hoad Bros.
Schooner, 117 registered tons. 90.0 x 19.2 x 11.0. Oak, elm, beech, ash.
Owners: Edwin Griffiths, 4th February 1864. Edward Griffiths.
Master: Edward Griffiths.
This vessel was bought from Rye on the 3rd February 1864, and it was insured with the Whitstable Star Mutual Maritime Assurance Association for £650. She was wrecked off the coast of Ireland on the 22nd June 1872.

42581 **LAURA**
Built in 1861 at Quaybach, Cardiganshire.
Brig, altered to Brigantine, 174 registered tons. 100.0 x 24.0 x 13.5.
Signal Code T.K.J.Q.
Owners: Charles C. Fowle, William Kemp, 25th May 1883. Abie Anderson, Stanley Anderson, 27th October 1906.
Master: George Fowle.
This vessel was altered from a brig to a brigantine in July 1886. She foundered off Whitby on the 30th October 1914.

29522 **LAURA**
Built in 1861 at Ipswich.
Brig, altered to Brigantine, 201 registered tons. 105.9 x 23.1 x 11.9.
Signal Code Q.G.B.P.
Owners: A. Anderson, The Whitstable Shipping Company, James Robert Daniels, 30th September 1886.
Masters: C. Shuter, W. Wilson.
This vessel was altered from a brig to a brigantine in October 1886. On the 17th September 1896 she was in the Thames Estuary bound for Whitstable with coal from Newcastle. The wind was W.S.W. force 4. When she was near the Swin Light Vessel she was run into the by the Swedish steam-ship "Astrea" and she soon sank. The crew of seven were all saved.

5292 **LAURA ANN**
Built in 1842 at Ipswich.
Schooner, 91 registered tons. 81.4 x 19.0 x 10.0. Signal Code J.H.B.S.
Owners: Alfred J. Anderson, 19th December 1889. William Murton.
Master: Austin.
On the 28th December 1889 she was insured for £320. On the 2nd February 1890 she stranded on the Gunfleet Sand. On the 6th February the Master of the tug "Harwich" claimed on behalf of the owner, J. Saul, £100 for towing LAURA ANN off the sand-bank, and J. Elven, of the cutter "Providence" claimed £10 for getting the tug. It was stated that the value of the cargo was £170, and the value of the ship was £150. On the 24th July 1891 it was reported that the LAURA ANN had been run into by a steamer off Shoreham, Sussex. She was finally broken up in 1897.

59698 **L.C. OWEN**
Built in 1868 at Grand River, Prince Edward Island, by William Welsh.
Brigantine, 204 registered tons. 104.2 x 24.8 x 12.8. Signal Code J.T.B.C.
Owners: J. Reeves, W. Flint, David Carlton, 30th May 1877. J. Reeves, 30th September 1891.
Master: Woodcock.
This vessel was insured on the 18th October 1889 for £460. She was broken up in April 1889.

60660 **LEADER**
Built in 1869 at Salcombe.
Brigantine, 185 registered tons. Signal Code J.D.N.Q.
Owners: Charles Hoult, Alfred Daniels.
Master: Groombridge.
On the 16th September 1892 she was insured for £700 at a valuation of £900. She was eventually unrigged at Exeter and used as a coal hulk.

77687 **LENA**
Built in 1878 at Prince Edward Island by Carroll and John Yeo.
Barquentine, 289 registered tons. 123.6 x 25.8 x 14.9. Signal Code W.J.F.Q.
Owners: George Holden, The Whitstable Shipping Company.
Masters: Sandy, Hammond.
This vessel was insured on the 21st October 1890 at a valuation of £2130, for £450.

56635 **LENA**
Built in 1867 at Dartmouth.
Schooner, 171 registered tons. 99.9 x 22.7 x 12.5. Signal Code H.S.K.V.
Owners: F.W. Fairbrass, 9th November 1889. The Whitstable Shipping Company, 1st December 1892.
Master: G. Hammond.
This vessel was noted for her female bust figure-head and for her semi-elliptical stern. On the 8th December 1898, she sailed from Leith with a cargo of coal for Whitstable and she was never heard of again, consequently the crew of six were also lost.

66376 **LENORE**
Built in 1873 at Summerside, Prince Edward Island by Angus MacMillan.
Brigantine, 199 registered tons. 105.2 x 24.2 x 13.9. Signal Code M.P.H.C.
Owners: J.R. Reeves, George Henry Pout, Henry Pout, 13th February 1888. W.H. Reeves, 28th November 1918.
Master: J. Pout.

This vessel was insured on the 18th October 1889 for £640, and she was lost on the 13th February 1919.

LEONIE

This vessel was registered as Whitstable owned, 24th November 1866.
Master: F.E. Gaskin.

5224 LEONORA

Built at Shoreham in 1853.
Brig, 128 registered tons. 87.9 x 23.1 x 11.2. Oak, red pine, elm.
Owners: Amanda Mary Ann Gaskin, Louisa Alice Gaskin, 20th April 1866.
Master: Gaskin.

This vessel was bought from Shoreham on the 18th April 1866. In December 1866 she was altered to a brigantine. She foundered near the West Ouse Buoy on the 8th January 1870.

24493 LIGHT OF THE HAREM

Built at Yarmouth in 1842.
Schooner, 156 registered tons. 79.5 x 22.2 x 13.6.
Owners: Henry Baker, George Baker, James Allen, John Nicholls, 20th March 1858.

This vessel was bought from Yarmouth on the 18th March 1858. On the 23rd November 1864 with a strong S.W. wind and driving rain all night she was driven on shore on Castor Beach near Great Yarmouth and was reported lost, the crew being saved by rocket apparatus. However she was got off and was eventually sold to Lowestoft on the 25th September 1865.

67256 LILY

Built at Millwall in 1873.
Ketch, 105 registered tons. 95.7 22.9 x 7.2.
Owners: Abbie Anderson, Stanley Anderson, Charles James Perkins, Thomas Rigden, 7th February 1919.

This vessel was reputed to have been the first real boomy to have been built on the London river. In company with her sister boomies, "Alice Watts" and "Malvoison" she was often engaged in salvage and diving operations, and all three were noted for their clipper bow. She was broken up in September 1936.

54682 **LOCH AWE**
Built in 1866 at Inverness.
Barque, 245 registered tons. 125.2 x 25.4 x 12.7.
Owner: C. Hoult, 16th March 1872.
Masters: Carvell, G.A. Hoult.
This vessel traded regularly to the ports of South America. Capt. Scott sailed in her on his way from Batavia. On the 4th October 1875 when she was off Cape St Francis she ran into a school of whales, and sustained damage to her bows and cutwater, she lost her long-boat, started her bulwarks and stantions. Fortunately she was insured with the Whitstable Star Mutual Maritime Insurance Association. On the 28th May 1880 she was at the entrance to St Johns Harbour, Porto Rio, being bound for St Johns with a cargo of sugar from Arigo, Porto Rio. In trying to enter the harbour she stranded, and on the 1st June 1880 she was condemned as a total loss. The crew of ten were all saved.

17855 **LONDESBOROUGH**
Built in 1856 at Coxgreen, Durham.
Snow, 165 registered tons. Altered to a Brig. 92.1 x 23.5 x 13.1.
Owners: R. Blaxland, T.W. Blaxland, G. Harris, W. Harris, 21st November 1863. G. Harris, 1876. Robert Frend, 1887.
Masters: Tritton, H. Jordan.
This vessel was bought from Hull on the 19th November 1863. On the 31st December 1889 she was off the coast of Norfolk bound from Seaham to Portsmouth, loaded with coal, when she stranded on the Hasborough Sands and was a total loss. The crew of six were all saved.

LORD FOLKESTONE PACKET

Built in 1823 at Folkestone.
Sloop, 58 registered tons. 50.0 x 18.6 x 8.4.
Owners: Thomas Henry Warner, sold to John Andrews, 29th March 1856.
This vessel was lost in 1856.

73900 LORD MARCH

Built in 1876 at Kingston-on-Spey, Morayshire, Elgin, by Duncan.
Schooner, 160 registered tons. 98.8 x 23.3 x 12.1. Signal Code P.N.L.H.
Owners: A. Nicholls, 14th January 1890. Frank Nicholls, 11th October 1917. Blaxland and Frank Nicholls.
Masters: W.T. Clothier, S. Clothier, J. Jeffery.
This vessel was noted for carrying a very large topsail. She was insured on the 7th January 1890 for £700 at a valuation of £875.
On the 24th December 1918 she sailed from Hull with a cargo of 300 tons of coal. At 4 p.m. she struck a submerged wreck on the Sand Hale Flats and was unable to get free. With the rise and fall of the tide she eventually became holed. At 6 p.m., with the deck under water, the Master and crew decided to leave her, and if possible to row to the Bull Light Ship, but the blizzard of snow and sleet made it impossible to find her. Their only hope of being saved was to keep rowing with the help of a sea anchor and the use of the oil bag.
When the pale winter dawn at last broke at 7 a.m. they were sighted by the Swedish steam-ship "Tyr" which was loaded with timber, and six of the crew were saved. During the night they had rowed and drifted over twenty miles.

50903 **LOUISA**

Built in 1864 at New London, Prince Edward Island, by W.W. Lord & Co.

Brigantine, 125 registered tons. 108.1 x 24.8 x 10.2. Signal Code L.H.R.K.

Owners: S. Holden, 13th February 1865. William Holden, George Holden, R.J. Wheeler, R.L. Wheeler, H. Rowden, H. Goldfinch, 22nd April 1872. G. Adams, G. Goldfinch.

Masters: Wheeler, Harris.

This vessel was bought on the 6th December 1864, and she was insured for £550.

From the Whitstable Times of the 3rd January 1885 we learn that she had run ashore on the Caul Sand, and there was little hope of getting her off. Her owners made several attempts to get her off, so Messrs. A. Gann & Co were instructed to disperse the wreck on the spot. However where others had failed they succeeded in raising the wreck. She was brought back to Whitstable, patched up and after serving her owners for another four years she was sold to Skien, Norway on the 31st August 1889.

783 **LUCINDE**

Built in 1830 at Darmsgarten Prussia.
Galliot, 154 registered tons. 78.4 x 24.1 x 12.4. Zinc.
Owners: George Harris, William Harris, Richard Blaxland, James Stamp, 26th December 1865. Blaxland, 1876.

On the 23rd October 1880 she was off the north pier, Lowestoft, bound for Seaham in ballast from London, when she was driven on to the pier by an east wind, force 6, where she stranded and became a total loss. The crew of five were saved.

51747 **L.W. YOUNG**

Brigantine.
Owner: Thomas Gann sen.
Master: Browning.

On Sunday the 27th April 1873, when anchored in the Yarmouth Roads, this vessel was run into by the schooner "Clementine" of Woodbridge, and she was severely damaged.

77646 **MAGGIE A.**

Built in 1877 at St Peters Bay, Prince Edward Island by J.A. McLaine.
Brigantine, 211 registered tons. 103.5 x 24.6 x 13.0. Signal Code T.Q.B.G.
Owners: The Whitstable Shipping Company.
Masters: F.J. Baker, F. Frend, E.W. Woolley, J. Joiner.

71491 **MAGIC**
Built in 1876 at Prince Edward Island by L.C. Owen and William Walsh.
Brigantine, 182 registered tons.
Owner: Frederick Charles Clothier.
Master: Seymour Clothier.

17067 **MAJESTAS**
Built in 1856 at Morell, Prince Edward Island.
Brigantine, 198 registered tons. 105.8 x 22.7 x 12.9. Built of birch, hackmatack, oak, spruce, red pine, felt and yellow metal.
Owners: W. Kemp, J. Goldfinch, David Waters, Herbert Tritton Sankey, 8th August 1864.
Master: H. Walker.
This vessel was insured with the Whitstable Star Mutual Maritime Assurance Association for £800.
On the 7th November 1880 when bound from Swansea to Gravesend with a cargo of coal a gale, force 8, blew her across the channel to Etaples, France, where she stranded and was a total loss. The crew of seven were saved.

87176 **MALVOISON**
Built in 1883 at Maldon by J.T. Howard.
Ketch, 113 registered tons. 101.0 x 22.8 x 8.5.
Owner: Charles W. Marshall.
Master: Horace Lawson.
Like her sister ships, the "Alice Watts" and the "Lily" this vessel was a boomie, and she was mostly engaged in salvage and diving operations.

17066 **MARCELLA**
Built in 1856 at Morell, Prince Edward Island.
Brigantine, 201 registered tons. 105.1 x 23.1 x 13.0. Yellow metal.
Owner: George Baker, 29th August 1864.
Masters: Kemp, G.D. Frend.

This vessel was bought from Plymouth on the 10th August 1864. She was insured with the Whitstable Star Mutual Maritime Assurance Association for £850.

The year 1885 was a time of commercial depression. Many vessels were laid up as it was not possible to get cargoes. MARCELLA was one of the fleet moored off Whitstable and after a time she became so neglected that it was considered that it was not worth the money to have her repaired. She was consequently broken up on the beach during the summer of 1885. Her figure-head is preserved in the Whitstable Museum.

5244 **MARCHIONESS OF LONDONDERRY**
Built in 1850 at Seaham.
Brigantine, 183 registered tons. 86.4 x 24.9 x 13.2.
Owners: Amanda Mary Ann Gaskin, Louisa Alice Gaskin, 23rd December 1875.
This vessel was wrecked off Bamburgh on the 6th February 1879.

MARGARET
Built in 1792 at Irvine, Ayre.
Schooner, 78 registered tons. 74.8 x 16.0 x 10.8.
Owners: John Graves, 1845. Robert Brows, James Hayward, Henry Nicholls.
Masters: John Graves, 27th September 1845. George Adams, 24th August 1847.
Although only a small vessel she was noted for having 3 masts. This vessel as bought from Yarmouth in 1845. After the death of Robert Brows we have the following note:

MARGARET
Bill of Sale, 24th August 1847.
John Giles and William Robertson, Executors, of Robert Brows, deceased, in consideration of the sum of £96.0.0. have sold to William Dyason.
John Graves, Henry Nicholls, and George Adams, all of Whitstable declare that they are with Robert Brows of Seasalter, and James Hayward, shipwright, owners of the Schooner MARGARET, built at Irvine, County Ayre in 1792, 106³⁄₈ tons, George Adams, master. 74.8 x 16 x 10.8.

34908 **MARGARET JANE SWIFT**
Built in 1855 at Port Elgin, New Brunswick, by Archibald McLallam.
Brigantine, 186 registered tons. 100.5 x 25.4 x 11.6. Signal Code R.M.K.D.
Owners: Henry L. Daly, H.A. Clarke, T. Andrews, J. Reeves, R. Young, 28th February 1856.
Masters: Swift, R. Fitall, Daly, 1869.
On the 20th February 1885 she was trying to enter Poole Harbour with a cargo of coal from Sunderland. The east wind, force 6, caused her to become stranded and a total loss. The crew of eight were all saved.

24504 **MARIA**
Built in 1845 at Limerick.
Schooner, 173 registered tons. 75.5 x 18.0 x 12.6.
Owners: George Austin, Stephen Rigden, 9th November 1860.
Master: William Allen, 7th July 1852.
This vessel was bought on the 13th October 1851. On the 3rd December 1864 it was reported that in a storm off Plymouth she had lost her bowsprit and masts. She was wrecked on the Bass Rocks on the 10th October 1876.

75280 **MARIA MELANIE**
Built in France.
Ketch, 99 registered tons. 69.4 x 21.8 x 10.5.
Owners: Henry Gann, George Herbert Gann, 31st October 1876. The Whitstable Shipping Company.
Masters: E. Parriss, W.R. Clothier, Adams.
This vessel was bought as a wreck in 1878 and repaired. On the 4th November 1888 she was trying to enter Broadstairs Harbour, the wind being S.E. force 4, when being heavily laden with coal from the Tyne, and the tide falling rapidly, she became stranded in the Bay. The crew of five were saved, and the ship was then broken up.

12525 **MARIE JOSEPHINE**
Built in 1855 at Lynn.
Brig, 165 registered tons.
Owner: William Kemp jun.
Masters: Bright, Smith, 1872.

56624 **MARION**
Built in 1867 at Sunderland.
Brigantine, 137 registered tons. Signal Code L.B.J.G.
Owners: W. Butler, Henry John Cornelius.
Masters: R. Field, J. Slingsby.
On the 27th January 1884 she was forty miles east of Sunderland when bound for Shields from Faversham in ballast. A gale, west force 10, dismasted her and she sprang a leak. The crew of six decided to abandon her and they were saved. MARION did not sink and she was towed into port. After an examination it was decided that she was unseaworthy and she was condemned to be broken up.

MARION
Owner: George Holden.
On the 24th September 1889 she was insured with the Whitstable Star Mutual Maritime Assurance Association for £650. The newspapers of the day reported that she sailed from Shields on the 23rd February 1891 and that she was last seen by Capt Sandy of the Whitstable ship "Lena" on the 10th March 1891 when she was near Start Point. She was then considered to have been lost, being at the time insured for £700. Among the crew lost was John Thomas Burtenshaw, a lad of sixteen years.

23787 **MARK BREEDS**
Built in 1827 at Hastings.
Schooner, 124 registered tons. 71.0 x 19.4 x 12.5.
Owners: James Daniels, Thomas Walker, James E.M. Williams, 22nd November 1844.
Masters: Thomas Walker, 22nd October 1844. Edward Jarrett, 25th August 1853.
This vessel was bought from Weymouth by James Daniels on the 19th February 1844. Her figure-head, which was a man's bust was removed on the 28th August 1855. She was lost in the North Sea, 2nd November 1863.

MARTHA
Built in 1800 at Plymouth.
Sloop, 66 registered tons. 52.1 x 17.1 x 7.0.
Owner: Thomas Fairbrass sen.

20032 **MARY**
Built in 1851 at Sandwich by Hoad Brothers.
Schooner, 132 registered tons. 82.2 x 19.9 x 11.6.
Owners: James Rigden, Richard Saffery, William Crofts, 20th December 1851.
Master: James Rigden.
The newspapers of the day reported that she was a respectable specimen of naval architecture, evidently light of heel, and well adapted for foreign as well as home trade. Unfortunately she was wrecked on Felixstowe Ridge on the 2nd July 1852.

50889 **MARY A. McKAY**
Built in 1864 and launched on the 18th August at New London, Prince Edward Island by Donald and George McKay.
Brigantine, 191.88 registered tons. 103.9 x 24.1 x 12.5. Signal Code W.Q.P.B.
Owners: W. Kemp, W. Gann, 30th January 1865.
Masters: W. Digby, 1869. Gibbons, W. Joiner, 1899-1900.
This vessel was bought on the 28th October 1864. On the 18th October 1889 she was insured for £600. On Thursday 20th December 1900 she was dismasted in a gale in the North Sea, and was towed into Grimsby by the s.s. "Viola". Being in a very bad condition it was considered that it would not be worth while to attempt to repair her. On Thursday 24th January 1901 she was put up for sale by auction and was bought by Mr Paul of Ipswich for £215.

23300 **MARY ANN**

Built in 1832 at Whitstable.
Dandy, 52 registered tons. 69.7 x 15.3 x 7.8. Felt and yellow metal.
Owners: George H. Gann, Thomas Gann, 22nd June 1854.
Masters: George Lott, 22nd June 1854. Gann, C. Fogg.
This vessel was noted for her tiller steering.
For some years she regularly traded to the Mediterranean ports. On the 22nd March 1882, when bound from Sunderland to Herne Bay with coal, she was driven by a gale, force 8, on to the Blakeney West Sands, off Norfolk, where she became a total loss. Her crew of four were all saved.
A newspaper article gives the following interesting information.

September 15th 1853.
On Saturday se'night a little dandy-rigged vessel, nine tons burthen, arrived in Whitstable Harbour, having only one person on board, who had performed, during a voyage of eight days, from Cromarty, in the north of Scotland, the duties of captain, mate and crew, he alone having navigated the little vessel through all the difficulties of a dangerous coasting voyage of upwards of 500 miles.

2640 **MARY ANN**

Built in 1851 at Rye by Hoad Bros.
Schooner, 143 registered tons. 89.2 x 22.2 x 12.3. Signal Code H.P.W.V.
Owners: F. Nicholls, Mary Blaxland, W.T. Blaxland, G. Blaxland, Thomas Terry, 25th September 1858.
Masters: Nicholls, E.J. Camburn, C. Taylor, Stephen Jarman, 1911. Taylor, G. Blaxland, 3rd November 1851.
A newspaper published the following enthusiastic report on Thursday, 18th December 1851.

The Mary Ann – Last week, the snug Harbour of Whitstable was visited by a beautiful new schooner, bearing the above name. She is the property of some gentlemen residing in the town, and is of a superior mould, excellently calculated for speed, as well as adapted for carrying cargo, in fact she is a pleasing proof that ship building is looking up. The experienced say that there are but few of her class that can surpass the sea-going qualities of the Mary Ann.

This was one of the smallest of the Whitstable deep sea craft. Although she was so small she was well able to carry 300 tons of coal, and sometimes she had 305 tons on board.
On the 18th October 1889 she was insured for £600.
On the 10th January 1914 she was wrecked on the Gun Fleet Sand, within sight of home.

Mary Ann (2640)

11212 **MARY ANN**

The particulars of this vessel have not been found but it is certain that she was purchased by William Camburn and George Barton on the 2nd March 1863.

22928 **MARY ANN GANN**

Built in 1847 at Whitstable by Thomas Gann.
Schooner, 177 registered tons. 84.3 x 21.8 x 12.8. Felt and yellow metal.
Owner: Thomas Gann sen.
Masters: William Thomas Bell, 24th August 1847. William Robertson, 12th February 1849. David Charosin, 23rd February 1849. Thomas Bedwell, 9th October 1849. George Clothier, May 1850. William Kemp, 18th November 1851. William Watts, 23rd March 1853. George Gaskin, 2nd March 1855. R. Foreman, F. Warboys, 1860. Kean, 1864.

It is thought to be of particular interest to record this long line of Masters as it would appear that MARY ANN GANN for some unknown reason had a different Master for almost every voyage.
She was lost after she was abandoned at sea on the 16th November 1864.

18396 **MARY GRACE**

Built in 1852 at Durham by Southwick.
Snow altered to Brigantine, 176 registered tons. 86.3 x 23.8 x 13.6.
Owners: D. Frend, Thomas Blakeley, Thomas Giles Rigden, John Foad, 2nd December 1863.
Masters: Frend, J. Lucas.

This vessel was bought from Shoreham on the 7th November 1863. On the 5th March 1878 she was off the coast of France, bound for London with a cargo of small stones from Guernsey, when she was struck by a squally N.W. wind and was driven ashore under the cliffs of Jobourg, near Cherbourg. Here she became a total loss, but the crew of six were saved.

8180 **MARY MAC**

Built in 1852 at Weymouth, Nova Scotia.
Brig, 189 registered tons. 101.7 x 24.2 x 11.4.
Owners: Frederick Kemp, William Camburn, William Bedwell, William How, Mary Ann Hammond, 9th April 1862.
Master: Stoner, 1864.

This vessel was bought from Londonderry on the 16th December 1861. She was sold away to Newcastle in April 1867.

15800 **MARY STEWART**

Built in 1857 at Garmouth, Moray.
Brigantine, 116 registered tons. 82.2 x 21.3 x 10.7. Fir, oak, and larch.
Signal Code L.T.S.G.
Owners: D. Daniels, Henry Holden, William Weir, James H. Butcher, E. Nicholls, 28th March 1865.
Master: Fullager.

This vessel was bought from Banff on the 28th March 1865 and was insured for £600. She was offered for sale by auction as a hulk in 1883. From the Whitstable Times of the 20th October 1883 we learn the following.

On Thursday last Mr J.T. Reeves submitted for sale by public auction at his Auction Mart, the hull of the brigantine "MARY STEWART" together with her masts, spars, rigging, anchors and chain, etc, as she now lies in Whitstable Bay. The lot was knocked down to Mr Solly for £35.

MARY STUART

Built in 1857 at Perth.
Schooner, 130 registered tons.
Owner: William Holden.
Masters: W. Gardner, 1866. Butcher.

19773 **MASONIC**
Built in 1857 at Jersey.
Brig, altered to Brigantine, 156 registered tons. Felt and yellow metal.
Signal Code M.T.J.D.
Owner: George H. Cann.
Masters: Freeman, George Foreman.
MASONIC was registered at Whitstable on the 15th May 1870. She met her end in an unusual manner. Having been repaired she was on the slipway waiting to be launched on the next spring tide. Eager to get another ship on to the slipway the owners allowed her to be launched when there was not enough water to float her and consequently she broke her back and never sailed again.

48607 **MATILDA CALDER**

Built in 1862 at Banff.
Schooner, 154 registered tons. 101.0 x 23.8 x 11.5. Signal Code V.T.L.J.
Owners: John A. Johnson, George H. Gann, H. Gann, 2nd November 1885.
Master: W. Joiner, 13th August 1895.

The Whitstable Times of the 20th October 1883 informs us that the MATILDA CALDER had sustained some damage in the Harbour through being hung up by the "Osiris" and the "Rapid". In June 1897 MATILDA CALDER was laid up for repairs and she was moored off the slipway.

On the 29th November 1897 there occurred a great tidal surge and gale. MATILDA CALDER broke adrift and was lifted inland on to the Salts. In order to refloat her it was necessary to dig a special channel, also to pass great bulks of timer under her. Those who witnessed the operation claimed in 1953 that the bulks of timber and the course of the channel were still to be seen.

5129 **MAY FLOWER**

Built in 1846 at Maitland, Nova Scotia.
Brig, 122 registered tons. 72.6 x 23.2 x 10.6.
Owners: James Reeves (timber merchant), William Madams (grocer), Edward Richard Laraman, William Hollaway, 27th October 1854.
Master: Edward Richard Laraman, 5th January 1855.

This vessel was bought from Liverpool on the 27th October 1854. She was altered to a Brigantine in November 1856.

39243 **MERGHEE**

Built in 1857 at Wood Island, Prince Edward Island.
Brigantine, 118 registered tons. 94.0 x 22.3 x 10.9.
Owners: Henry Wooton Nicholls, John Nicholls, John Johnson, 31st December 1859.
Masters: Adams, 1860. Nicholls, 1864.

This vessel was bought on the 11th July 1859. She was lost off Shields on the 6th January 1867.

36826 **MERIDIAN**

Built in 1860 at Pisquid, Prince Edward Island, by McDonald.
Brig, 226 registered tons. 100.0 x 24.2 x 13.8.
Owners: George Holden, Thomas Gann jun., William Blackman, 16th March 1861.
Masters: D. May, 1860. Burton, Daniels, 1869.

This vessel was bought on the 8th December 1860. She was sold to Holland on the 11th April 1876.

Matilda Calder

12927 **MERTON**
Built in 1825 at Swansea.
Schooner, 104 registered tons. 71.2 x 20.4 x 11.0.
Owners: George Herbert Gann, Henry Gann, 18th April 1878.
This vessel was announced as missing on 8th November 1878 while on a voyage from the north with coal.

35139 **MILO**
Built in 1856 at Stittsborough, New Brunswick, by Albert Co.
Brig, 210 registered tons. 109.4 x 26.0 x 11.9. Birch, spruce and tamarack.
Owner: James Gann, 6th December 1864.
This vessel was bought from Glasgow on the 2nd December 1864. She was lost off Orfordness on the 8th December 1866.

29678 **MILO**
Built in 1861 at Plymouth by J. Banks.
Brigantine, 114 registered tons. Signal Code Q.G.P.L.
Masters: Harrison, W. Dodson.
On the 28th December 1889 she was insured for £450. On the 10th December 1891, when off the coast of Essex, she was caught in a W.S.W. gale, force 8, and was driven on to the Long Sand on the 11th December, and the crew were rescued by the Broadstairs Lifeboat. On the 23rd December, there being no hope of getting her off the sand-bank, she was sold by Messrs Duinker and Goedkoop for £80. This amount the agent's charges reduced to £62.15.7, which amount was handed to the Owners on the 5th July 1892, who paid on account of total loss £200. On the 9th August 1892 they found that the balance in hand from this involved transaction was £169.16.7. During her eventful career, on the 9th February 1865 she had made the newspaper headlines by being nearly destroyed by fire in the Harbour.

MINERVA
Built in 1826 at Jersey.
Brig. 115 registered tons. 73.8 x 18.3 x 11.8.
Owners: Charles Lawson, James Camburn, William Kemp.
Masters: Charles Lawson, 20th May 1852. James Camburn, 13th April 1853.
This vessel was bought on the 30th March 1852, and sold to Sunderland in March 1855.

Moneta

The MONETA at Sandwich, circa 1885. She would be delivering coal to the gas-works, to the left of the picture. Captain Gann ('Moneta Tommy') is on the left; the central figure is believed to be Henry Cosby Solly, a Whitstable shipwright and barge owner.

MIRANDA

Built in 1826 at Cross House, Southampton.
Schooner, 84 registered tons. 71.1 x 19.6 x 9.1.
Owners: Philpot Wood, James E.M. Williams, John Deane, William Edwards.
Masters: William Kemp, 3rd November 1848. Richard Keys, 4th January 1849. John Livingston, 27th June 1849.
This vessel which came into Whitstable ownership in 1849 was wrecked at Teceire on the 15th November 1851.

27629 **MONETA**

Built in 1859 at Prince Edward Island, by Cox.
Brigantine, 158 registered tons. 101.0 x 22.3 x 11.5. Signal Code P.S.C.V.
Owners: Josiah Reeves, Thomas Gann, John Gann, James Reeves, John Collar 2nd February 1860. She was insured 18th October 1889 for £500.
Masters: John Collar, 1860. Thomas Gann, 1860-1894. John Dyason, 1894.

This vessel was bought from Plymouth on the 31st January 1860. At the time of purchase she was called the "Union". Owing to her being damaged Thomas Gann took out the jibboom and put in a standing bowsprit. He also altered her from a double to a single top-sail brigantine. These changes made the MONETA one of the fastest vessels in the Whitstable fleet. She actually held the record from the north of England to Whitstable with coal, doing the journey in twenty-eight hours. Her nearest rival was the "Pinta" which took thirty-two hours. One reason for her fast passages was that of the superb seamanship of Thomas Gann, who took full advantage of the eleven foot draft of his vessel and used a short cut across the Thames Estuary. In the local vernacular "he slammed her through the Swatch Way", and this enabled him to get to the Harbour before the deeper draft vesssels which were compelled to go round the "Mouse" light ship.

On his death-bed in October 1894, Thomas Gann gave the command to Captain John Dyason. Afterwards he said, "I should never have done it; she's not an old man's ship, she'll take him down with her." Two months later, on 19th December 1894, when about four miles south of Dungeness, the wind being N.W. by W., force 4, MONETA being bound for Ouistreham, France, with a cargo of coal from the Tyne, was run into by the Danish steam-ship "Ella". The stricken vessel sank so fast that Capt Dyason and two members of the crew were drowned, only three being saved by the "Ella".

71496 **MORAVIAN**

Built in 1875 at Prince Edward Island, by F.W. Hyndman.
Brig, 249 registered tons. 112.5 x 25.4 x 13.9.
Owners: Thomas Gann jun., George Holden, W.J. Bronger, 6th June 1879.
Masters: Allen, Fred Attwood.

On the 30th October 1885 this vessel was seen off Harborough, being bound for Devonport with coal from South Shields. After that time she was never seen again, but the register records that she was lost on the Sizewell Bank with her crew of seven.

1659 **MYRTLE**
Built in 1848 at Garmouth, Banff.
Schooner, 89 registered tons. 71.0 x 19.4 x 10.1.
Owners: Thomas Ougham, Edward Gaskin, 2nd May 1863.
Master: Edward Gaskin.
This vessel was bought from Hartlepool on the 29th April 1863.

47861 **MYSTERY (original name THATIGKEIT)**
Brigantine, 162 registered tons. 93.3 x 23.4 x 10.7.
Owner: George Peters, 25th September 1863.
This vessel was lost on the 7th September 1868.

75271 **NELLIE S.**
Built in 1876 at Whitstable.
Brigantine, 282 registered tons. 131.0 x 26.0 x 12.8. Signal Code P.T.K.Q.
Owner: George Henry Gann, 5th July 1876.
Masters: Tilley, P.L. Francis, 1887.
This was the largest vessel ever built at Whitstable. She was built of English oak and African hardwood obtained from ships broken up in Chatham Dockyard, had a flat bottom, square chine, and a flush deck, but was never fitted with lee-boards. She was mostly engaged in transporting mahogany from Mexico. This fact led her to being chartered to transport railway rails to that country, and gaining eternal fame. During the captains absence the stevedores loaded her until the deck was awash, and they flatly refused to unload her despite the plimsoll line being well under the surface, and the captain pleaded in vain. The result was the captain and his crew faced almost certain death and sailed the overloaded vessel across the Atlantic to Mexico, and won the admiration of thousands. She was registered to carry 530 tons on a draught of 12.6.
This brave ship was sold to London on the 20th April 1883 and was bought by Messrs Thorburn Bros of Cornwall.

70702 **NEREID**
Built in 1858.
Brigantine, 417 registered tons.
Owners: Hoult & Co., Charles Hoult.
Masters: A. Anderson, Coleman, Thomas Clark, 1877.

NEWCASTLE TRADER
Built in 1811 at Yarmouth.
Brig, 110 registered tons. 70.0 x 19.3 x 9.11.
Owner: James Greenland, 6th May 1834.
Master: James Greenland.

NEW SPECULATION

Built at Whitstable in 1825 by Fairbrass.
Owner: Fairbrass.
Master: Thomas Ely sen.

This vessel was mentioned at the Kent Assizes 11th March 1861. She traded from Whitstable to London and Devonport.

16519 **NEW UNION**

Built in 1800 at Cowes.
Ketch, 54 registered tons. 74.2 x 18.9 x 7.2. Signal Code M.B.T.G.
Owners: George Herbert Gann, Henry Gann, 18th May 1877.
Masters: W. Usher, S. Igglesden.

This vessel was mostly engaged in the cross channel trade. On the 22nd January 1884 she was in the Thames Estuary off the Gantlet waiting for the tide to turn, with a general cargo from London. A strong W.N.W. wind force 5 caused her to roll and overturn an oil stove, which caught her on fire. The crew of three made a desperate effort to save her, but it was hopeless, and she was a total loss. The crew were all saved.

NONPAREIL

Built in 1831 at Hastings.
Schooner, 97 registered tons. 77.0 x 17.7 x 11.0.
Owners: Thomas Gann, James E.M. Williams, Thomas Bedwell.
Masters: Thomas Bedwell, 1st December 1846. J. Souden, 13th August 1849. Thomas Bedwell, 12th September 1850. W. Watts, 7th November 1851.

This vessel was bought from London on the 20th November 1846, and sold back to London again in July 1854.

52739 **NORTHERN LIGHT**

Built in 1864 at New London, Prince Edward Island, by U. MacKay and R. Taylor.
Brigantine, 172 registered tons. 101.7 x 23.0 x 11.9. Signal Code L.J.R.B.
Owners: George Waters, 31st July 1865. George Waters, Charles Holman Nicholls, Thomas Pettman Bell, Rev. Thomas Drawbridge, Thomas Wells, George Daniels, William Kemp, 17th October 1872.
Masters: Thomas Dadd, Hoult 1873.

Bought from London on the 26th July 1865, and insured with the Whitstable Star Mutual Maritime Assurance Association for £900. She was sold as a hulk in 1900, and was broken up in 1908.

OCEAN QUEEN

Owner: Aaron Kemp.
Master: Whorlow.
This vessel stranded on the Longsands on the 14th December 1867 and after a time was towed off and into Harwich Harbour. Since then all trace of her was lost.

50310 **OLD GOODEY**

Built in 1865 at Sandwich.
Schooner altered to Brigantine, 174 registered tons.
100.4 x 24.3 x 12.3. Signal Code H.Q.W.G.
Owners: Edwin Rigden, J. Rigden, A.T. Rigden, D. Rigden, 20th May 1868. Frederick Charles Ashby, 24th May 1902.
Masters: Ashby, D. Rigden, W. Sidders.
This vessel came to Whitstable in 1865 and was then insured for £650. She was altered to a brigantine in January 1866. At one period in her life she survived a remarkable series of accidents. On the 3rd August 1889 she was in collision with the dandy "Rosabel", when Messrs Small & Co claimed £12.5.10 for damage, and £12 for loss of fishing. The agreed compensation was £16.10.0.
On 5th August 1889 OLD GOODEY ran into Ramsgate Pier and broke her bowsprit and her cutwater was carried away. On the 7th September 1889 she stranded on the bar when being towed into Sunderland Harbour, but was got off at two hours flood tide. She was pulled up on Thompson's slip-way, a piece of elm keel 45 feet long by 15 inches by 12 inches was renewed.
On the 24th March 1890, when being in ballast with chalk, OLD GOODEY was in collision with the steam-tug "Gleanor" off Fort Yar. The tug had eight passengers on board and although both vessels were damaged they both managed to make port.
Finally in April 1910 she was dismasted and converted into a hulk. Her lovely figurehead was secured by a Faversham butcher and fixed up over his shop door. After some years she was bought by Captain Silver and restored with the intention of putting her on permanent exhibition in the "Cutty Sark" at Greenwich.

23779 **OLIVE LEAF**

Built in 1854 at Rye by Hoad Bros.
Schooner, 167 registered tons. 86.0 x 21.7 x 13.4. Signal Code N.T.C.G.
Owners: Edward Adams sen., Edward Adams jun., George Kennet Baker, 24th August 1871. F. Baker.
Masters: Edward Adams sen., 1860. A. Beal, Edward Adams jun., 1864.
This vessel was bought when quite new, on the 3rd July 1854. She was insured by Mr G. Baker for £850. She was last seen on the 25th January 1883 when she sailed from Sunderland with coal for Spithead, and nothing more was ever seen or heard of her.

45559 **OLIVIA**

Built in 1863 at Sandwich.
Schooner, 157 registered tons. 90.5 x 23.5 x 12.7. Signal Code V.D.S.G.
Owners: John Nicholls jun., 25th August 1863. John Alfred Johnson.
Master: A. Newman.

On the 13th October 1881 she was seen passing through the Downs, bound for Sunderland from Portsmouth in ballast, with a crew of seven. The Shipping Register informs us that she was lost off Yarmouth on the 14th October 1881, with all hands.

45557 **ONWARD**

Built in 1863 at Ipswich.
Schooner, 161 registered tons. 98.0 x 23.0 x 12.4.
Owners: E. Nicholls, Henry Holden, 15th April 1863.
Masters: W. Earle, R. Court, Allen.

This vessel was insured for £965. She foundered 11th April 1874.

42985 **ONYX**

Built in 1863 at Hillsborough River, Prince Edward Island by Robert Longworth.
Brigantine, 131 registered tons. 95.2 x 22.7 x 10.2. Signal Code T.M.C.P.
Owners: Thomas Gann jun., William Gann, Frederick Gann, Henry Pout, 23rd October 1866. Whitstable Shipping Company 10th May 1893.
Masters: Putwain, 1864. E. Pout, 1870.

This vessel was bought 19th October 1866. On the 30th April 1891 she was in collision with the Grimsby fishing ketch "Magna Charter" when nine miles south of Flamborough Head, and while she suffered little damage herself the ketch was a total loss. The wind was S.W. force 4. ONYX was broken up in December 1898.

Onward, see previous page

50950 **ORION**
Built in 1864 at West Point, Prince Edward Island.
Brigantine, 159 registered tons. 95.8 x 23.8 x 11.1.
Owners: Frederick Kemp, 24th April 1865. Waters & Kemp.
Masters: G.F. Boucher, 1873. Thomas Camburn.
This vessel was bought on the 18th January 1865. She was wrecked at Arnland on the 11th December 1872.

719 **ORMSBY HALL**
Built in 1839 at Stockton.
Schooner, 86 registered tons. 70.6 x 21.2 x 9.1
Owners: Valentine Court, Robert Harrison, 19th November 1866.
This vessel was insured with the Whitstable Star Mutual Maritime Assurance Association for £300.
She foundered off Lowestoft on the 20th June 1871.

45709 **OSIRIS**
Built in 1862 at Prince Edward Island.
Brigantine, 185 registered tons. 109.5 x 22.5 x 12.3.
Owners: George Herbert Gann, Henry William Madams, 6th November 1863.
Masters: J.E. Pearce, Thomas Clark, 1865-1870. Stone.
This vessel was bought from Plymouth on the 4th November 1863. She was wrecked on the Spaniard Sand in June 1871, but the wreck was bought by George Herbert Gann, and repaired. She was eventually broken up in December 1885.

82856 **OSPREY**
Built in 1886 at Whitstable.
Schooner, 32 registered tons. 70.8 x 13.3 x 6.3. Signal Code K.F.W.D.
Owner: Frederick William Fairbrass, 21st May 1886.
Master: Morris.
This vessel was sold to Egypt in August 1914.

812 **PARAGON**
Built in 1842 at Aberdeen.
Schooner, 153 registered tons. 100.2 x 20.7 x 12.5.
Owners: William Griffiths Lawson, Henry W. Nicholls, Edward Kitchinham Lawson. Sold to John Livingston, 20th July 1853. Sold to John Camburn, 1860.
Masters: John Livingston, 16th July 1853. Gaskin, John Camburn, 1860. S. Flowers.
PARAGON was bought from Aberdeen on the 1st June 1853 and she was destroyed by fire on the 21st February 1862.

11298 **PARA PACKET**
Brigantine altered to Schooner, 131 registered tons. 72.2 x 20.5 x 12.1.
Owners: Stephen Rigden, George Austin, 8th June 1842. Ebenezer Cotton, Thomas Reeves, 9th July 1851.
Masters: Ebenezer Cotton, 8th June 1842. Edward Allen, 4th March 1851. James Allen, 15th February 1854. William Allen, 15th December 1855. Pelfrey.
This vessel was bought in 1842. She was reputed to carry an average cargo of 210 tons of coal.
She was condemned and was broken up by the 21st April 1876.

20144 **PEARL**

97 registered tons. Signal Code M.V.T.S.

This vessel was insured with the Whitstable Star Mutual Maritime Assurance Association for £400 at a valuation of £500 on the 11th November 1889. Particulars of her history are not known.

10423 **PEGGY**

Built in 1844 at Garmouth, Banff.
Ketch, 52 registered tons. 56.7 x 17.4 x 8.0.
Owners: Absolom Anderson, Morris, 5th July 1880.
Masters: Morris, W.G. Joiner.

In 1874 PEGGY was insured for £200 and it is interesting to see the cost of this action.

December 5th	*To entry Charge*	*£1.0.0*
	Policy Duty	*1.0*
	Survey	*5.0*
February 8th	*Call*	*2.1.4*
May 5th	*Call*	*1.7.6*

29749 **PERSEVERANCE**

Built in 1861 at Cardiff.
Ketch, 72 registered tons. Signal Code Q.G.W.F.
Owners: Abie Anderson, J. Rogers, Alfred J. Anderson.
Master: George Dunn.

Engaged for most of her life round the coasts of Britain, on a certain day in 1871 this small craft was in Falmouth Harbour, with a cargo of lead and her deck stacked high with esparto grass, when she caught fire. Efforts to save her were hopeless and in dramatic manner she was sunk by gun fire. After a time divers went down to her, cleared the grass from her decks, and the lead from her fore-hold, stopped up the shot holes, pumped the water out of her with a steam pump, and successfully raised her.

11268 **PETREL**

Built in 1842 at Montrose, Forfar.
Schooner altered to Dandy, 58 registered tons. 76.0 x 18.9 x 8.8. Yellow metal.
Owners: E. Allen, R.S. Newing, T. Allen, 5th July 1856. T. Hoult.
Masters: Thomas Clark, Thomas Allen, 15th July 1851.

It would appear that this vessel came here about 1850. In 1851 she was lengthened and sundry repairs carried out. In 1856 she was still further lengthened, a new keelson was fitted, and sundry repairs carried out.
This little vessel, valued at £300, was one of the Whitstable fleet that regularly sailed via the Azores, up the Mediterranean to Patras in Greece. She was sold to Dundee in October 1871.

73938 **PINTA**

Built in 1875 at Prince Edward Island, by Angus MacMillan.
Brigantine, 199 registered tons. Signal Code S.D.W.V.
Owners: T.W. Fairbrass, The Whitstable Shipping Company.
Masters: G. Witnall, 1889. George Sperry Nicholls.
Sperry Nicholls gained for this vessel the reputation of being one of the fastest in the Whitstable fleet, only the "Moneta" was faster, but she held the record for racing over from Norway with ice.
She was lost on the 28th October 1880.

PLATO

Built in 1822 at Philadelphia, in the State of Pennsylvania.
Barque, 310 registered tons. 98.6 x 22.6 x 16.9.
Owners: Robert Young, George Cox, James Goodwin, Robert Walker.
Master: David Charosin, 8th December 1853.
A newspaper of the period had the following announcement.

1853 Whitstable. Another fine bark, of 310 tons burthen was last week added to the Whitstable fleet. Her name is the Plato, Captain David Charosin, and is the property of Messrs Robert Young and Co.

33315 **POLLY**

Built in 1857 at Quebec.
Brigantine, 173 registered tons. 96.6 x 23.0 x 12.4. Tamarac, oak, spruce, felt and yellow metal. Signal Code R.D.S.W.
Owners: George Holden, Thomas Gann jun., Mary Blaxland, W.T.Blaxland, G. Blaxland, J. Theobald, 23rd November 1877. The Whitstable Shipping Company.
Masters: Gardner, John Rowland, W.R. Clothier.
On the 18th October 1889 she was insured for £430. On the 16th November 1889 at 5.15 p.m. POLLY was two miles east of Cromer bound for Whitstable with a cargo of coal from Seaham, when she was run into by the steam-ship "Angelus" of Newcastle and soon sank. The crew of seven were rescued.

50916 **PRIMROSE OF IRELAND**

Built in 1864 at New London, Prince Edward Island.
Brigantine, 168 registered tons. 96.3 x 24.3 x 11.8.
Owners: Thomas Gann jun., George Holden, J. Blackman, Fanny Blackman, 26th November 1866.
Master: Woodcock.
This vessel was bought on the 16th February 1865. She was sold foreign in June 1875.

24594 **PRINCE ALBERT EDWARD**

Built in 1842 at Whitstable by William Madams.
Schooner, 83 registered tons. 70.0 x 17.5 x 9.9.
Owner: Thomas Gann (sailmaker).
Masters: John Collar, 14th October 1842. W. Charosin, 25th September 1844. William Kemp, 29th October 1844. G. Clothier, 14th July 1847. J. Stroud, 31st July 1849. W. Clothier, 26th October 1849. W. Ranson, 24th May 1850. E. Gaskin, 3rd November 1852. J. Lott, 15th June 1856.
This vessel was lost in the Black Sea in 1856.

44435 **PRINCE CONSORT**

Built in 1862 at Aberdeen by I. Duthie & Sons.
Brigantine, 192 registered tons. 107.3 x 23.8 x 13.5.
Owners: John E. Pierce, 3rd January 1881. F. Pierce.
Masters: F. Pierce, E. Camburn, Wallace Bell, 1888.
On the 18th October 1889 she was insured for £680. On the 1st February 1890 she was damaged by a gale while lying in dock at Shields and she then, in turn, damaged the brig "Hare Belle" of Yarmouth. On the 12th February 1901 she became stranded on the South Gare Breakwater, River Tees, and was a total loss.

11026 **PROMISE**

Built in 1847 at Howden Pans, Northumberland.
Brigantine, 168 registered tons. Signal Code K.Q.W.B.
Owners: Frederick William Fairbrass, The Whitstable Shipping Company.
Masters: Huson, Day, J.J. Joiner jun., 1904. R. Coleman, Ericson, 1907.

Prince Consort, see previous page

13221 **PROPITIOUS**
Built in 1825 at Boston, Lincs.
Schooner, 52 registered tons. 58.4 x 16.9 x 7.6.
Owner: Charles Hoult, 30th June 1860.
This vessel was bought from Hull on the 25th May 1860. She was sold to Sunderland on the 22nd November 1862.

PROVIDENCE
Built in 1813 at Masborough, Yorkshire.
Sloop, 54 registered tons. 55.1 x 15.0 x 7.0.
Owner: Samuel Shepherd.
Master: William Morris, 14th May 1832.
This vessel foundered off Circo in 1850.

11245 **PRUDENCE**
Built in 1826 at Berwick-on-Tweed.
Schooner, 163 registered tons. 75.0 x 20.4 x 14.0.
Owner: John Tassell.
Master: Thomas Edward Laraman, 30th April 1855.
This vessel was lost off the Dudge Light-Ship on the 31st October 1863.

PSYCHE
Owners: W. Foreman and Dadd.
Master: Barden.
Although owned, manned, and well-known at Whitstable, it has not been possible to discover facts about her.

55393 **PURVEYOR**
Built in 1867 at Portsmouth.
Ketch, 60 registered tons.
Owner: James Camburn.
Bought from Arbroath.

452 **QUEEN**
Built in 1853 at Prince Edward Island.
Brigantine, 149 registered tons. 87.2 x 22.3 x 12.6.
Owners: George Harris, William Harris, Richard Blaxland, 17th October 1862.
Masters: Hovenden, 1864. Cooper, 1875.
This vessel was bought from Swansea on the 23rd August 1862. She was broken up in October 1884.

56454 **QUEEN OF THE ISLES**
Built in 1867 at Newburgh, Perthshire.
Schooner, 173 registered tons. 97.7 x 22.3 x 12.3.
Owner: William Goldfinch, 12th September 1870.
This vessel came to Whitstable in 1870, and was lost in December 1874.

43968 **QUICKSTEP (ex JEHOSSIN)**

Schooner, 163 registered tons. 97.7 x 23.7 x 10.8.
Owners: John Lane Page, Henry Epps Larkin, John Ginder, 14th March 1862.
This vessel was bought from London on the 10th February 1862. She was broken up in September 1879.

124365 **R.A.G.**

Built in 1904 at Malta.
Ketch, 82 registered tons. 77.9 x 17.4 x 8.7.
Owners: Fred Rigden, Henry Gann, 1st November 1923.
This small vessel was named after those who had a financial interest in her, namely, Rigden, Anderson, and Gann. She came to Whitstable in November 1923, and was broken up in July 1929.

RAMBLER

Owner: A. Gardner.
Masters: Taylor, W.S. Joiner.

RANGER

Owner: Thomas Gann.
Master: Thomas Winder.
This vessel was mentioned at the Kent Assizes, 11th March 1861.

29578 **RAPID**

Built in 1861 at Shoreham by May.
Brigantine, 191 registered tons. 100.4 x 24.8 x 12.4. Signal Code Q.G.F.T.
Owner: H.J. Digby.
Masters: R. Claringbold, H. Digby, J. Joiner jun., 1911. W.G. Joiner, 1915.
This vessel was sold to Ireland in November 1916 but was lost off the Scilly Isles with all hands, Daniel Court, master.

RAVEN
Built in 1849 at Quaco, New Brunswick.
Brigantine, 121 registered tons. 74.4 x 20.1 x 10.3.
Owners: Charles Hoult, Alfred Hoult.
Masters: Alfred Hoult, 26th November 1851. Sacar Hoult, 2nd April 1852. Thomas Hoult, 3rd June 1853.
This vessel was bought from London on the 26th November 1851. The *Kentish Independent* of the 20th December 1856 informs us that the RAVEN, a ship of Whitstable, was damaged in Robin Hood's Bay by being run into by an unknown vessel. She was damaged, dismasted, and cut to the water line. Captain Thomas Hoult in command. She was finally lost on the Haisboro Sand on the 29th December 1867.

66357 **RAVEN**
Built in 1873 at Bay Fortune Bridge, Prince Edward Island, by James Duncan.
Brigantine, 177 registered tons. 106.5 x 24.2 x 12.9. Signal Code M.N.V.F.
Owners: George Camburn, 10th April 1884. T.R. Dadd, George Gann, Pout, J.G. Gann, 1915.
Masters: E. Blaxland, H.W. Beesley.
This vessel was sold to London on the 12th May 1916.

74196 **RAYMOND**

Built in 1876 at Summerside, Prince Edward Island, for D. Evans. Brigantine, 199 registered tons. 104.8 x 24.3 x 12.9. Signal Code Q.M.T.G.

Owners: S. Evans of New Quay, 1884. E. Davies of New Quay, 1888. W. Foreman, T.R. Gadd, 1890. Thomas R. Dadd, Emily Foreman, G. Hall, F.C. Ashby, 28th May 1895. W. Joiner, J. Keeler, 1912.

Masters: J. Joiner jun., W. Dadd.

This vessel, bought for Whitstable in 1895 was mainly used in the coasting trade, and was sold away to J. Murdock of Poole in 1916. Although her future history does not concern Whitstable it is well worth noting. In 1917 she had an unpleasant encounter with a German submarine off Ushant, and was saved by the timely arrival of a patrol boat. On the 1st April 1927 she had the misfortune to sit on the anchor of another ship in Fowey Harbour, and suffered damage. In 1928 she was engaged for the training of young men as pilots by a syndicate, under the direction of Edward M. Tumilty and George Dean, the P&O river pilot. In the autumn of 1929 she was sold to Mr Charles Quirk the carbide manunfacturer, and was re-named Lady Quirk to be used as a training ship. On her first voyage she stranded on the Bembridge Ledge, Isle of Wight, but she was got off and was given a mooring in Poole Harbour where she was used as a training ship in 1930, and was then dedicated by the Bishop of Stepney.

After her husband's death Lady Quirk presented the RAYMOND to the Battersea Sea Cadet Corps to replace the "Nelson" which had been recently sunk, and she was then towed round to the Thames. After a time she was used as a boat-house by the Leigh-on-Sea Yacht Club. With the outbreak of war in 1939, she was left to the destructive powers of vandals, who did so much damage that on the return of peace it was decided to break her up. Her figurehead found a resting place in the garden of the Leigh-on-Sea Yacht Club.

17920 **RECKLESS**
Built in 1857 at Rye.
Schooner, 149 registered tons. 91.3 x 22.1 x 12.4.
Owners: George Albert Cox, William White Foreman, William H. Randall, 8th January 1859.
Master: George Merritt.
This vessel was bought from Rye on the 7th January 1859, and she was wrecked off Cleethorpes in 1880.

36431 **RECOMPENSE**
Built in 1859 at Prince Edward Island, Lot 49, by Bollem.
Brigantine, 213 registered tons. 106.0 x 23.2 x 12.9. Felt and Zinc.
Owners: Henry Epps Larkin, 5th November 1861. William Bate Knight, 19th November 1870. Gann, Cox & Co.
Masters: Dunn, Burniston.
This vessel was bought from Liverpool on the 2nd November 1861. She was insured with the Whitstable Star Mutual Marine Assurance Association for £1,000.
The *Whitstable Times* of the 14th August 1869 announced that RECOMPENSE had foundered in Tenby Roads by springing a leak, she went down at 5.00 a.m. on Wednesday 11th August, and that divers had been sent down to devise a means of raising her. This was successfully achieved, and she was repaired and went into service again.
The *Whitstable Times* announced that on Monday 29th November 1875 she had collided with the yawl "Ann" breaking her Mast and Bowsprit, and doing damage estimated at £260.
She was finally wrecked off Cromer on the 19th December 1878.

39272 **REMEDY**
Built in 1857 at Prince Edward Island, Lot 49, by Bollem.
Brigantine, 139 registered tons. 96.0 x 22.0 x 10.2. Black birch, spruce, pine, juniper, and maple.
Owners: Thomas Giles Rigden, John Foad, 25th March 1861. J. Goldfinch.
Master: Thomas Rigden, 1861.
This vessel was bought from Bideford, on the 11th March 1861. She was lost in Mount Bay on the 11th April 1869.

45560 **RENA**
Built in 1859 at Grossfelin near Emden.
Schooner, 70 registered tons. 72.7 x 16.0 x 7.8.
Owner: Thomas Butcher jun., 9th September 1863.
This vessel was sold to Yarmouth on the 20th May 1867.

58881 **RESOLUTE**
Built in 1869 at Aberdeen by Duthie.
Barquentine, altered to a Schooner, 198 registered tons.
116.6 x 24.6 x 13.2. Signal Code J.F.G.P.
Owners: W.S. Pearce, G.H. Gann, 17th May 1884. The Whitstable Shipping Company.
Masters: Herbert Whitnall, G.M. Beer, A. Fryer.
This vessel was sold to Blyth in April 1919.

RESOLUTION
Built in 1787 at Strood.
Sloop, 47 registered tons. 52.9 x 15.0 x 8.0.
Owner: James Reeves (timber merchant).
Masters: Thomas Edward Laraman, 3rd November 1849. George Samson, 18th April 1853.
This vessel was sold to Sunderland in March 1855.

11211 **RESOLUTION**
Built in 1809 at Cowes.
Schooner, 80 registered tons. 62.2 x 17.9 x 9.1.
Owner: Stephen Rigden.
Masters: Thomas Lott, 6th April 1853. Stephen Cornelius, 28th December 1854.
This vessel was lost off the coast of France on the 12th March 1863.

47312 **RESULT**

Built in 1863 at St Helier, Isle of Jersey.
Brig, 163 registered tons. 106.2 x 23.3 x 12.1. Signal Code D.L.H.B.R.
Owners: Joseph Pettman, 19th July 1866. W. Franklin, E. Nicholls.
Masters: Joseph Pettman, Court, T. Rigden.

This vessel was bought from London on the 17th July 1866, and was insured with the Whitstable Star Mutual Maritime Assurance Association for £1,000. She was sold foreign in June 1877.

46857 **RETRIEVER**

Built in 1863 at Belfast, Prince Edward Island, by William McGill.
Brigantine, 190 registered tons. 106.0 x 23.8 x 12.9. Signal Code V.L.F.R.
Owners: Ozias Ougham, William Carlton, Josiah Reeves, Agnes Taylor, 4th February 1880 from George Butcher, Marshall, 23rd October 1865.
Master: W. Carlton.

This vessel was bought by George Butcher on the 4th October 1865. On the 18th July 1889 when off Beachy Head she ran into the Danish schooner "Afma". The claim for assistance and damage was settled at £145.5.0, and her owners then insured her for £560. She was turned into a hulk on the 27th February 1891.

124364 **RHODESIA (ex SEMPER SPERA)**
Built in 1909 at Delkgyl, Holland.
Ketch, 119 registered tons. 97.4 x 19.4 x 7.2.
Owners: Abbie Anderson, Thomas Rigden, Stanley Anderson, Charles James Perkins, 18th November 1920.
Master: Lawson.
This vessel was a familiar craft as she was moored off the beach here in a neglected state, often referred to as the "old iron pot"

3919 **RINGLEADER**
Built in 1853 at Sandwich by Hoad Bros.
Brig altered to Brigantine, 180 registered tons. 100.6 x 23.0 x 12.0. Zinc. Signal Code H.W.J.F.
Owners: William Holden, John Foad, James Henry Butcher, John Spenceley, James Henry Lott, 25th July 1853. William Griffiths Lawson, E. Allen, James Kemp, 13th January 1870.
Masters: James Henry Butcher, 25th July 1853. William T. Bell, 25th April 1854. James H. Butcher, 13th July 1855. Barden, N. Allen, 1861.
In July 1853 the local newspapers published the following.

A beautiful Brig, 180 tons register, named the "Ringleader", for the Whitstable trade, was launched from the Ship-yard of Messrs Hoad, Sandwich, on Saturday 16 July. Her singular name has excited some curiosity here; and if any dependance is to be placed in the opinion of those who profess to be judges of ship's models, the Ringleader will not be a sluggard as to sailing qualities.

This generous prophecy was destined to become true, for without delay she was added to the Mediterranean fleet in company with the "William" and the "Petrel". She was altered to a brigantine in November 1887. On the 16th October 1903, when off Folkestone, she was run down by the barque "Hawthornbank" and she quickly foundered.

Rose

20207 **ROBERT**
Built in 1820 at Dundee.
Schooner, 87 registered tons.
Owners: Vidler & Co.
This vessel was insured with the Whitstable Star Mutual Maritime Assurance Association. On the 29th November 1897 she was endeavouring to ride out a gale in the North Sea when she became dismasted, and was in collision with another vessel. She did not sink and was towed into Lowestoft.

ROB ROY
Registered at Whitstable 2nd November 1863.
182 registered tons.
Owner: James Holden.
Masters: Ashby, 1864. R. Wraight.
This vessel was insured for £840.

ROCHFORD
Built in 1787 at Vauxhall, Surrey.
Boomsail, 57 registered tons. 68.2 x 18.2 x 7.2.
Owner: Thomas Fairbrass, 2nd October 1922.
Masters: Richard Wraight, 14th September 1836. Thomas Fairbrass, 2nd October 1839.
This vessel was broken up in July 1840.

63321 **ROSE**

Built in 1870 on the Isle of Whithorn, Sunderland, and registered at Sunderland.
Brigantine, 164 registered tons. Signal Code L.T.R.C.
Owners: George Holden, Belmont, Whitstable, and Pout Brothers.
Masters: A. Pout, Sandy, A. Fryer, 1890. George Frend, 1891.

On the 18th October 1889 she was insured for £400. Few stories of shipwreck can be more thrilling than the tragic loss of the brigantine ROSE. She left Sunderland on Monday 25th March 1901, and as she approached the Thames Estuary she became unmanageable in the north-east gale. At 1.45 a.m. on Thursday 26th March she struck on the Red Sand and in a few minutes she sank. George Frend, the master was in his cabin at the time, and it was only with the greatest difficulty that he fought his way out, and climbed with the rest of the crew into the rigging. With marvellous presence of mind one of the crew managed to grasp a bucket with some paraffin and about six pounds of cotton waste. As soon as possible they set fire to this, hoping that the Girdler Lightship would see them, it being scarcely two miles away. Although the signal burned for a quarter of an hour it was not seen. Hour after hour the men clung to the rigging, and when at last the dawn broke it revealed seven men, George Frend the master, Wallace Adams, John Stevens, Darky Thomas, a boy from the Cornwall Training Ship, and two others. Darky Thomas, who had come out of the "Eagle" especially for this trip, was the first to fall off exhausted, and was swept away by the fast running tide. Shortly afterwards the two unknown men went mad. One went overboard at 8.00 a.m., and soon afterwards the other man lost his grip, and hung by the foot from the yard arm. His frantic struggles at last released him and he too was swept away. The next to go was the young lad who lost consciousness and fell. Although the masts of the vessel were seen from the shore it was not realised that there were living men in the rigging.

Late in the afternoon, Capt J.R. Daniels, with the aid of his powerful telescope saw signs of life in the rigging, and at once telephoned the Margate and Clacton Life-boats. Here the story is best continued by *The Life-Boat* published on 1st November 1901.

THE LIFE-BOAT
1st November 1901

MARGATE – About 4.40 p.m. on the 21st March, a telegram was received from Lloyd's agent at Whitstable stating that a brigantine had stranded on the Red Sand and that her crew were apparently in jeopardy. A strong gale was blowing from N.E. and the sea was rough. The crew of the Life-boat ELIZA HARRIET were summoned and in ten minutes from the receipt of the telegram the boat was launched and was on her way to the scene of the casualty. On reaching the West Last a vessel was observed about N. by W. and thinking she was the one reported to be in distress the boat made for her, but found she was a brig riding at anchor. As darkness had now set in, the Life-boatmen boarded her to ascertain if her crew could give any information respecting the stranded vessel. They were informed that a sunken vessel had been seen in a S.W. direction about a mile and a half distant but no men had been observed either on the vessel or on her masts. Proceeding in the direction indicated, the Life-boat searched until 9.30 when the strong tide rendered it prudent to put into Whitstable for a time. About 4.00 a.m., having received fresh directions, she again put off, resumed the search, and at daylight found she was close to the vessel which was sunk between the Red and Middle Sands. Her foreyard was just under water and on running in nearer to her men were seen in the top. The Life-boat having sailed to windward of the wreck lowered her foremast and with the help of oars got alongside with her head right under the vessel's foretop, this being the only way of getting the men off, as they were perfectly helpless. They numbered three men: the survivors of a crew of seven. Having taken the men, one of whom was almost lifeless, on board, the boat was, with some difficulty, got clear of the wreck and at once sailed for Whitstable. The tide being low when she arrived, a dinghy was procured by means of which the rescued men were landed, and they then received proper attention. At high water the Life-boat left for her station, arriving home about 4.30 p.m. The wrecked vessel was the brigantine "Rose" of Whitstable, laden with coal.

THE WHITSTABLE TIMES
March 30th 1901

TERRIBLE SUFFERINGS OF THE CREW
Nearly Thirty Hours in the Rigging

Last week we briefly reported the loss of the brigantine Rose on the Red Sand, and the rescue of three of the crew of seven who were on board. Subsequent enquiries lead us to characterise the casualty as one of the most appalling and distressing cases of shipwreck that has ever occurred to our local vessels. It will be remembered that on Thursday the masts of a vessel were observed on the Red Sand, but as a man of war was seen to pass close by no one ever dreamed that anyone could be in the rigging. In the afternoon, just after four o'clock, Captain J. R. Daniels was informed that a vessel had gone down on the sand which, by the way, is seven and a half miles distant from the shore. He at once had a look through his telescope and observed that there were human beings in the rigging. He at once telephoned to the Margate and Clacton lifeboat stations informing them of his fears that there was someone in the wreck and the Margate boat put out. Darkness, however, set in before she could reach Whitstable, and it was impossible for them to locate the vessel that night. As soon as daylight dawned the boat was launched from Whitstable Harbour, and at six o'clock the wreck was reached. It was then found that the Captain, George Frend, the mate, Wallace Adams, and an able bodied seaman, named John Stevens, were still hanging in the rigging, and that four of the crew had perished. The survivors were brought ashore. Captain Frend and his mate, in spite of having for nearly thirty hours been exposed to the fury of the gale walked to their homes, but Stevens was so exhausted and in such a serious condition that he had to be carried on a stretcher to Rolfe's Harbour Street coffee tavern, and it was at first thought he would not pull through. Under the careful treatment of Dr Hayward and skillful rubbing and nursing, however, he regained consciousness, and on Saturday was able to go to his own lodgings in the town.

On Friday night our representative was able to obtain an interview with Captain Frend, who is a brother to the skipper who lost his life a month or two ago. He was at his sister's house in Harbour Street, where he had been very carefully looked after. His statement was to the following effect: "We left Sunderland on Monday morning, and although the weather was somewhat bad we did not experience anything very dreadful until we were nearing home. On Thursday morning, at about a quarter to two, we went ashore on the Red Sand. I was in the cabin at the time, the vessel went down in five minutes. Before I could get out of the cabin, water was coming in, and I only had time to shout to the crew to look out for themselves and take to the rigging. Fortunately one of them was able to get a bucket containing some paraffin and about six pounds of cotton waste. As soon as we got in the rigging we set fire to the waste, which burnt for quite a quarter of an hour. We made quite sure that the men on the Girdler Lightship would see us, as the vessel was not two miles away. They apparently did not, and we had to hang on until daybreak, having full confidence that when daylight came help would soon be at hand. Wearily the time drew on, and hour after hour passed by. There were altogether seven on board, myself, and the mate, Wallace Adams, John Stevens, the man who was saved with us, Darkey Thomas, and three others, including a boy who was formerly in the Cornwall training ship. For the life of me I cannot tell you their names. I generally addressed them by nick names. When I engaged them they of course signed the papers, which have been unfortunately lost. I know Darkey came out of the Eagle, while the boy had been working at Canterbury in a tannery yard, which he left on the day of the Queen's funeral. I never gave up hope myself, but when not a soul came near us and we had nothing to eat or drink, the others began to lose heart. The wind was very biting and seemed to go right through us. Darkey was the first to go. He dropped off exhausted, and we saw him washed away. Later on two of the others went mad. Their sufferings were most agonising. First they laughed, and they gave way to despair, foaming at the mouth. One went overboard about eight o'clock on Thursday evening, and he was followed soon afterwards by the other one. The lad went sometime afterwards in the early hours of the morning not long before help reached us. One of the men fell from the crossyard and hung by his foot just in front of us for some time. I shall never forget his distorted features with foam coming from his mouth. How we three who were saved managed to hang so long as we did I cannot tell. I kept shouting to them to hang on saying that while there was life there was hope. When the Margate boat did come, so excited were we in spite of our exhausted condition that we could hardly contain ourselves. In all my life I have never gone through such an experience. I hope I never may again. We were thirty hours without food or drink."

Great indignation is felt in Whitstable that four men should lose their lives within sight of three coastguard stations, but as far as can be ascertained no one saw that the rigging contained any sailors. If the thought had only occurred that life was to be saved, many would have been willing to go out to their succour. Thee Rose was insured in the Whitstable Mutual Marine Association.

EDITORIAL COMMENT

There has been plenty of excitement in the town during the past week. First and foremost perhaps was the loss of the brigantine "Rose" on Wednesday in last week. In another column is given an interview which our representative had with the Captain on the night of Friday, from which it will be seen that the sufferings of the crew, who were exposed to the biting bitter blast of the north easterly gales, which were experienced on Thursday were terrible. The masts of the vessel were observed throughout Thursday by numerous persons on shore, but it never occurred to anyone that human beings were in the rigging. Late in the afternoon, however, when Captain J. R. Daniels brought his telescope to bear on the wreck he saw signs of life, and at once telephoned to Margate and Clacton for the lifeboats to be launched. The Margate men came to Whitstable as soon as practicable, but owing to darkness setting in they were unable to locate the Rose's position and had to wait until the morning before they set out again. When they reached the ill fated vessel, there, crouched in the rigging, were the Captain, mate, and one seaman out of a crew of seven. The survivors were more dead than alive, but we are pleased to say, owing to prompt attention when they reached shore, they are now fast recovering from the effects of their exposure.

All the talking and writing in the world will not alter the fact that assistance did not come to the crew in time for the whole seven to be saved, but the awful truth that four lives were lost within a distance of about seven miles from the land, and within the sight of three coastguard stations is a terrible thing. The captain avers that as soon as the vessel struck a quantity of paraffin oil and waste were burned for twenty minutes, and yet those on board the Girdler lightship, a distance of only two miles did not see it. This denotes lack of observance on the part of the men on the lightship, but no doubt further light will be brought to bear on the subject. At any rate it is to be hoped that a strict enquiry will be made by the proper authority as to whether or not a sharp lookout was kept.

The statement that "The Rose was insured in the Whitstable Mutual Maritime Association" is somewhat strange as that organisation had apparently ceased to exist some eight years earlier. The minute book of the Association records the following.

"A General Meeting of the Members of the Whitstable Star Mutual Marine Assurance Association was held at the Auction Mart Whitstable on Tuesday April 4 1893 at 11.30.

The Liquidator Mr J.T. Reeves laid before the Meeting a Balance Sheet of the Society which showed a balance due to him of £3.18.5. and reported that the Society had been duly wound up according to law.

Present, Messrs J.T. Reeves, A. Nicholls, W. Bronger, C. Hoult, H. Pout. Mr J.T. Reeves in the chair.

Proposed by Mr W. Bronger, and seconded by Mr C. Hoult, that the sum of £5.5.0 be paid to the Liquidator for his services in winding up and that a notice be sent to the members applying for the amount together with the above balance of £3.18.1 viz at 4/6 per ship."

The minute book confirms that the Rose was insured with the Association for £400 class 2, and that the only claim made for her was on January 6th 1891 for £16.5.9 for loss of anchor.

6489 **ROWENA**
Built in 1856 at Arbroath, Forfar, Scotland.
Snow Brig, 195 registered tons. 101.5 x 23.6 x 13.5. Felt and yellow metal. Signal Code J.P.B.N.
Owners: William John Bronger, Stephen Richards, Edward Thomas Jarrett, 24th January 1865.
This vessel was bought from Dundee on the 21st January 1865. She was altered to a brigantine on the 29th April 1876, and she foundered off Lowestoft on the 12th July 1883.

61 **ROYAL GEORGE**
Built in 1826 at Dover.
Schooner, 94 registered tons. 83.3 x 14.9 x 9.2.
Owners: Philpot Wood, James E.M. Williams, William Edwards, John Deane, 27th April 1845.
Masters: John Livingston, 27th August 1845. William Kemp, 13th November 1847. John Livingston, 29th March 1848. William T. Bell, 22nd June 1849. Charles Harris, 2nd July 1852. William Edwards, 2nd May 1854. Edward Gaskin, 3rd October 1854.
The *Kentish Gazette* of 14th March 1854 informs us that the ROYAL GEORGE was the first vessel to be fitted with "Prighs Patent Water Ballasting Machine" as exhibited at the Crystal Palace.
This little vessel was famous for the number of long voyages which she made, which may be the reason for the number of masters which she had. She was wrecked off the coast of Georgia on the 18th October 1856.

60834 **RUBY**
Built in 1868 at Rotherhithe, London, by Salisbury.
Barque, 267 registered tons. Signal Code H.D.C.G.
Owner: Abie Anderson.
Master: D. Court.
This vessel was altered to a barquentine and was sold away.

56642 **RUPERT**
Built in 1867 at Hempstead, Gloucester.
Brigantine, 163 registered tons. 99.0 x 23.0 x 12.5. Signal Code H.J.B.K.
Owners: Thomas Gann jun., W. Gann, T. Gann, John Pout, Henry Pout, 4th May 1867. William Foreman.
Masters: L. Pout, 1891. Barden.
This vessel was insured on the 18th October 1889 for £325. She was quite new when purchased in April 1867.
On the 24th December 1895 she stranded off North Shields and was

Rupert, *see previous page*

Sancho Panza

wrecked with the loss of all hands. A subsequent newspaper report of a Whitstable Council meeting reveals the sympathy that was felt as the result of this tragic loss, when Councillor J.R. Daniels stated that since the last meeting there had been a development of the RUPERT relief matter. He stated that a sum of £169.11.0 had been received from the Mayor of Tynemouth on behalf of the Barden family. The amount was divided over the whole family, with restrictions as to the three younger children's shares. The committee at the north wished that the money should not be under the mother's control, but invested in the Post Office Savings Bank. The local committee did not think this should be so as the baby was entitled to £75. If invested in the Post Office and the child died, there would be a lot of trouble caused in getting the money for the mother. With regard to the girl aged eleven, she was entitled to £25.1.10. Would it not be wrong to let the child have that money invested in her own name so that she could draw it out the next day. The Whitstable Council decided to send their objection and hoped that the conditions would be modified. The Whitstable fund had amounted to over £54 and the Council agreed to hand that sum over to Mrs Barden together with £52.1.10, her portion from Tynemouth. Councillor Foreman said that he would also give the widow £21.1.6 which he had received from Sunderland.
So it was that our forefathers managed the affairs of our town.

58057 SALACIA

Built in 1867 at Sunderland by W.H. Pearson jun.
Brigantine, 243 registered tons. 104.6 x 25.4 x 15.3. Signal Code H.N.P.T.
Owners: R.J. Wheeler, Emeline Camburn, G. Peters, S. Lissenden, H. Rowden, J.H. Camburn, G. Holden, J.C. Brown, 8th March 1881. G. Holden jun., George Camburn.
Masters: A. Fryer, Sandy.
On the 9th February 1889, in a gale, she stranded near Hunstanton, and was a total wreck.

2536 SANCHO PANZA

Built in 1828 at New Shoreham, Sussex.
Schooner, 146 registered tons. 85.2 x 12.1 x 15.5.
Owners: Walter Foreman, Richard John Foreman, John Spenceley, C. Lawson, Adams, 1861.
Masters: Foreman, 1861. Harnett, 1864. Baker, 1870. Carlton.
This vessel was bought from London on the 19th December 1848 and was insured for £760. One mast and her figurehead were removed on the 18th September 1855. On the 23rd January 1897 she stranded on the Pye Sand near Harwich and was wrecked.

26631 **SANDFORD**

Built in 1844 at Guernsey.
Brig, 157 registered tons. 92.8 x 21.9 x 12.3.
Owners: James Kemp jun., Richard Wheeler, William Cornelius, John Jutson, John West, 1857.
Master: Nicholls, 1861.
This vessel was bought from Plymouth on the 31st October 1857. The *Whitstable Times* shortly afterwards records the following.

While the shipwrights connected with Mr Gann's yard were attempting to launch the schooner Sandford, belonging to Messrs Wheeler, Kemp, and Jutson, something in the Slip gave way, and the vessel fell suddenly to the ground, after going about 40ft. Although there were several persons on board and others close to the schooner, fortunately they all escaped sustaining any injury from the mishap. A hole, however, was knocked through the vessel, and other damage done to her, which is now being repaired on the Slip.

At the same time she was altered from a brig to a schooner. SANDFORD was lost in Morte Bay on the 1st December 1867.

SARAH

Built in 1826 at Hastings.
Sloop, 42 registered tons. 50.0 x 15.3 x 7.0.
Owners: Thomas Butcher jun. She was sold to Edward Butcher on 19th April 1852.
Masters: William Allen, 3rd April 1850. Thomas Shepherd, 4th September 1851. Wallace Harris, 12th August 1850. Thomas Lott, James Stroud.
This vessel was bought from Deal on the 2nd February 1850.

25949 **SARAH HORNE**

Built in 1846 at Pictou, Nova Scotia.
Brig altered to Brigantine, 199 registered tons. 93.0 x 21.2 x 12.8. Felt and yellow metal.
Owners: William Amos, Benjamin Harris, John Gann, 11th November 1862.
This vessel was bought from Shields on the 7th October 1862, and she was sold to London in October 1867.

35556 **SARAH JANE**

Built in 1857 at Bathurst, New Brunswick.
Brig, 165 registered tons. 94.2 x 24.3 x 11.3. Tamarac and birch. Felt and yellow metal.
Owners: Richard Blaxland, George Harris, William Harris, 2nd May 1868.
This vessel was altered from a brig to a brigantine in June 1871. She was lost off Dudglow, 5th March 1876.

20355 **SCYLLA**

Built in 1857 at Prince Edward Island, by Coffin.
Brigantine, 125 registered tons. 85.2 x 22.0 x 11.1.
Owners: George Peters, Henry Holden, William Holden, James Henry Butcher, Henry Holden jun., 30th October 1859.
Masters: Butcher, 1861. Witten, Maxted.

This vessel was bought from Plymouth on the 30th September 1859, and she was insured with the Whitstable Star Mutual Maritime Assurance Association for £150. She was lost off Shields on the 29th November 1874.

28451 **SEAHAM**

Built in 1860 at Rye by James Collins and Hoad Bros.
Schooner, 144 registered tons. 94.0 x 22.6 x 12.1. Signal Code P.W.L.Q. Zinc. 1862.
Owners: George Morrell, Henry Clothier, Jarrett, 29th August 1860.
Masters: H. Clothier, 1861. J. Pettman, G. Boumer.

This vessel was engaged in the slate trade, and she was wrecked in South Roads, off Lowestoft on the 28th October 1882.

27833 **SELA**

Built in 1859 at Hillsborough, Prince Edward Island, by Hayon.
Brig altered to Brigantine, 198 registered tons. 109.7 x 24.7 x 12.0. Signal Code P.S.W.K.
Owners: George Holden, Thomas Gann jun., William Blackman, 1st November 1859. George John Drury, Frederick William Fairbrass, 17th April 1890. The Whitstable Shipping Company, 1st December 1892.
Masters: Ougham, William Brunger, 1861. Hills, J. Sinclair, J. Pettman, H. Pout 1877.

This vessel was bought after her maiden voyage over the Atlantic in October 1859. She was altered from a brig to a brigantine in August 1884, and she was sold to the Greeks in September 1919. Nevertheless her impressive remains were photographed by D. Owen of Fishguard in April 1959 as she laid on the sea-shore at Neyland, Milford Haven.

Sesame

Sela, see previous page

39249 **SELEKA**
Built in 1857 at Prince Edward Island.
Brigantine, 165 registered tons. 96.5 x 22.2 x 12.7.
Owners: George Blaxland, Thomas Terry, John Graves, Osborne Nicholls, Alfred Nicholls, 17th November 1859.
Masters: Sandy, Bell, 1869.
This vessel was bought from London on the 16th November 1859. She was condemned to be broken up on the 28th August 1879.

63562 **SESAME**
Built in 1870 at Sunderland.
Brigantine, 175 registered tons.
Owner: George H. Gann.
Master: Sayers, 1882.

50890 **SEVEN SONS**
Built in 1864 at Egmont Bay, Prince Edward Island.
Brig, 194 registered tons. 101.7 x 24.3 x 12.4.
Owners: Edward Kemp, 26th May 1865. J. Andrews.
Master: Jutson.
This vessel was bought after her first voyage on the 30th November 1864 and was insured for £1,000. She was lost off North Shields in a S.W. gale on the 2nd December 1876.

26603 **SHAMROCK**
Built in 1840 at Grand Lake, New Brunswick.
Brigantine, 91 registered tons. 66.0 x 19.9 x 8.6.
Owners: William Woodward, William Dutaillis, Charles Thomas Pelfrey, David Waters, Thomas Richard Culver, Robert Young, 28th May 1852.
Masters: Charles Thomas Pelfrey, 29th May 1852. William Fearn, 7th July 1854. William Court, 27th November 1854.
This vessel was lost off Scarborough in March 1856.

37687 **SHOOTING STAR**
Built in 1854 at New Glasgow, Nova Scotia.
Barque, 267 registered tons. 111.8 x 26.0 x 14.1. Birch, spruce, and yellow pine, felt and zinc.
Owner: J.T. Goldfinch, 6th September 1865.
Master: Laraman.
This vessel was bought from London on the 3rd May 1861, and sold back to London on the 3rd July 1866.

27628 **SILOAM**
Built in 1859 at Prince Edward Island by Coffin.
Brigantine, 165 registered tons. 94.6 x 22.1 x 11.1. Signal Code P.S.C.T.
Owners: E. Nicholls, J. Reeves, H. Nicholls sen., H. Nicholls jun., T. Nicholls sen., 28th February 1860.
Master: H.R. Nicholls, 1860.
This vessel was bought from Plymouth on the 27th February 1860 and she was insured with the Whitstable Star Mutual Maritime Assurance Association for £600.

58024 **SILVER HILL**
Built in 1868 at Kingston, Shoreham, Sussex.
Brig altered to Brigantine, 192 registered tons. 102.0 x 24.6 x 12.8. Signal Code K.T.B.W.
Owner: James Goldfinch sen., 16th April 1874.
Master: Rogers.
This vessel suffered a truly spectacular end for she was burnt on Collar's Slip on the 29th March 1878.

53045 **SIR ROBERT McLURE**
Built in 1866 at Aberystwith.
Brig, 197 registered tons. 102.9 x 24.1 x 13.1.
Owners: William Lane, John Wallace Taylor, John Seatter, 15th August 1884.
Master: Charles Putwain.
This vessel was run down when she was thirteen miles S.E. from the Owers Light on the 4th February 1886, and was lost.

23804 **SNOWDROP**
Built in 1845 at Prince Edward Island.
Brigantine, 81 registered tons. 65.5 x 17.3 x 10.3.
Owners: Frederick William Fairbrass, Thomas W. Fairbrass, bought from Swansea on 4th September 1851. Sold to Henry Saffery, and John Saffery, 23rd December 1854.
Masters: Henry A. Collar, 11th September 1851. William Maxted, 7th October 1854. Henry Saffery, 28th December 1854. Bright.
This vessel was lost at the entrace to Seaham Harbour on the 13th October 1867.

2746 **SOPHIE**
Built at Mytilene in the Archipelago.
Barque, 335 registered tons. 99.5 x 25.7 x 15.5.
Owner: Thomas Fairbrass, 1851.
Master: Edward Vincer, 17th December 1851.
This vessel was broken up in 1861.

60232 **SPARKLING FOAM**

Built in 1868 at Sandwich by Henry Pain.

Brigantine, 199 registered tons. 115.8 x 24.4 x 12.8. Signal Code H.J.L.W.

Owners: Charles Hoult, Alfred Hoult, A.W. Daniels, 5th October 1868.

Masters: Charles Hoult, G.A. Hoult, 1888. Tilley, J.W. Miller.

Captain J.W. Miller was her master for thirty-eight and a half years, and he was known more by the name of his ship than by his own name.

On the 24th September 1889 her figurehead and cut-water were damaged by a steamer in the Commercial Dock, and this event would seem to have moved the owners to think seriously about insurance, for on the 18th October 1889 they insured the ship for £700. She was sold to Fowey on the 21st December 1915.

SPECULATION

Built in 1811 at Sandwich.
Sloop, 50 registered tons. 46.9 x 16.1 x 7.2.
Owners: Thomas Fairbrass jun., Charles Alexander Friend.
Master: Thomas Fairbrass jun.

After sailing as a sloop for some time she was altered to a schooner. Her average cargo was 90 tons of coal. She was sold away in 1825.

SPECULATION

Built in 1824 at Stone House, Plymouth.
Sloop, 78 registered tons. 55.2 x 18.1 x 8.8.
Owners: Stephen Rigden, Ebenezer Cotton, Thomas Fairbrass sen., Thomas Fairbrass jun., Charles Alexander Friend.
Masters: Thomas Ely, James Acors, 25th October 1847. William Allen.

This vessel was bought at Dover on the 18th October 1847.

76573 SPEEEDWELL

Built in 1878 at Kingston-on-Spey, Scotland, by Alexander Spencer.
Barquentine, 198 registered tons. Signal Code R.N.V.H.
Owner: On 3rd April 1900 she was bought by Abbie Anderson for £925.
Master: Daniel Court.

On the 12th November 1913 she was going from London to the Tyne with a cargo of ore when she was run down by the s.s. "Caspian", and was totally lost in the North Sea.

60238 **SPINDRIFT**
Built in 1870 at Seacombe.
Brigantine, 223 registered tons. 120.7 x 24.0 x 12.9.
Owner: Thomas Gann jun., 12th July 1870.
Master: A. Sykes.
This vessel came to Whitstable in July 1870 and she was wrecked off the Island of St George's on the 6th December 1870.

27832 **SPITFIRE**
Built in Hamburg.
Dandy, 31 registered tons. 64.8 x 15.8 x 5.5.
Owners: Thomas Gann jun., William Blackman, George Holden, 11th October 1859. John Wells Flick, 14th May 1870.
This vessel broke up and sank in Ramsgate Harbour in January 1890.

39153 **SPRAY**
Built in 1856 at Georgetown, Prince Edward Island.
Brig, 217 registered tons. 110.0 x 23.0 x 13.6.
Owners: George Holden, Thomas Gann jun., George Blaxland, Thomas Terry, 8th June 1857.
Three months after she came to Whitstable she foundered in a S.S.W. gale, but all the crew were saved.

Stag, see overleaf

65484 **STAG**
Built in 1871 at Dartmouth.
Barquentine, altered to Brigantine 214 registered tons.
111.4 x 24.2 x 12.9. Signal Code K.F.C.H.
Owners: George Henry Goldfinch, H. Gann, G.H. Gann, D. Stephens, E.J. Gann, 21st December 1883. The Whitstable Shipping Company.
Masters: Burniston, Attwood.
This vessel was lost on the Sunk Sands, off Harwich, on the 1st January 1908.

STAR
Owner: T. Attwater.
Master: W. Murton.
This vessel was registered at Whitstable on the 31st March 1865, and she was then insured with the Whitstable Star Mutual Maritime Assurance Associaton for £360. Apart from these few particulars it has not been possible to find out anything about her. While there may be an opinion that she is the same vessel as that next described it is difficult to appreciate how, with different owners she could be confused with another craft which was insured with the same company on the following day.

23657 **STAR**
Built in 1857 at Sunderland.
Brigantine, 157 registered tons. 76.2 x 23.2 x 13.4.
Owners: Charles Lawson, James Jutson, 1st April 1865. George Gann.
Masters: George Gann, Sandy, John Parker.
This vessel was bought from Sunderland as a wreck in January 1864, towed back to Whitstable and put in a thorough state of repair. Having been re-launched she was insured with the Whitstable Star Mutual Maritime Assurance Association for £700 and she continued to sail from here until 10th January 1872, when she was lost on the Hasborough Sand.

11267 **STAR OF THE NORTH**
Built in 1853 at Bathurst, New Brunswick.
Brigantine altered to Schooner, 165 registered tons.
86.8 x 22.4 x 11.9. Signal Code K.R.W.C.
Owners: F.W. Fairbrass, W. Cannon, 16th August 1853.
Masters: H. Adams, 2nd January 1855. Baldock 1870. Newman, Fryer, C. Carlton 1891. Henman.
This vessel was bought from Henry McCullough, of St Johns, New Brunswick, on the 16th August 1853. She was altered to a schooner in August 1856, and was broken up in December 1913, when she was owned by the Whitstable Shipping Company.

44912 **STAR OF THE OCEAN**

Built in 1863 at Southampton.
Brigantine, 186 registered tons. 100.4 x 22.6 x 13.0.
Owners: Sophia Fairbrass, 15th October 1878. Mrs Vernon Fairbrass, F.W. Fairbrass, The Whitstable Shipping Company, 1st December 1892.
Master: Uden.

This vessel was bought as a wreck from Plymouth in September 1878. She was towed round to Whitstable and put in a thorough state of repair. She was lost by collision in the North Sea in 1893.

28940 **STATESMAN**

Brig, 144 registered tons. 90.4 x 21.8 x 11.5. Signal Code Q.C.N.H.
Owners: George Baker, Richard Baker, Edward Baker, John Camburn, Joseph Bolton, 10th August 1876. C. Putwain.
Master: Joseph Bolton.

This vessel was bought from Dover on the 8th October 1862, and insured with the Whitstable Star Mutual Maritime Assurance Association for £800. She was run down off Beachy Head on the 3rd February 1884.

Star

John T. Parker (Capt. Jack), skipper of the 'Star'. He was also a diver and it was reported he died of 'wear and tear' associated with his work.

John Thomas Parker, his son, was also a diver.

25657 **STEPHEN AND SARAH**

Built in 1854 at Rye by Hassell & Holmes.
Brig altered to Brigantine, 177 registered tons. 96.5 x 32.0 x 13.4.
Felt and yellow metal. Signal Code P.G.V.K.
Owners: David Waters sen., David Waters jun., Stephen Rigden, Herbert Tritton Sankey, Henry A. Clarke, 28th February 1854. W. Kemp, Dadd & Co.
Masters: E. Allen, 8th February 1854. C. Harris 27th April 1854, C. Fowle, Bowman, Johnstone, 1861.

It was boasted that this vessel was built entirely of seasoned oak, and was therefore considered to be very sturdy. In 1860 she was altered to a brigantine and insured with the Whitstable Star Mutual Maritime Assurance Association for £800.

On the 29th November 1897 she was endeavouring to ride out a gale in the North Sea, but owing to continual rolling she lost her masts, and in an effort to save her the crew cast her adrift, and thereby she lost her anchors and chains. She was eventually caught and towed into Yarmouth, but before they reached safety the ship's boy and Captain Bowman had been washed overboard and drowned.

Her future life was very short for on the 29th October 1898 she stranded on the Gunfleet Sand and was a total wreck.

27419 **STRATHSPEY**

Built in 1860 at Garmouth, Moray, by Stewart.
Schooner, 126 registered tons. 89.0 x 22.2 x 11.4.
Owners: Henry Holden, David Daniels, 3rd May 1865. E. Nicholls.
Masters: Goodwin, J. Wood, Lacey.
This vessel was bought from Banff on the 28th April 1865, and insured with the Whitstable Star Mutual Maritime Assurance Association for £700. She sailed from Sunderland bound for Plymouth on the 12th February 1872, and was never heard of again.

29291 **SUNBEAM**

Built in 1860 at Hartlepool by Blumer.
Schooner, 102 registered tons. Signal Code Q.F.B.R.
Owner: T. Mortley.
Master: T. Mortley.
This vessel was insured with the Whitstable Star Mutual Maritime Assurance Association for £750.

89864 **SUNSHINE**

Built in 1890 at Whitstable by the Whitstable Shipping Company.
Ketch, 119 registered tons. 95.8 x 23.3 x 9.0. Signal Code M.K.W.S.
Owners: James Thomas Goldfinch, 22nd October 1890. T. Rigden, A. Anderson, J. Anderson, 19th June 1918. Fred Goldfinch.
Masters: E. Camburn, G.H. Pattenden.
This vessel was insured with the Whitstable Star Mutual Maritime Assurance Association for £600 at a valuation of £1,500, on the 22nd October 1890. It would appear from her log book that she spent most of her life as a collier bringing coal to Ramsgate and Margate.
She was wrecked in Zeebrugge Harbour on the 5th April 1920.

6963 **SUSAN**

Built in 1842 at Miramichi, New Brunswick.
Brig, 168 registered tons. 91.6 x 22.7 x 12.6. Signal Code J.R.B.F.
Owners: W. Kemp, D. Waters, J. Goldfinch, H.T. Sankey, Thomas Gann, 20th September 1860.
Master: T. Walker.
This vessel was bought from London on the 18th September 1860, and she was insured with the Whitstable Star Mutual Maritime Assurance Association for £700. She was lost on the 21st February 1882.

Sunshine, see previous page

Sunshine

39184 **SUSAN GRAY**

Built in 1857 at Vernon River, Prince Edward Island.
Brig, 223 registered tons. 103.0 x 24.3 x 13.6. Black birch, spruce, pine, maple.
Owners: Thomas Gann jun., George Holden, George Blaxland, Thomas Terry, 29th March 1859.
Master: Blaxland.
This vessel was bought from London on the 24th March 1859, and it was sold to South Shields on the 21st October 1863.

27688 **SUSAN HENDRY**

Built in 1860 at Perth.
Schooner, altered to Brigantine. 84.0 x 21.1 x 11.6. Spruce, cedar, pine, teak. Signal Code P.T.F.D.
Owners: James Kemp jun., William Kemp, Thomas Humphrey, 16th June 1865.
Master: W.M. Care.
This vessel was bought from Kirkaldy on the 11th June 1865 and was insured with the Whitstable Star Mutual Maritime Assurance Association for £720. The *Whitstable Times* reported that she sank eight miles S.E. of Aldebury in 1884.

11266 **SUSANNAH**

Built in 1810 at Sandwich.
Schooner, 166 registered tons. 86.9 x 20.3 x 11.0.
Owners: William Blackman, Thomas Gann, 30th October 1858.
Masters: S. Harrison, 17th May 1839, and 14th March 1844. G. Clothier, 15th October 1845. Edward Bell, 3rd November 1845. T. Gaskin, 18th November 1846. G. Richardson, 8th May 1847. W. Bedwell, 4th November 1850. A. Marr, 15th March 1854. Singer 1856. Woodcock, 1864.
This vessel was bought from Sandwich on the 15th April 1839, but the names of her original purchasers have been lost. From the long list of her masters may be judged the great variety of her voyages, long and short, in which she was employed.
On the 19th December 1879 she was sold by auction and was afterwards converted into a lighter.

SUSANNAH ANN

Built in 1841 at Deptford, Durham.
Brig, 165 registered tons. 76.4 x 21.5 x 12.6.
Owners: James Reeves, Edward Kemp, John Lawson, John Graves, December 1850.
Masters: Thomas Edward Laraman, 28th June 1851. Henry Richard Nicholls, 25th September 1853. Richard Gaskin, 5th April 1854.
This vessel was bought from Rochester on the 27th December 1850. Her end is not known.

6787 **SWIFT**

Built in 1817 at Woolwich Dockyard.
Dandy, 82 registered tons. 58.7 x 16.8 x 10.5.
Owners: Philpot Wood, James E.M. Williams, William Edwards, John Deane, 8th August 1853.
Masters: Richard Keys, 22nd August 1848. Edward Vincer, 4th January 1849. George Nicholls, 4th January 1850.

It has not been possible to find out the names of the original owners of this little vessel, but her new owners in 1853 had her lengthened and a new keelson built. In June 1857 she was altered from a dandy to a schooner, and a female bust was added as her figure-head.
In September 1862 the female figure-head was removed and replaced by one depicting a swift, as being considered to be more in keeping with her name. She was sold to Ipswich on the 2nd November 1864.

60241 **SYRINGA**

Built in 1871 at Seacombe.
Barquentine, 248 registered tons. 130.0 x 24.2 x 12.7. Signal Code K.W.C.S.
Owners: George Holden, Thomas Gann jun., W. Gann, H. Gann, F Gann, Herbert Gann, 23rd August 1871.

This vessel was registered at Whitstable on the 14th August 1871. It should be noted that the "Gann" owners were the five sons of Thomas Gann sen., of the Manor House.
This vessel was sold to Glasgow on the 10th November 1883.

TAMERLANE

Built in 1817 at Southdown, Suffolk.
Square, 121 registered tons. 69.4 x 20.4 x 11.1.
Owners: Walter Foreman, George Mommer, William Robinson.
Master: Sacar Hoult, 7th February 1831, and 29th September 1836.
This vessel probably came to Whitstable in 1831, and she was sold to Clay on the 31st October 1836.

89852 **TANKERTON TOWER**

Built in 1884 at Whitstable by Goldfinch Bros.
Schooner, 118 registered tons. 95.0 x 20.5 x 9.1. Signal Code J.N.R.B.
Owner: A.J. Anderson, 7th August 1884.
Masters: W. Cox, J. Anderson, Holsen, Bailey.
In 1884 the vessel the "Good Intent", which had been built by John Collar in 1844, was drawn up on Goldfinch Brothers' slipway, cut in halves, lengthened, and launched, named the TANKERTON TOWER, on the 31st July 1884.
On the 11th November 1891, when twenty five miles off Souter she suffered considerable damage in a gale. She was rescued and towed into Newcastle by two tugs for £110. On the 2nd February 1892 the insurance was settled at £239.16.1.
In 1893 she was wrecked at Salt Fleet, but was re-floated, brought back to Whitstable, where she was drawn up on Fairbrass's slip and repaired. She was launched in July 1894, taken over by Capt Bailey, and was sold to Middleton, Gloucestershire.

47270 **TARTER**

Built in 1864 at Rye.
Brig altered to Brigantine, 176 registered tons. 100.6 x 22.9 x 12.8. Signal Code V.M.W.G.
Owners: F.C. Clothier, W. Clothier, Elizabeth A. Clothier, James R. Clothier, 18th May 1881.
Master: H. Clothier.
The Whitstable Times informs us that on the 10th January 1885 the TARTER was run into by a steamer at the entrance to Tyne Dock, that the vessel was insured with the Whitstable Star Mutual Maritime Assurance Association, and that Mr James Daniels was investigating. On the 23rd January 1900 TARTER was sunk in collision off the North Foreland.

68346 **THAMES**

Built in 1875 at Plymouth by Marshall.
Brigantine, 176 registered tons. 103.7 x 24.0 x 12.7. Signal Code M.B.N.P.
Owners: The Whitstable Shipping Company, 4th November 1887.
Masters: K.W. Ericson, 1917. C. Cooper, 1919. G. Goldfinch.
This vessel had foundered in Swansea Bay in November 1880, but her previous name was not known. In 1887 she was raised by the Trinity House authorities and sold as a wreck to the Whitstable Shipping Company. When she was at Antwerp in 1917 she was impounded by the Germans, but Capt Ericson managed to escape. She foundered in the Bay of Biscay in 1923.

51924 **THIRZA**

Built in 1865 at Prince Edward Island by Robert Longworth.
Brigantine, 199 registered tons. 104.4 x 23.8 x 12.7. Signal Code H.J.W.M.
Owners: Thomas Gann jun., William Gann, Frederick Gann, George Holden, Henry Pout, James Pout, The Whitstable Shipping Company, 23rd October 1866.
Masters: F. Baker, George Frend, Blaxland, L.J. Ballands, Arnold, 1879. Silk, 1880. Frederick Maxted, 1891. Gibbons, 1899.

The Gann brothers bought this vessel in 1866, and they boasted that they did not mind if she paid or not providing she made fast passages. No expense was spared to keep her in tip top condition and make her safe when "cracking on". Her proud master during this period was George Wilkinson Frend, and he could tell many stories of her speed and the trips she made to all parts of the world. Later Henry Pout objected so strongly that she should ever be run at a loss that Captain George Frend left in protest and disgust.

In August 1915 the Great War was raging, the menace of the German U-boats was growing every day and THIRZA was lying in the Tyne. The Admiralty saw in her just the type of vessel that they needed to fight the German submarines. So they purchased her, fitted her with an auxillary motor, and armed her with two 12 pounders and two six pounders. It should be noted that she was not just an armed Merchantman which is armed for defensive purposes only, but a properly commissioned war-ship carrying cargo as well as her offensive armament.

During the time that she was engaged in this adventurous task her name was changed from THIRZA to "Ready", then to "Elixir", followed by "Probus", and lastly to "Q.30". In May 1917, under the name of "Probus", having loaded up with coal at Granton, she left there on the 4th May and sailed for Treguier. Having unloaded her coal she sailed for Swansea with a load of pit props. Her next port of call was Falmouth from where, at 3.30 p.m. on the 30th June she set sail for Morlaix in company with twelve other sailing ships, and one armed steam-trawler, the "Harlech Castle" as escort. It was the purpose of the "Probus" to act as decoy so that when the little fleet became strung out over a distance of three miles, four miles astern of the last ship was to be found the decoy. At 2.15 p.m. on the 21st June a distance of eight miles separated the decoy from the armed steam trawler. The "Probus" was heading on a course south-east by south, the wind being S.W. force 3 and she was sailing at four knots. Suddenly the master observed what appeared to be a ketch-rigged vessel steering the same course four miles away on the starboard quarter; but from the speed with which the bearing altered it was quickly seen that the ketch was not under sail alone.

At 2.30 p.m. the ketch revealed her true identity by opening fire. The first shot fell ten yards short of the brigantine. This prompted the crew to go to action stations and get the boat ready to be launched. Meanwhile the U-boat kept up a rapid fire from about 4,000 yards. The PROBUS then ran up the White Ensign, and at 3,500 yards opened fire with her starboard 12-pounder. The first shot fell 500 yards short, but the second shot seemed to be a hit, for the enemy which was lying across the brigantine's bows stopped and a large cloud of smoke went up and caused him to temporarily cease fire. The PROBUS then went on the other tack and brought her port 12-pounder into action, with the result that her fourth shot was a direct hit, for it dismantled the German's mast and sails, and raised a cloud of smoke from the fore part of the conning tower. This was too hot for the German and he was compelled to submerge, leaving the PROBUS to follow the convoy to Morlaix, where she arrived safely on the 25th June.

As far as Whitstable is concerned, the register of the THIRZA was closed on the 15th May 1920 when she was converted into a lighter.

91820 **THISTLE**

Built in 1887 at Plymouth.
Ketch, 62 registered tons. 70.5 x 19.2 x 8.5.
Owners: The Whitstable Shipping Company 10th May 1893.
It would appear from the 1911 register that she was sold to Minehead, Somerset.

19067 **TRIO**

Built in 1857 at Jersey.
Brig altered to Brigantine, 156 registered tons. 102.5 x 21.0 x 12.0. Felt and yellow metal.
Owners: T.G. Rigden, W.J. Goodwin, 31st March 1865. Ethelbert Idenden, E. Coleman.
Masters: Stone, Harlow.
This vessel was bought from London on the 28th March 1865, and was insured with the Whitstable Star Mutual Maritime Assurance Association for £870. She was altered to a brigantine in October 1865.

57007 **TRUE**

Built in 1866 at Fifteen Point, Prince Edward Island.
Brigantine, 218 registered tons. 104.0 x 25.3 x 12.9.
Owners: Charles Hoult, 29th July 1872. H.P. Coleman.
Master: H.P. Coleman.
This vessel was lost off Newhaven on the 14th January 1879.

127024 **TUBAL CAIN**

Built in 1871 at Essex, Mass, U.S.A.
Schooner, 80 registered tons.
Owner: George Foreman.
Master: George Foreman.

51906 **T.W. DODD**

Built in 1865 at New London, Prince Edward Island.
Brigantine, 177 registered tons. 97.0 x 23.7 x 12.3. Signal Code J.L.K.N.
Owners: Henry Wooton Nicholls, John Nicholls jun., George R. Johnson, John A. Johnson, Richard Johnson, Henry J. Baker, 21st May 1874. The Whitstable Shipping Company, 3rd July 1900.
Masters: G. Knight, G. Lacey.
This vessel was bought from Liverpool on the 12th June 1866, and was insured with the Whitstable Star Mutual Maritime Assurance Association for £1000. On the 29th November 1897 she tried to ride out a gale off Yarmouth, but having lost her tackle and anchors she had to be rescued and towed into Yarmouth. She was converted into a lighter in April 1909.

29508 **TWEED**

Built in 1865 at Newburgh, Fife, by Scrimgeour.
Brigantine altered to Schooner, 199 registered tons.
107.6 x 24.4 x 12.6. Signal Code S.W.Q.T.
Owners: G. Blaxland, 19th March 1873. Frank Nicholls, Alfred Nicholls.
Master: G. Clark.

On the 18th October 1889 she was insured for £620.

On the 16th November 1889 she was in collision with the Tug "Rescue", and Mr Nicholls had to pay £6.10.0 in compensation. In September 1915 she sailed from Whitstable with a cargo of burnt ore for the Tyne. Then she sailed from the Tyne on the 8th November with a cargo of clay for Dunkirk. She was last seen on the 13th November in Yarmouth Roads, after which she completely disappeared.

TWO SISTERS

Built in 1823 at Limehouse.
Sloop, 35 registered tons. 58.0 x 14.2 x 4.6.
Owners: William Kemp, Robert William Laraman.
Master: Thomas Laraman, 17th December 1847.

This vessel was sold by William Kemp, (Inn Keeper) to Robert William Laraman, on the 4th November 1847. She was broken up in May 1848.

41845 **TYNE**

Built in 1858 at Tynemouth, St Johns, New Brunswick.
Brigantine, 173 registered tons. 91.9 x 24.5 x 11.9.
Owners: William Griffiths Lawson, Charles Lawson, 20th November 1861.
Masters: Charles Lawson, Fuller, 1870.

This vessel was bought from Liverpool on the 2nd May 1861, and was insured with the Whitstable Star Mutual Maritime Assurance Association for £800.

William Griffiths Lawson showed more preference for this leaky ship than for any of the better vessels which he owned. She was always reputed to be a floating coffin, but she never sank. The crew were called the "sail and bail crew" because they were only engaged if they supplied their own personal bucket with which to bail her out. Lawson used her mostly in salvaging the cargoes of vessels which had been wrecked round the coasts of Devon, Cornwall, and Wales. Every night it was the custom to run TYNE ashore in order to prevent her sinking, and to enable the crew to have a good night's rest. The story was often told of a very successful salvage operation which involved golden sovereigns. When Lawson went to the bank to place his treasure in safe custody the clerk was at once suspicious and informed the police. But when the rough sailorman proved his just ownership to the two great bags of sovereigns he was only too pleased to accept them.

TYNE was eventually sold foreign.

56644 **UNCLE NED**

Built in 1867 at Ipswich by Ebenezer Robertson.
Brigantine altered to a Schooner in February 1892, 198 registered tons. 116.7 x 23.5 x 12.8. Signal Code H.Q.C.W.
Owners: James Robert Daniels, Edward Nicholls sen., Edward James Nicholls, Thomas Goldfinch, George Goldfinch, Robert Court, John Wyatt Court, Charles Stephen Beal, 21st May 1867.
Masters: W. Kearon, E. Court.

This vessel was bought when she was new and was insured with the Whitstable Star Mutual Maritime Assurance Association for £1000.

She was mostly engaged in the sugar trade, and she made a reputation for fast passages to and from the West Indies. The story was often told of the Royal Mail Steam Packet leaving Kingston Harbour on the day before the UNCLE NED, and when she was steaming up the Channel off Southampton there was the UNCLE NED in front of her.

Her outstanding speed was attributed to the fact that she had what was considered to be the ideal lines, namely, "a cod's head and a mackerel's tail".

Her connection with Whitstable was severed in June 1928, when she was sold to Dublin. She was eventually broken up in the river at Arklow in 1944, and the bearded figure-head was left to adorn a nearby garden.

69850 **UNDINE**

Built in 1875 at Fowey by Butson.

Brigantine, 174 registered tons. 104.1 x 24.0 x 13.2. Signal Code N.V.G.R.

Owners: W. Eois, F. Nicholls, Osborne Nicholls, Alfred Nicholls, 22nd May 1894.

Masters: E. Blaxland, Osborne Nicholls.

This vessel was planned and built with the definite intention that she should be a "flyer". Her mission in life was to transport pineapples from America in perfect condition for the English market. With this object in view she was fitted out with mahogany trays on which to lay the pineapples. In order to increase her powers of speed her boom was of the extraordinary length of seventy two feet, and her yards were correspondingly long. This made it necessary to tow her up to Gravesend to be loaded with chalk as ballast, it being nearly impossible to sail her in confined waters. Consequently when the pineapple trade decreased it was found necessary to cut nine feet off her boom, and two feet off the ends of her yard arms.

In February 1917 she became lost in a dense fog in the Wash, being at the time loaded with spent bark from the Tannery at Canterbury. In the light wind she just drifted until she was five miles off Flamborough Head. at 3.00 a.m. on the 25th February she was run into by the Welsh steam-ship "Emlyn", of 370 tons, owned by the Mailen Line Ltd. She wasw hit on the port bow and was cut right into the port side of the foremast, and sank rapidly.

Uncle Ned

Undine, see previous page

Undine

UNITY

Built in 1785 at Shoreham.
Square, 190 registered tons. 83.9 x 23.9 x 19.5.
Owner: Thomas Fairbrass.
Masters: Edward Hoult, 10th April 1839. Henry Hoult, 29th December 1842. Henry Tilley, 25th November 1843.
This vessel was wrecked off Hartlepool on the 1st March 1844.

Utopia

28769 **UTOPIA**

Built in 1860 at Rye, by Hoad.
Brig, 160 registered tons. 105.0 x 23.5 x 12.6. Signal Code Q.B.T.V.
Owner: George Henry Goldfinch.
Master: T. Minter.
The photo was taken when UTOPIA was driven ashore at Whitstable. She was sold away to Gillingham.

23008 **VECTIS**

Built in 1832 at Cowes by White.
Schooner, 74 registered tons. Signal Code N.P.T.S.
Owner: William Burniston.
This vessel spent all her life here as a collier.

Utopia

29388 **VENILLA**

Built in 1841 at Medford, United States.
Brigantine, 148 registered tons. Signal Code Q.F.L.D.
Owner: John A. Anderson.
Master: Warner.
This vessel was originally named the "John A. Page" and she was insured with the Whitstable Star Mutual Maritime Assurance Association for £750.

VENUS

Built in 1817 at Rye.
Brig, 80 registered tons. 55.7 x 18.1 x 9.3.
Owners: William Blackman, Thomas Fairbrass, James Greenland.
Masters: James Allen, 4th September 1827. James Randall, 8th October 1827. James Greenland, 28th February 1832.
This vessel was seized, condemned, and sold by auction on the 27th August 1827. William Blackman sold his share to Thomas Fairbrass on the 27th August 1828.

20040 **VENUS**

Built in 1847 at Elliot River, Prince Edward Island.
Brig, 175 registered tons. 98.0 x 22.5 x 13.6. Signal Code M.V.K.W.
Owners: Joseph Somers Randall, Ozias Kemp, David Waters, Frederick Kemp, I. May, J. Flick, 31st May 1864.
Masters: J. White of Seasalter, 8th March 1848. W. Bedwell, 20th March 1852.
This vessel was bought after her maiden voyage on the 22nd February 1848. She was broken up in August 1885.

34253 **VENUS**

Built in 1856 at St Peters, Prince Edward Island.
Brig, 181 registered tons. 104.9 x 24.6 x 12.0.
Owners: William John Collar, James Gann, 19th June 1861.
This vessel was bought on the 13th June 1861, and she was lost on the Pakefield Flat on the 26th October 1865.

44127 **VENUS**

Built in 1862 at Wexford.
Brig altered to Brigantine, 225 registered tons. 113.0 x 24.1 x 13.0. Signal Code T.R.S.P.
Owners: Frederick William Fairbrass, William Cannon, 7th March 1863. The Whitstable Shipping Company.
Master: Henry Adams.
This vessel was bought from Wexford on the 4th March 1863. She had the misfortune to collide with and sink the "Jane 9791" on the 30th April 1866. She was lost on the 27th December 1911.

Venus (44127)

52897 **VESTA**

Built in 1864 at New London, Prince Edward Island.
Brig, 222 registered tons. 107.7 x 25.4 x 13.6.
Owners: John Stephen Sharp, William Charles Gibbens, John Hatton, 5th February 1866.
This vessel was bought on the 11th September 1865.

VICTORIA

Built in 1837 at Inverness.
Schooner, 82 registered tons. 56.1 x 17.1 x 10.6.
Owner: John White.
Masters: Joseph White, 16th February 1846. Henry Collard, 8th March 1848.
This vessel was bought from Chatham on the 2nd February 1846. The newspaper described one of her adventures as follows:

March 1857. **THE GALE**

There was sad havoc amongst the anchors and chains of the vessels belonging to this place last week. They were riding at anchor in the Yarmouth Roads, with a great many other vessels, when a strong wind sprung up from the north-east, and obliged them to slip their anchors and seek a better place of refuge. The consequence was, that the Agnes, the Abbeyony, the Alice, and the Victoria, belonging to this port, lost an anchor and chain each.

Vivid, see overleaf

Capt. Humphrey and mate Ted Maxted on board the 'Vivid' – Whitstable Harbour 1893.

26392 **VICTORIA**
Built in 1838 at Mayland, Pembroke.
Schooner, 140 registered tons. 77.2 x 22.4 x 12.8.
Owners: Charles Lawson, James Camburn, William Griffiths Lawson, William Kemp, 28th June 1858.
This vessel was bought from London on the 17th June 1856, and it was wrecked on the 17th December 1860.

11739 **VIVID**
Built in 1852 at Rye.
Brigantine, 168 registered tons. 91.4 x 22.9 x 13.3. Signal Code K.T.V.M.
Owners: T. Blakeley, H. Clothier, 20th April 1863. Fred C. Clothier, H.W. Clothier, 31st October 1913.
Masters: H. Carvell, Burton, Humphrey.
This vessel was bought from Dover on the 15th April 1863. She was lost in the North Sea in July 1914 by being run down.

22742 **VIXEN**
Built in 1833 at Saltcoats, Yorkshire.
Schooner, 106 registered tons. 78.7 x 20.0 x 10.6. Signal Code N.M.S.C.
Owners: James Reeves, 11th July 1857. Robert Frend, George Frend.
Master: George Frend.
This vessel was insured with the Whitstable Star Mutual Maritime Assurance Association on the 18th October 1889 for £320. In January 1896 she was wrecked and sold as a hulk.

Wallards

26076 **VOLUNTEER**

Built in 1840 at Ilfracombe, Devon.
Schooner, 79 registered tons. 66.3 x 18.9 x 10.8.
Owner: Samuel Hills, 11th June 1858.
This vessel was bought from Liverpool on the 9th June 1858. She was lost between Lowestoft and Southwold on the 12th April 1866.

24650 **VULCAN**

Built in 1854 at Rye by Hoad Brothers.
Brig, 190 registered tons. 89.6 x 21.9 x 13.5.
Masters: Joseph White, 2nd May 1854. George Taylor, 19th November 1855.
This vessel came to Whitstable when she was quite new in 1854. She was wrecked at Great Yarmouth on the 12th November 1876.

60249 **WALDEMAR**

Built in 1871 in Russia.
Brigantine, 311 registered tons. 125.5 x 28.8 x 13.7. Signal Code N.T.G.R.
Owners: George Holden, Thomas Gann jun., James Pout, 20th April 1875.
This vessel came here in 1875, and she was sold to Holland in December 1887.

50316 **WALLANDS**

Built in 1866 at Lewes to the order of James H. Goldfinch.
Schooner, 99 registered tons. Signal Code N.T.R.M.
Owners: James H. Goldfinch, William Isaac Robinson, 1866.
Masters: H. Carvel, T. Burtonshaw.
When Mr Robinson went to live at Newhaven he sold his share in her for £105. She was then altered to a ketch.
She was mostly engaged in the timber trade and was so engaged in 1912 when she grounded on the bar at the entrance of Rye Harbour, and was sold as a hulk.
A painting of her is preserved in Littlehampton town hall.

557 **WARRIOR**

Built in 1842 at Carleton, New Brunswick.
Barque, 174 registered tons. 88.0 x 22.7 x 13.0.
Owners: Thomas Gann, William Blackman, George Holden, 18th November 1856.
Master: James Allen.
This vessel was altered to a brig in September 1857, and was insured with the Whitstable Star Mutual Maritime Assurance Association for £800. She was sold to Sunderland on the 11th March 1861.

19054 **WATCHFUL**
Built in 1857 at Sandwich.
Brig, 162 registered tons. 96.2 x 22.0 x 12.6. Oak, ash, elm.
Owners: E. Adams sen., E. Adams jun., E. Adams the younger, Walter Adams, 10th June 1863.
This vessel was wrecked off Cape St Mary's on the 22nd October 1870.

187 **WATERWITCH**
Built in 1846 at Newport, Mon., by Richard Roberts.
Schooner altered to Brigantine, 158 registered tons. 83.0 x 2.7 x 13.0.
Signal Code H.B.S.L. Yellow metal in 1862.
Owners: W. Robertson, J. Gann, W.J. Gann, T.J. Gann, J. Camburn, Isabella Camburn, Eliza Camburn, W. Blaxland, Henry Nicholls, 7th April 1858.
Master: Gibbens.
This vessel was bought from London on the 5th April 1858, and was insured with the Whitstable Star Mutual Maritime Assurance Association for £325.
She was first registered at Newport, Mon. on the 23rd July 1846, and was broken up at Whitstable in 1881. This last piece of information was evidently not reported to Mr J.T. Handly, the Registrar of Shipping at Faversham, as it should have been. An interesting letter has survived, evidently written in response to an enquiry four years later, which gives the following information.

WATERWITCH *Whitstable July 13th 1885*

In answer to yours I write to inform you this vessel was broken up at Whitstable 1881. The Certificate of Register was lost.

Yours truly, Thos Jas Gann

It is certain from this that Thomas James Gann was a master of brevity.

WENSLEYDALE
Built in 1813 at Paule, Yorkshire.
Schooner, 55 registered tons. 59.4 x 14.5 x 8.1.
Owners: William Madams, Thomas Hoult, William Robertson, William Dyason, William Henry Madams.
Masters: William Robertson, 3rd June 1840. Thomas Holmes, 9th March 1849.
This vessel spent all her time here as a collier and she was sold to Clay in April 1849.

WILLIAM
Built in 1825 at Folkestone.
Schooner, 83 registered tons. 61.2 x 16.4 x 10.1.
Owner: William Blackman.
Masters: William Soans, 9th February 1843. Henry Clothier, 11th October 1847.
This vessel was bought from Yarmouth 27th January 1843, and she was lost in 1849.

23753 **WILLIAM**
Built in 1851 at Prince Edward Island.
Brig, 151 registered tons. 84.2 x 19.8 x 12.4.
Owners: William Gann, Porter, 10th November 1852.
Master: William Gann, 10th November 1852.
This vessel was bought from Dennis Reddin of Charlotte Town, Prince Edward Island, on the 26th October 1852. She was altered to a brigantine in March 1856, and she was sold to Colchester on the 15th September 1858.

11269 **WILLIAM**
63 registered tons.
Owner: E. Allen.
Master: Philip Newman.
This little vessel was the smallest of the fleet which sailed from Whitstable regularly via the Azores and the Canary Islands to the Mediterranean ports. She was insured with the Whitstable Star Mutual Maritime Assurance Association for £250.

44895 **WILLIAM & ANTHONY**
Built in 1862 at Charleston, Cornwall.
Brig altered to Brigantine, 196 registered tons. 97.0 x 24.0 x 13.3.
Owners: J. Rigden, W. Crofts, A.J. Rigden, Edwin Rigden, D.J. Rigden, 19th November 1872.
Master: H. Wendman.
This vessel came into Whitstable ownership in 1872 and was then altered from a brig to a brigantine. In 1873 she was insured with the Whitstable Star Mutual Maritime Assurance Association for £1000. She was sold away to Folkestone on the 20th June 1880.

28017 **WILLIAM DYER**
Built in 1865 at Monkswearmouth.
Brigantine, 160 registered tons. Signal Code H.D.G.M.
Owner: Fred Frend, 43 Harbour Street, Whitstable.
Master: F. Frend, 1912.
This vessel was described by Captain Peterson in *Sea Breezes* February 1955 as being, "A rakish old craft which leaked like a sieve."

William Dyer, see previous page

WILLIAM THE FOURTH

Built in 1830 at Blackwall.
81 registered tons. 114.0 x 14.0 x 9.0. One of the earliest steam vessels. As there was no appropriate class she was described as a Trysail.
Owners: A small company of Whitstable men consisting of Thomas Minter, John Sanders, Thomas T. Pope, William Sharp, and William Kitchingham (landlord of the Duke of Cumberland, Whitstable), who registered themselves as, the Whitstable and Canterbury Steam Packet Company.
Master: Captain Thomas Minter.

This unique vessel is depicted in advertisements as "having two masts, fore and aft, and in between an enormous smoke stack as high as the masts, held in position by stays fore and aft to the two masts and on each side by shrouds, she is also fitted with a bowsprit and a jibboom. At her stern is slung a small boat on derricks, over which flies an enormous ensign. Her white painted ports give her a distinguished appearance."

As far as is known this vessel was the first instance of a combined railway and steam-boat transport.

Interesting particulars of her use and employment are to be found in the *Railway Companion* published in 1836. She was advertised to leave

Whitstable at 12 o'clock every Monday, Wednesday and Friday, under the command of Captain Thomas Minter, on the way calling at Gravesend for passengers and sail to Dyer's Hall Steam Packet Wharf better known as Thompson's Iron Wharf, Upper Thames Street, near London Bridge. The ship would then return to Whitstable every Tuesday, Thursday and Saturday.

Fares from Canterbury (including the railway charges) Chief Cabin 6s, children 4s, Fore Cabin 5s, children 3s 6d. From Whitstable, Chief Cabin 5s 6d, children 3s 6d. Fore Cabin, 4s 6d, children 3s.

The combined Road, Rail, and Water transport between Dover and London, —— The Railway Carriages leave Canterbury Station every morning at 11 o'clock, to meet which, coaches will run from the Ship Hotel, Dover, returning to Dover on the arrival of the Packet in the afternoon.

The *Kentish Gazette* on April 19th 1836 gives the following interesting information. *We are now able to announce to our readers that the Canterbury and Whitstable Steam Packet Co have purchased the WILLIAM THE FOURTH as a passage boat between London and Whitstable. She is now lying in Whitstable Harbour and appears to be admirably suitable for the purpose.*

In order to cater for the comfort of waiting passengers an inn was built at Whitstable Harbour and another in North Lane Canterbury, both being named the Steam Packet Inn.

On Tuesday last the "William the Fourth", Canterbury and Whitstable Steamer to London, sailed with a large party from Whitstable Harbour on an excursion of pleasure to Sheerness, where, through the friendly interposition of Mr Sicklemore, R.N. of this city, they obtained admission to the Dock Yard and inspected the capacious regions of a Man of War. On Wednesday a numerous party took a trip to Harwich. Many of them being fresh water sailors, found the heaving of the majestic waves far from conducive to their anticipated enjoyment. On Thursday the vessel again visited Sheerness, but on Friday, the roughness of the water and the briskness of the gale, prevented any of the party leaving the Harbour, and the boat did not sail.

Sad to relate the ambitious project for which the vessel had been purchased was a complete failure and after twelve months, on 29th June 1837 she was sold to Joseph Hickey Grose and Thomas Street, of Sydney, New South Wales. Then followed one of the greatest sailing achievements of all time. Captain Thomas Minter with his brave crew of Whitstable men, long before the advantage of the Suez Canal was made, sailed the little steam vessel from Whitstable to Sydney, New South Wales, where she achieved fame by being the first such ship to be entered on the Shipping Register there as No. 3, (Nos 1 and 2 being sailing ships).

To complete the picture, on 22nd January 1839 Thomas Street sold his share to Joseph Hickey Grose, and Edward Stamp was registered as her master.

WILLIAM THE FOURTH met her end when she ran ashore on Nobby's Island, New Castle, N.S.W., and became a total loss.

WILLIE

Built in 1860 at Kingsbury by Date.
Brig altered to Brigantine, 204 registered tons. Yellow metal 1861.
Owner: William James Camburn.
Master: William James Camburn.
This vessel had a discouraging stay at Whitstable as all her profits were taken up in keeping her fit for sea. Also she was owned here at a time of industrial depression.

71438 WILLIE

Built in 1874 at Grand River Bridge, Prince Edward Island, by William Welsh and R. Burdett.
Brigantine, 185 registered tons. 104.1 x 24.7 x 12.5. Signal Code P.M.L.G.
Owners: T. Gann jun., George Holden, W.J. Bronger, H. Pout, J. Blackman, Fanny Blackman, 15th February 1876. A.W. Daniels, John Thomas Reeves, the Whitstable Shipping Company 14th August 1913.
Masters: Thunder, J. Grigg, Sidders, T. Goodwin, J. Joiner jun.
In order to avoid confusion with the other "Willie" owned here this vessel was always referred to as "Thunders Willie". She was noted for the fact that she had a scroll figurehead. She was insured with the Whitstable Star Mutual Maritime Assurance Association on the 18th October 1889 for £400. She was sunk by a German submarine on the 16th March 1916.

Willie (71438)

48565 **WINIFRED**
Built in 1863 at Lowestoft.
Schooner, 99 registered tons. Signal Code V.T.H.N.
Owner: Charles William Marshall, 45 & 46 Court Street, Faversham.
Master: James Spencer Sweetman.
Although this vessel was part owned by a Faversham man she was sailed and crewed by Whitstable men and sailed from Whitstable Harbour. She was engaged in the North Sea and Channel trade. She disappeared from the register before 1911.

60245 **ZEBRINA**
Built in 1873 at Whitstable by Gann.
Schooner, 169 registered tons. 109.1 x 24.5 x 9.9. Signal Code M.G.C.S.
Owners: George Holden, Thomas Gann jun., Henry Saddleton, F. Gann, W. Gann, G.H. Gann, H. Gann, 3rd September 1873.
Masters: Jeffreys, J. Phillips, A. Cornhill.
ZEBRINA enjoyed the distinction of being the last of the Whitstable fleet to be recorded in Lloyd's Shipping Register. She was built especially for the River Plate meat trade, and sailed on her first voyage on the 5th September 1873, but after several voyages, proving too slow, she was transferred to the Mediterranean trade.
Her second claim to fame was that she had a flat bottom, being often referred to as "Gann's Barge ship", which feature made her famous in the first Great War as the unsinkable ship, when to the amusement of her crew the German torpedoes passed harmlessly under her.
Her third claim to fame was the unsolveable mystery which caused her to be called the "Mary Celeste" of Whitstable, owing to the fact that on the bright sunny morning of the 17th October 1917 she was found drifting off Rozel Point near Dielette with not a soul on board.

Zebrina

She had left Falmouth on the 15th October 1917 with a cargo of soft coal bound for Cherbourg. Her master at the time was Captain Martin who had under him a mate and the unusual number of twenty three men. There would seem to be no obvious reason for this extraorindary number of men when the usual number necessary for the crew was six. The only explanation that can be offered is that ZEBRINA was really a Q ship, and the extra men were the crews of the guns, usually 8- and 12-pounders.

One account of the 17th October says that she was observed by the French coastguards to be on the rocks of Rosel Point opposite the Island of Guernsey. Another account claims that she was observed with her sails all set drifting aimlessly off Rozel Point Dielette. However when the coastguards boarded her they found everything in perfect order, the table set for breakfast, the Captains log book in his cabin, with the entry of the date when they had left Falmouth, in the galley-stove a fire was burning, all ropes and chains in tidy order, the boats on the chocks, in fact everything very much like that when the "Dei Gratia" found the "Marie Celeste", but the twenty-three men crew had completely disappeared. Naturally several solutions to the mystery were considered, such as that a German submarine had taken off all the men in an effort to solve the mystery of the unsinkable ship, and that before any more could be done a British destroyer was seen approaching and the submarine quickly dived. Perhaps the best solution to the mystery may be found from the evidence given by the Master of the Ipswich schooner 68313 "Lucy Richmond" owned by Charles W. Marshall, Court Street, Faversham. When the "Lucy Richmond" arrived at Cherbourg the Master reported that he had heard a sound like unto that of rusty old tins grinding one against the other. He had heard that noise before: it was made by a German submarine as it surfaced. Going on deck and peering into the darkness he had seen a little distance away the outline of a German submarine. It was therefore surmised that the submarine had suddenly dived, and as it was destroyed shortly afterwards nothing more could be learned. A fresh crew was put on board, and after she had discharged her cargo at Cherbourg she was sailed round to Ramsgate Harbour and used as a store ship. Then after the war she was fitted with motors. The story would appear to end when as a hulk she was used as a coal store in Velder Creek, Langstone Harbour, Portsmouth.

42998 **ZUMA**

Built in 1863 at Cardigan, Prince Edward Island.
Brigantine, 184 registered tons. 100.0 x 23.2 x 12.8.
Owner: Charles Hoult, 11th January 1864.
Master: T. Hoult.

This vessel was insured with the Whitstable Star Mutual Maritime Assurance Association for £500.

She was in collision and foundered in December 1871.

William White Foreman (1825-1912) c1867. He was owner of the vessels Anenome and Isis and part owner of the Anne (ex Johannes), Cautious, Greenwich, Hilda, Impetuous and Reckless.

Whitstable Ships built at Prince Edward Island

It should be explained that these vessels were built especially for the transport of soft wood timber with wooden trunnels. The timber was passed into the hold through trap hatches situated on either side of the bow, and they thus became solid floating logs. Accommodation for the crew was provided by a specially built deck house. After being unloaded at Liverpool and similar ports they were put up for sale, and inasmuch as they did not conform to the regulations governing sea-going vessels they could be purchased cheaply. Those vessels which were purchased by Whitstable people were drawn up on one of the twenty eight slipways here, the trunnels were bored out, iron bolts inserted in their place, and the ships' bottoms covered with copper. This enabled them to qualify for the necessary certificate of seaworthiness. While being chartered for almost any type of cargo a number were regularly engaged in transporting coal from the Tyne to London. Then in the summer they would have the holds scrubbed out and transport ice from the fiords of Norway. A number sailed regularly to the Canaries, Patras, and Alicante, while others were engaged in the tobacco and sugar trade to Jamaica.

It should be noted that the information and dates given regarding the owners has been gathered from many different sources, and inasmuch as no complete source of the history of each vessel exists it must be accepted that the information given can only apply in many cases to the brief mention available.

For full details of the following vessels see the main listing (Pages 57 – 276).

42160 ACADIAN
66314 ADA
29062 ALBERTA
71405 ALBERT T. YOUNG
39012 ALICE
71447 ALICE H.
53682 AMANDA
39225 AMORET
66423 ANEROID
ANN
21577 ANN WHYTE
54125 ARABIAN
71436 AUBREY PEAKE
28111 BETHESDA
77928 BRENDA
73939 CARMENTA
39195 CAROLINE
5748 CESAR
42934 CHARLES
71420 CHARLES P. KNIGHT
39178 CHEBUCTO
42894 CHRISTINA
29065 COLLINA
71454 CONSUS
39257 CONTEST
36413 CORA
71408 CRAIGH ALVAH
22067 CYRUS
26353 DIANA
37747 DUCHESS
71445 EAGLE
20555 EDITH
42893 EDITH
969 ELIZA
ELIZABETH
23951 ELIZABETH
21888 ELIZA GANN
107761 EMPRESS
28460 EROS
42907 ETHEL
573 EVA
46873 EXPERT
22997 FAIRY
28601 FANNY
41738 FANNY FORESTER
59757 FLIRT
42960 FLORA
39130 FLORA

36411	GANNEMEDE
60644	GILPIN
59779	GUIDE
39207	HELEN
66288	HENRY
42165	HERO
77667	HILDRED
73934	IBIS
5221	INDUSTRY
45058	INTERNATIONAL
18720	ISABEL
22463	ISABELLA
42999	JAMES
38989	JOHN DOUSE
50884	JOHN PITCAIRN
77945	JOSEPH
46868	JUNO
39165	KATHLEEN
39035	KINBURN
57018	LADY ROWENA
59698	L.C. OWEN
77687	LENA
66376	LENORE
50903	LOUISA
77646	MAGGIE A.
71491	MAGIC
17067	MAJESTAS
17066	MARCELLA
50889	MARY A. McKAY
5129	MAY FLOWER
39243	MERGHEE
36826	MERIDIAN
27629	MONETA
71496	MORAVIAN
52739	NORTHERN LIGHT
42985	ONYX
50950	ORION
45709	OSIRIS
73938	PINTA
50916	PRIMROSE OF IRELAND
452	QUEEN
66357	RAVEN
74196	RAYMOND
36431	RECOMPENSE
39272	REMEDY
46857	RETRIEVER
20355	SCYLLA
27833	SELA
39249	SELEKA
50890	SEVEN SONS
27628	SILOAM
23804	SNOWDROP
39153	SPRAY
39184	SUSAN GRAY
51924	THIRZA
57007	TRUE
51906	T.W. DODD
20040	VENUS
34253	VENUS
52897	VESTA
23753	WILLIAM
71438	WILLIE
42998	ZUMA

The names of the Whitstable owners are the first of those so far discovered, and need not be accepted as those of the original local owners.

Whitstable Ships built at Nova Scotia

For full details of the following vessels see the main listing (pages 57–276).

5067	ACTIVE
41395	ANENOME
38940	DARING
5202	DOLPHIN
5127	DOVE
1981	HARRY CLEM
2954	HELENA
41797	IANTHE
35177	IRIS
2180	MARY MAC
25949	SARAH HORNE
37687	SHOOTING STAR

Whitstable Ships built at New Brunswick

Adjacent to and divided from Prince Edward Island by the Northumberland Strait we have New Brunswick where nine Whitstable ships were built, as follows:

For full details of the following vessels see the main listing (pages 57 – 276).

52151 BOXER
37162 ELIZA B.
35139 MILO
RAVEN
35556 SARAH JANE
26603 SHAMROCK
11267 STAR OFTHE NORTH
6963 SUSAN
557 WARRIOR

Vessels registered as having been built at Whitstable

1775 FRIENDS GOODWILL smack
1777 ENDEAVOUR yawl
1778 WHISTABLE No. 9756 smack
1780 WILLIAM AND MARY smack
1781 JAMES AND ELIZABETH smack
1782 CALCUTTA yawl
WILLIAM AND MARY smack
1783 GOOD INTENT smack
1784 SWALLOW smack
1785 HOPE smack
1786 ENDEAVOUR smack
KENT smack
PROVIDENCE smack
1787 FRIENDSHIP smack F133
SPEEDWELL smack
SPRIGHTLY yawl
UNITY smack
1788 CUCKOO smack
POLYDAMUS smack
RAINBOW smack
SALISBURY smack
1795 THREE FRIENDS smack
1803 FOX smack
ROSE smack F14
WATCH smack No. 10991
1811 MATCHLESS yawl
1820 ELIZA yawl F15
ELIZA yawl No. 9772
1821 FAME yawl
PROVIDENCE smack
FLORA yawl
1821 HOPE yawl
cont MARY yawl
1822 FRIENDS yawl
MARIA yawl
1823 DELIGHT cutter
ELEANOR yawl
VIGILENT yawl No. 10982
1824 ALERT sloop F84
HOPE yawl 8258
1825 DOVE cutter
MARY yawl
NEW SPECULATION by Fairbrass
STAR yawl
1826 JANE yawl
ELIZABETH F5
1827 FIDELITY smack
KENT yawl
SUPERB yawl
SUPERIOR yawl
1828 ALBION smack F246
PEARL yawl F27
SIDNEY yawl F110
SYDNEY cutter
1829 DARE yawl
JOHN cutter No. 7542
1830 ANN smack F43
BRITANNIA smack F68
EAGLE smack F260
1832 MARY ANN cutter No. 28300 by Henry Madams
MARY ANN dandy No. 23300

Vessels registered as having been built at Whitstable *(continued)*

1835 HOPE yawl No. 8270
COMET smack
1836 FAVOURITE smack by Samuel Holloway
HARMONY No. 11214
JANE smack No. 10990
1837 PLANET smack by Samuel Holloway
1838 PROVIDENCE smack No. 9789
1840 ROCHFORD spritsail by William Madams
1841 EXPEDIENT smack No. 11263 by William Madams
HANNAH schooner No. 11259 by William Blackman
1842 ELLEN JANE yawl No. 9759 by James Daniels
PRINCE ALBERT EDWARD No. 24594 by William Madams
1843 ALLAN cutter F77 by Madams
1844 ALICE dandy
GOOD INTENT yawl by Henry Madams
JANE yawl
JANE boomsail No. 9791
1845 CZARINA smack by Thomas Gann
1846 GOOD INTENT smack by Henry Madams
1847 EQUIVALENT schooner No. 2704 by James Daniels
LUCY smack No. 9792 F46
MARY ANN GANN schooner No. 22928
TOURIST smack by William Madams
1848 ALARM cutter by Thomas Gann
1849 MYSTERY cutter by William Henry Madams
1850 FANNY GANN schooner by Thomas Gann
1852 SELINA No. 11239
1857 SERAPH cutter No. 19094
1861 ROMP smack No. 28454
1865 ABRAHAM AND JOHN smack No. 48896
1866 ALFRED AND ELIZABETH spritsail No. 55185
1867 EDITH ANNIE smack No. 56648
1869 ALFRED F6
ALFRED AND MARY F62
EXCEL F61
1873 FAIRY F63
ZEBRINA schooner No. 60245 by Gann
1875 GRATITUDE barquentine No. 67094 by Dyason
SEASALTER smack F223 No. 67094
1876 NELLIE S. brigantine No. 75271
ELLIDA cutter
1878 LAVINIA yawl by Madams
PHANTOM by Collar Bros
SYDNEY AND CLARA smack No. 79188
1879 ADIEU ketch No. 81924
ALPHA ketch No. 81922
IBEX ketch No. 80512
1884 EVA F21
TANKERTON TOWER schooner No. 89852 by Goldfinch Bros
1885 ALFRED F30
1886 OSPREY schooner No. 82856
1888 POST BOY cutter by Goldfinch Bros
QUICKSILVER F36 by Madams
1889 INVICTA F58
VICTORY yawl
1890 FAVOURITE cutter by Whitstable Shipping Company
IBIS F52
SUNSHINE ketch No. 89864 by Whitstable Shipping Company
1894 CEREAL spritsail No. 104931

Vessels registered as having been built at Whitstable *(continued)*

1895 BELMONT schooner No. 104933
DULUTH spritsail No. 104935
1897 HILDA F86
1898 AZIMA spritsail No. 104941
1900 BLUE BELL F109 by Collar
PAMELA MARY cutter No. 24167
1901 GRACE STUART F123
1902 IRIS F126
1906 IRENE F42
ST AGNES yawl F6
1907 EMMELINE F40 by Collar
GAMECOCK F76 by Collar
JENNIE F70
MONARCH F80
1908 ROSE AND ADA F105
1913 EUCRATE spritsail No. 124326
1913 SEASALTER F322
ROYAL NATIVE F230 built by Holloway but date unknown

A Whitstable First

Francis Petit Smith, who was born at Hythe in 1808 and educated at Ashford, invented propulsion by screw. In 1837, while being tested at Whitstable, the propellor was broken by a floating log, and the broken propellor drove the vessel faster at 10 knots.

On the mud at Whitstable

Lloyd's Agency at Whitstable

In 1811 the Committee of Lloyd's established the Lloyd's Agency system to collect information on the arrival and sailings of ships and casualties to them. Another duty was the inspection of damage to ships and cargo, and the issue of reports detailing the extent and cause of damage to enable assured to submit their claims to the underwriters.

An agency was not established at Whitstable until 1832 when Ralph Leggett was appointed, and he was succeeded the following year by Philpot Wood. Wood held the Agency until 1875 when he tendered his resignation.

On the 11th August 1875 the committee of Lloyds appointed Captain James Robert Daniels, aged 40, and he held the post until his death was reported in November 1904. The Committee, on the same day (16th November 1904) appointed his son Captain Alfred William Daniels, aged 45, to the Agency.

Following the death of Alfred William Daniels in June 1927 the Committee appointed his company, Daniels Bros (Whitstable) Ltd, on the 7th December 1927. The firm of Daniels Bros was established in 1869, and became a limited liability company in 1916.

The records at Lloyd's mention amongst the directors of Daniels Bros (Whitstable) Ltd, James D. Daniels, aged 68 in 1927, died 1940. Henry Kingsford Daniels, aged 78 in 1927, and E.F. Daniels aged 78 in 1940.

James D. Daniels was the brother of Alfred, and it is assumed that the others were his also.

The company was sold to the London & Rochester Trading Co. Ltd in 1958, and changed its name to the Crescent Shipping Co. in 1969.

In 1974 the rationalisation of Lloyd's agencies in England saw the disestablishment of the Whitstable Agency, which had a district extending from Warden Point to Reculver Church, and the inclusion of the area in a larger agency at Dover. However a sub-agency was maintained and the Crescent Shipping still hold that appointment.

The records at Lloyd's indicate that James Robert Daniels was agent of the Whitstable Mutual Maritime Insurance Company Ltd, and his son Alfred William Daniels was secretary. The importance of Whitstable as a port and the number of ships locally owned can be gauged by the fact that they were able to support such a local mutual insurance association.

Lloyd's
Lime Street
London EC3M 7HA.

Master Mariners in Whitstable

1851	17	**1859**	37	**1862**	30	**1866**	83	**1867**	84
1870	100	**1874**	65	**1875**	60	**1878**	68	**1887**	72

Master Mariners in Whitstable in 1851

James Acors, High Street
George Adams, 6 Hartsfield Terrace, Oxford Street
William Butcher, 2 Hartsfield Terrace, Oxford Street
David Charosin, 4 Hartsfield Terrace, Oxford Street
William Gann, High Street
Robert Grimson, *Master of the Revenue Cutter* 5 Hartsfield Terrace, Oxford St.
William Hoult, Harbour Street
Edward Larraman, 3 Hartsfield Terrace, Oxford Street
Steed Larraman, 2 Hartsfield Terrace, Oxford Street
Thomas Larraman, 1 Hartsfield Terrace, Oxford Street
Thomas Minter, Harbour Street
William Ransom, Harbour Wall
George Richards, Swan Street
William Robinson, High Street
George Sharp, 8 Hartsfield Terrace, Oxford Street
William Sheepwash, Marine Street
Joseph White, Swan Street **17 in all.**

Master Mariners in Whitstable in 1859

James Acors, Sydenham Street
John Adams, 8 Hartsfield Terrace, Oxford Street
Edward Allen, Sydenham Street
James Allen, Sydenham Street
Robert Anderson, High Street
Edward Appleton, Swanfields
William Bedwell, Swan Terrace
James Bell, The Wall
Richard Blaxland, Swanfields
William Butcher, 2 Hartsfield Terrace, Oxford Street
James Camburn, Sydenham Street
Henry Clothier, Sydenham Street
William Court, Sydenham Street
Joseph Day, Swan Terrace
William Earl, Sydenham Street
Edward Gaskin, Sydenham Street
Thomas Gaskin, Sydenham Street
William Goodwin, Swanfields
Robert Grimson, Sydenham Street
Cornelius Henry, Harbour Place

Charles Jutson, Sydenham Street
Thomas Laraman, 1 Hartsfield Terrace, Oxford Street
Alfred Mann, Horse Bridge
Charles Nicholls, Seasalter
Henry Nicholls, High Street
William Page, High Street
Francis Putwain, High Street
William Randle, Sydenham Street
Thomas Rigden, Swan Terrace
Robert Sayers, 4 Hartsfield Terrace, Oxford Street
George Sharp, 8 Hartsfield Terrace, Oxford Street
George Taylor, Sydenham Street
James Tunbridge, Sydenham Street
Philip Warner, Harbour Place
John Weatherley, High Street
Samuel Wells, 9 Hartsfield Terrace, Oxford Street
Joseph White, Swanfields **37 in all.**

Master Mariners in Whitstable in 1862

James Acors, Sydenham Street
Edward Adams, Oxford Street
Edwin Adams, Oxford Street
Edward Allen, Sydenham Street
James Allen, Sydenham Street
William Allen, Sydenham Street
Robert Anderson, High Street
Edward Appleton, Swanfields
William Bedwell, Swan Terrace
Richard Blaxland, Swanfields
James Henry William Butcher, Victoria Street
James Camburn, Sydenham Street
Henry Clothier, Sydenham Street
William Court, Sydenham Street
Joseph Day, Swan Terrace
William Earl, Swanfields
Thomas Gaskin, Sydenham Street
William Goodwin, Swanfields
Charles Jutson, Sydenham Street
Thomas Laraman, 1 Hartsfield Terrace, Oxford Street
Alfred Mann, High Street
Henry Nicholls, High Street
Francis Putwain, High Street
Thomas Rigden, Swan Terrace
Robert Sayers, 4 Hartsfield Terrace
George Sharp, Harbour Street

George Taylor, Sydenham Street
James Tunbridge, Sydenham Street
John Weatherley, Harbour Place
Joseph White, Swanfields **30 in all.**

Master Mariners in Whitstable in 1866

James Acors, 16 Sydenham Street
Edward Adams, Oxford Street
Edwin Adams, Oxford Street
Edward Allen, 13 Sydenham Street
James Allen, 14 Sydenham Street
James Thomas Allen, 54 Sydenham Street
Thomas Allen, Norfolk Street
Robert Anderson, Oxford Street
William Baldock, Albert Street
Alfred Beal, 14 Harbour Place
Edward Bell, Oxford Street
Wallace Bell, Middle Wall
George Blaxland, Oxford Street
Richard Blaxland, Swanfields
Thomas Blaxland, Middle Wall
William Blaxland, Swan Terrace
William Bronger, Harbour Place
John Brown, 7 Marine Parade
Matthew Browning jun., 6 Marine Parade
James Butcher jun., 13 Albion Place
James Butcher sen., 15 Albion Place
Thomas Butcher, Harbour Terrace
George Camburn, 50 Sydenham Street
James Camburn, 49 Sydenham Street
James Camburn, 51 Sydenham Street
William Camburn, Oxford Street
William Camburn, 52 Sydenham Street
George Chapman, Harbour Place
Thomas Clarke, Norfolk Street
Henry Clothier, 43 Sydenham Street
John Collar, Suffolk Street
William Court, Richmond Cottage, Oxford Street
Richard Curling, 4 Marine Cottages, Harbour Place
Joseph Day, Essex Street
William Henry Digby, 53 Sydenham Street
Stephen Duncan, Bexley Street
John Field, Bexley Street
Charles Fowle, 6 Marine Cottages, Harbour Place
George Friend, Albert Street

William Friend, Albert Street
John Gann, 2 Marine Parade
Alexander Gardner, Albert Street
Robert Gardner, 2 Sydenham Street
Thomas Gaskin, Norfolk Street
Thomas Goodwin, Swanfields
William Goodwin, Swanfields
Edward Harris, Oxford Street
George Hoult, Harbour Place
Thomas Hoult, 6 Sydenham Street
John Johnson, 12 Albion Place
Richard Johnson, High Street
Charles Jutson, 21 Sydenham Street
Frederick Kemp, 22 Sydenham Street
William Kemp jun., Swanfields
Thomas Lott, Albert Street
Alfred Mann, High Street
Edward Maxted, 19 Harbour Place
John Moon, Victoria Street
David Moyes, The Island
Henry Nicholls sen., 18 Albion Place
Henry Richard Nicholls, 5 Albion Place
John Nicholls, 11 Albion Place
Osborne Nicholls, Oxford Street
John Parker, Bexley Street
Joseph Pettman, 10 Albion Place
Henry Pout, Bexley Street
James Pout, 7 Bexley Terrace
John Pout, 7 Sydenham Street
Francis Putwain, High Street
George Richardson, Victoria Street
William Robinson, Harbour Place
John Rowden, The Wall
Thomas Sandy, Essex Street
George Taylor, Sydenham Street
William Tilley, 9 Sydenham Street
James Tunbridge, Sydenham Street
Frederick Ward, Marine Cottages, Harbour Place
William Waters, Rose Terrace
Edward Weatherley, Oxford Street
John Weatherley, Harbour Terrace
Thomas Wells, 3 Sydenham Street
William White, Albert Street
Frederick Woodcock, 1 Marine Cottages, Harbour Place

83 in all.

Master Mariners in Whitstable in 1867

James Acors, 16 Sydenham Street
Edward Adams, Oxford Street
Edwin Adams, Oxford Street
Edward Allen, 13 Sydenham Street
James Allen, 14 Sydenham Street
James T. Allen, 54 Sydenham Street
Thomas Allen, Norfolk Street
Robert Anderson, Oxford Street
William Baldock, Albert Street
Alfred Beal, 14 Harbour Place
Edward Bell, Oxford Street
Wallace Bell, Middle Wall
George Blaxland, Oxford Street
Richard Blaxland, Swanfields
Thomas Blaxland, Middle Wall
William Blaxland, Swan Terrace
William Bronger, Harbour Place
John Brown, 7 Marine Parade
Matthew Browning jun., 6 Marine Parade
James Butcher jun., 13 Albion Place
James Butcher sen., 15 Albion Place
Thomas Butcher, Harbour Terrace
George Camburn, 50 Sydenham Street
James Camburn, 49 Sydenham Street
James Camburn, 51 Sydenham Street
William Camburn, Oxford Street
William Camburn, 52 Sydenham Street
George Chapman, Harbour Place
Thomas Clarke, Norfolk Street
Henry Clothier, 43 Sydenham Street
John Collar, Suffolk Street, Oxford Street
William Court, Richmond Cottage, Oxford Street
Richard Curling, 4 Marine Cottages, Harbour Place
Joseph Day, Essex Street
William H. Digby, 53 Sydenham Street
Stephen Duncan, Bexley Street
John Eddenden, High Street
John Field, Bexley Street
Charles Fowle, 6 Marine Cottages, Harbour Place
George Friend, Albert Street
William Friend, Albert Street
John Gann, 2 Marine Parade
Alexander Gardner, Albert Street
Robert Gardner, 2 Sydenham Street
Thomas Gaskin, Norfolk Street

Thomas Goodwin, Swanfields
William Goodwin, Swanfields
Edward Harris, Oxford Street
George Hoult, Harbour Place
Thomas Hoult, 6 Sydenham Street
John Johnson, 12 Albion Place
Richard Johnson, High Street
Charles Jutson, 21 Sydenham Street
Frederick Kemp, 22 Sydenham Street
William Kemp jun., Swanfields
Thomas Lott, Albert Street
Alfred Mann, High Street
Edward Maxted, 19 Harbour Place
John Moon, Victoria Street
David Moyes, The Island
Henry Nicholls sen., 18 Albion Place
Henry R. Nicholls, 5 Albion Place
John Nicholls, 11 Albion Place
Osborne Nicholls, Oxford Street
John Parker, Bexley Street
Joseph Pettman, 10 Albion Place
Henry Pout, Bexley Street
James Pout, 7 Bexley Terrace
John Pout, 7 Sydenham Street
Francis Putwain, High Street
George Richardson, Victoria Street
William Robinson, Harbour Place
John Rowden, The Wall
Thomas Sandy, Essex Street
George Taylor, Sydenham Street
William Tilley, 9 Sydenham Street
James Tunbridge, Sydenham Street
Frederick Ward, Marine Cottages, Harbour Place
William Waters, Rose Terrace
Edward Weatherley, Oxford Street
John Weatherley, Harbour Terrace
Thomas Wells, 3 Sydenham Street
William White, Albert Street
Frederick Woodcock, 1 Marine Cottages, Harbour Place **84 in all.**

Master Mariners in Whitstable in 1870

James Acors, Canterbury Road
Edward Adams jun., Oxford Street
Walter Adams, 14 Albion Place, Canterbury Road
Edward Allen, 13 Sydenham Street

Thomas Allen, Norfolk Street
Robert Anderson, Oxford Street
Robert Thomas Argent, Argyle Road
William Baldock, Albert Street
Alfred Beal, 14 Harbour Place
Edward Bell, High Street
Edward Bell, Middle Wall
Wallace Bell, Middle Wall
George Blaxland, Oxford Street
Thomas Blaxland, Middle Wall
William Bronger, Harbour Place
John Brown, 7 Marine Parade
Matthew Browning jun., 6 Marine Parade
George Burton, 42 Sydenham Street
James Butcher jun., 13 Albion Place
James Butcher sen., 15 Albion Place, Canterbury Road
Thomas Butcher, Harbour Terrace
John Carlton, Argyle Road
George Camburn, 50 Sydenham Street
James Camburn, 51 Sydenham Street
Thomas Camburn, Argyle Road
William Camburn, Swan Cottage, Oxford Street
George Chapman, Bexley Street
Thomas Clarke, Norfolk Street
Henry Clothier, 43 Sydenham Street
John Collar, Suffolk Street, Canterbury Road
John Cooper, 18 Albion Place, Canterbury Road
John Wyatt Court, Oxford Street
Robert Court, Canterbury Road
Richard Curling, 4 Marine Cottages, Harbour Place
George Dawkings, Borstal Hill, Seasalter
Joseph Day, 2 Essex Street
William Henry Digby, 53 Sydenham Street
Stephen Duncan, Bexley Street
John Brown Dyason, 19 Sydenham Street
William Earle, 1 Sydenham Street
John Field, Bexley Street
Edward Foster, Swanfields
Charles Fowle, 6 Marine Cottages, Harbour Place
George Friend, Albert Street
William Friend, Albert Street
Thomas Gann, 3 Essex Street
Alexander Gardner, Sydenham Street
Edward Gaskin, 49 Sydenham Street
Richard Gaskin, Victoria Street

Thomas Edward Gaskin, Oxford Street
William Gibbons, Swanfields
Edwin Griffiths, Argyle Road
Edward Harris, Norfolk Street
Edward Harris, Suffolk Street
Thomas Hoult, 6 Sydenham Street
John Hughes, 2 Swan Cottages, Oxford Street
John Johnson, 12 Albion Place
Richard Johnson, Gorrell Road
Charles Jutson, 21 Sydenham Street
Cyrus Charles Jutson, Canterbury Road
Charles Lawson, Swanfields
John Lawson sen., Oxford Street
George Lissenden, 9 Bexley Terrace
Edward Maxted, Canterbury Road
George Merritt, Victoria Street
George Miller, Swanfields
David Moyes, Sydenham Street
Alfred Nicholls, Canterbury Road
Hammond Nicholls, Argyle Road
Henry Nicholls sen., Argyle Road
Henry Richard Nicholls jun., 5 Albion Place, Canterbury Road
John Nicholls, 11 Albion Place, Canterbury Road
Osborne Nicholls, Oxford Street
Thomas Orford, Canterbury Road
Thomas Ougham, Oxford Street
John Parker, Bexley Street
Joseph Pettman, 10 Albion Place
John Phillips, Victoria Street
Jacob Thomas Porter, Bexley Street
Henry Pout, Bexley Street
James Pout, 7 Bexley Terrace
John Pout, 7 Sydenham Street
Francis Putwain, High Street
George Richardson, Victoria Street
William Ritchie, Albert Street
William Robinson, Harbour Place
George Rogers, Argyle Road
John Rowden, The Wall
Thomas Sandy, Essex Street
William Sayer, Argyle Road
George Taylor, 56 Sydenham Street
William Tilley, Victoria Street
Edward Tritton, 6 Bexley Terrace
David Waters, Oxford Street

William Waters, Rose Terrace
Edward Weatherley, Essex Street
John Weatherley, Sydenham Street
William White, Albert Street
William White, Canterbury Road
Frederick Woodcock, 1 Marine Cottages, Harbour Place **100 in all.**

Master Mariners in Whitstable in 1874

James Acors, Canterbury Road
Edward Adams jun., Oxford Street
Walter Adams, 14 Albion Place, Canterbury Road
Thomas Allen, Norfolk Street
William Allen, 55 Sydenham Street
Robert Anderson, Oxford Street
William Baldock, Albert Street
Alfred Beal, 14 Harbour Place
George Burton, 42 Sydenham Street
John Carlton, Argyle Road
George Camburn, 50 Sydenham Street
James Camburn, Westcliff
Thomas Camburn, Argyle Road
George Chapman, Bexley Street
Thomas Clarke, Norfolk Street
Henry Clothier, 43 Sydenham Street
John Collar, Suffolk Street, Canterbury Road
John Cooper, 18 Albion Place, Canterbury Road
John Wyatt Court, Oxford Street
Robert Court, Canterbury Road
George Dawkins, Borstal Hill, Seasalter
William Henry Digby, 53 Sydenham Street
John Brown Dyason, 19 Sydenham Street
William Earl, 1 Sydenham Street
John Field, Bexley Street
Edward Foster, Swanfields
Charles Fowle, 6 Marine Cottages, Harbour Place
Frederick Gann, Canterbury Road
Thomas Gann, Oxford Street
Alexander Gardner, Sydenham Street
Robert Gardner, 11 Fountain Street
Edward Gaskin, 49 Sydenham Street
George Gaskin, Middle Wall
Richard Gaskin, Victoria Street
Thomas Edward Gaskin, Oxford Street
William Gibbons, Swanfields

Thomas Harford, Canterbury Road
George Hodges, Sydenham Street
Thomas Hoult, Norfolk Street
James Hudson, Bexley Street
Edward Joiner, Bexley Street
George Joiner, Harbour Place
John Joiner, Bexley Street
Joseph Jutson, Canterbury Road
Charles Jutson, West Avenue
Charles Lawson, Swanfields
Edward Maxted, Canterbury Road
Thomas Wood Minter, Sydenham Street
Alfred Nicholls, Canterbury Road
Hammond Nicholls, Argyle Road
Henry Richard Nicholls jun., 5 Albion Place, Canterbury Road
John Nicholls, 11 Albion Place, Canterbury Road
Osborne Nicholls, Oxford Street
Thomas Orford, Canterbury Road
Henry Pout, Bexley Street
James Pout, 7 Bexley Terrace
Francis Putwain, High Street
George Rogers, Argyle Road
Thomas Henry Rogers, Middle Wall
Henry Sandy, Sea Wall
George Sharp, Fountain Street
John Slater, Essex Street
William Tilley, Victoria Street
Edward Tritton, 6 Bexley Terrace
Frederick Woodcock, 1 Marine Cottages, Harbour Place **65 in all.**

Master Mariners in Whitstable in 1875

James Acors, Canterbury Road
Edward Adams jun., Oxford Street
Thomas Allen, Norfolk Street
William Allen, Sydenham Street
Robert Anderson, Oxford Street
William Baldock, Albert Street
Alfred Beal, Harbour Place
George Burton, 42 Sydenham Street
John Carlton, Argyle Road
George Camburn, Sydenham Street
James Camburn, Westcliff
Thomas Camburn, Argyle Road
Henry Clothier, 43 Sydenham Street

John Collar, Suffolk Street
John Cooper, 18 Albion Place
John W. Court, Oxford Street
Robert Court, Canterbury Road
George Dawkins, Borstal Hill
William Henry Digby, 53 Sydenham Street
John B. Dyason, 19 Sydenham Street
W. Earl, 1 Sydenham Street
John Field, Bexley Street
Edward Foster, Swanfields
Charles Fowle, Harbour Place
Frederick Gann, Canterbury Road
Thomas Gann, Oxford Street
Alexander Gardner, Sydenham Street
Robert Gardner, 11 Fountain Street
Edward Gaskin, 49 Sydenham Street
George Gaskin, Middle Wall
Richard Gaskin, Victoria Street
Thomas E. Gaskin, Oxford Street
William Gibbons, Swanfields
George Hodges, Sydenham Street
Thomas Hoult, Norfolk Street
James Hudson, Bexley Street
Edward Joiner, Bexley Street
John Joiner, Harbour Place
Joseph Jutson, Canterbury Road
Charles Jutson, West Avenue
Charles Lawson, Swanfields
Edward Maxted, Canterbury Road
Thomas W. Minter, Sydenham Street
Alfred Nicholls, Canterbury Road
Hammond Nicholls, Argyle Road
Henry Richard Nicholls, Canterbury Road
Osborne Nicholls, Canterbury Road
Thomas Orford, Canterbury Road
Henry Pout, Bexley Street
James Pout, Bexley Terrace
John Pout, Sydenham Street
Francis Putwain, High Street
George Rogers, Argyle Road
Thomas Henry Rogers, Middle Wall
Henry Sandy, Sea Wall
George Sharp, Fountain Street
John Slater, Essex Street
William Tilley, Victoria Street
Edward Tritton, 6 Bexley Terrace
Frederick Woodcock, Harbour Place **60 in all.**

Master Mariners in Whitstable in 1878

James Acors, Canterbury Road
Edward Adams jun., Oxford Street
Thomas Allen, Norfolk Street
William Allen, 55 Sydenham Street
William Baldock, Albert Street
Alfred Beal, 14 Harbour Place
George Burton, 42 Sydenham Street
John Carlton, Argyle Road
George Camburn, 50 Sydenham Street
James Camburn, Westcliff
Thomas Camburn, Argyle Road
George Chapman, Bexley Street
Thomas Clarke, Norfolk Street
Henry Clothier, 43 Sydenham Street
John Collar, Suffolk Street
John Cooper, 18 Albion Place
Robert Court, Canterbury Road
William Court, 17 Albion Place
George Dawkings, Borstal Hill, Seasalter
William Henry Digby, 53 Sydenham Street
John Brown Dyason, 19 Sydenham Street
William Earle, 1 Sydenham Street
John Field, Bexley Street
Edward Foster, Swanfields
Charles Fowle, 6 Marine Cottages
Frederick Gann, Canterbury Road
Thomas Gann, Oxford Street
Alexander Gardner, Albert Street
Robert Gardner, 11 Fountain Street
Edward Gaskin, 49 Sydenham Street
George Gaskin, Middle Wall
Richard Gaskin, Victoria Street
Thomas Edward Gaskin, Oxford Street
William Gibbons, Swanfields
John G. Harris, High Street
Thomas Hoult, Norfolk Street
James Hudson, Bexley Street
Edward Joiner, Bexley Street
George Joiner, Harbour Place
John Joiner, Bexley Street
George Jordan, Canterbury Road
Joseph Judson, Canterbury Road
Charles Jutson, West Avenue
Charles Lawson, Swanfields
George Lissenden, Bexley Street
Edward Maxted, Canterbury Road
Thomas Wood Minter, Sydenham Street

Alfred Nicholls, Canterbury Road
Hammond Nicholls, Argyle Road
Henry Richard Nicholls jun., 5 Albion Place
John Nicholls, 11 Albion Place
Osborne Nicholls, Oxford Street
Thomas Orford, Canterbury Road
Lewis Poate, Oxford Street
Henry Pout, Bexley Street
James Pout, 7 Bexley Terrace
John Pout, 7 Sydenham Street
George Rogers, Argyle Road
Thomas Henry Rogers, Middle Wall
Henry Sandy, Sea Wall
George Sharp, Fountain Street
Samuel Shilson, Oxford Street
John Slater, 8 Albion Place
William Smith, Canterbury Road
Henry Thompson, Albion House, Fountain Street
William Tilley, Victoria Street
Edward Tritton, 6 Bexley Terrace
Frederick Woodcock. **68 in all.**

Master Mariners in Whitstable in 1887

George Adams, Swanfields
William Allen, 13 Sydenham Street
Frederick Baker, Middle Wall
William Baldock, Albert Street
Edward Blaxland, Kitchingham Place
Henry Browning, Middle Wall
William Burniston, 3 Norfolk Street
George Burton, 43 Sydenham Street
James Butcher, Canterbury Road
Henry Byron, Canterbury Road
Edward Camburn, Middle Wall
George Camburn, 50 Sydenham Street
William Camburn, Sydenham Street
William James Camburn, 53 Sydenham Street
Charles Carlton, 6 Sydenham Street
George Carrell, Middle Wall
John Carvell, Kitchingham Place
Henry Clothier, 4 Sydenham Street
Henry William Clothier, Kitchingham Place
William Norman Court, 17 Albion Place, Canterbury Road
Alfred William Daniels, Kitchingham Place
John Digby, 47 Sydenham Street
John Brown Dyason, 19 Sydenham Street
Daniel Foster, Kitchingham Place

Henry William Gann, Argyle Road
Thomas Gann, Oxford Street
Robert Gardner, 11 Fountain Street
Richard Gaskin, Victoria Street
Thomas Gibbens, 10 Norfolk Street
John Gilbert, Swanfields
Charles Goldfinch, 16 Sydenham Street
George Goldfinch, Middle Wall
George Goodwin, Swanfields
William Goodwin, 57 Sydenham Street
William Gray, 2 Norfolk Street
Richard Groombridge, Middle Wall
John Harris, Oxford Street
George Hodges, Norfolk Street
William Hoult, Canterbury Road
James Hudson, Sidmouth Street
William Humphrey, 48 Sydenham Street
Edward Joiner, Fountain Street
Charles Jutson, Kitchingham Place
Joseph Jutson, Canterbury Road
Charles Kemp, 20 Sydenham Street
Harry Kemp, Canterbury Road
Mark Kemp, Fountain Street
George Lissenden, Horsebridge House
Hammond Nicholls, Argyle Road
Henry Richard Nicholls jun., 5 Albion Place
Osborne Nicholls, Oxford Street
Joseph Ougham, Kitchingham Place
Lewis Poate, Canterbury Road
Henry Pout, Bexley Street
James Pout, 7 Bexley Terrace
John Pout, 7 Sydenham Street
Frederick Putwain, Swanfields
Seymour Putwain, 7 The Grove
George Ritchie, Kitchingham Place
Henry Sandy, Sea Wall
Alfred David Sandy, Suffolk Street
Henry Setterfield, High Street
George Sharp, Fountain Street
Samuel Shilson, Oxford Street
James Smith, Suffolk Street
William Smith, Canterbury Road
Herbert Stroud, Middle Wall
James Tilley, 1 Sydenham Street
John Tilley, 17 Sydenham Street
Richard Waters, Middle Wall
William Wilson, Argyle Road
William Wilson, 2 Sydenham Street **72 in all.**

CERTIFICATES OF DISCHARGE

A number of 'Certificates of Discharge' from those early years have survived the passage of time and are reproduced here. They inform us of the name of

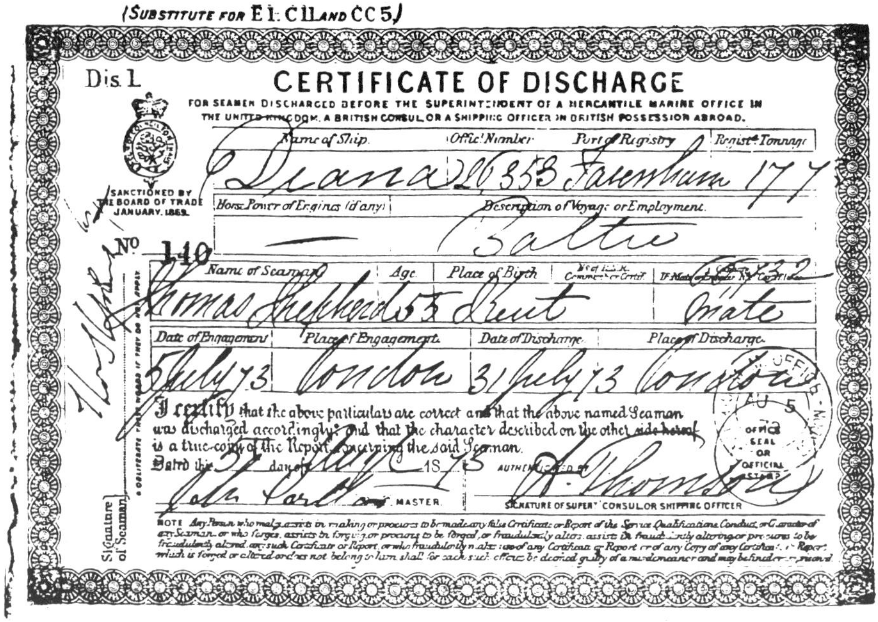
(SUBSTITUTE FOR E1. C11 AND CC5)

Dis. 1.

CERTIFICATE OF DISCHARGE

FOR SEAMEN DISCHARGED BEFORE THE SUPERINTENDENT OF A MERCANTILE MARINE OFFICE IN THE UNITED KINGDOM, A BRITISH CONSUL, OR A SHIPPING OFFICER IN BRITISH POSSESSION ABROAD.

SANCTIONED BY THE BOARD OF TRADE JANUARY, 1869.

Name of Ship	Offic! Number	Port of Registry	Regist! Tonnage
Diana	26353	Faversham	177

Horse Power of Engines (if any)	Description of Voyage or Employment
—	Baltic

No 140

Name of Seaman	Age	Place of Birth	No of R.N.R. Commiss. or Certif.	Capacity. If Mate or Engineer No of Certif. (if any)
Thomas Shepherd	55	Kent		Mate

Date of Engagement	Place of Engagement	Date of Discharge	Place of Discharge
5 July 73	London	31 July 73	London

I certify that the above particulars are correct and that the above named Seaman was discharged accordingly, and that the character described on the other side hereof is a true copy of the Report concerning the said Seaman.

Dated this 31 day of July 1873 AUTHENTICATED BY

MASTER

SIGNATURE OF SUPER! CONSUL OR SHIPPING OFFICER

OFFICE SEAL OR OFFICIAL STAMP

Signature of Seaman

OBLITERATE THESE WORDS IF THEY DO NOT APPLY

NOTE. Any Person who makes, assists in making or procures to be made any false Certificate or Report of the Service Qualifications, Conduct, or Character of any Seaman, or who forges, assists in forging, or procures to be forged, or fraudulently alters, assists in fraudulently altering or procures to be fraudulently altered, any such Certificate or Report, or who fraudulently makes use of any Certificate or Report or of any Copy of any Certificate or Report which is forged or altered or does not belong to him, shall for each such offence be deemed guilty of a misdemeanor and may be fined or imprisoned.

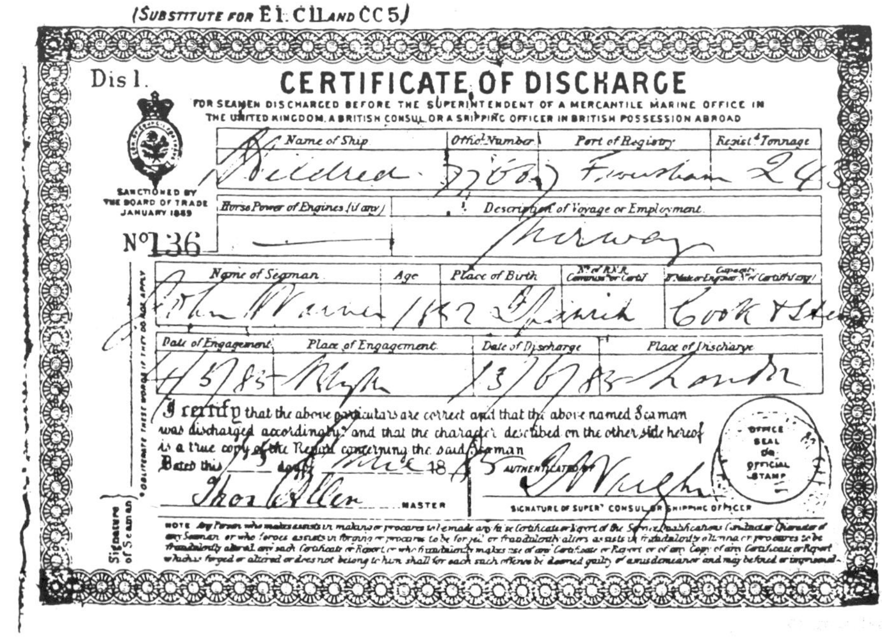
(SUBSTITUTE FOR E1. C11 AND CC5)

Dis 1.

CERTIFICATE OF DISCHARGE

FOR SEAMEN DISCHARGED BEFORE THE SUPERINTENDENT OF A MERCANTILE MARINE OFFICE IN THE UNITED KINGDOM, A BRITISH CONSUL, OR A SHIPPING OFFICER IN BRITISH POSSESSION ABROAD

SANCTIONED BY THE BOARD OF TRADE JANUARY 1869

Name of Ship	Offic! Number	Port of Registry	Regist! Tonnage
Mildred	77067	Faversham	243

Horse Power of Engines (if any)	Description of Voyage or Employment
—	Norway

No 136

Name of Seaman	Age	Place of Birth	No of R.N.R. Commiss. or Certif.	Capacity. If Mate or Engineer No of Certif. (if any)
John Warner	18	St Ipswich		Cook & Stew

Date of Engagement	Place of Engagement	Date of Discharge	Place of Discharge
4/5/85	Blyth	13/6/85	London

I certify that the above particulars are correct and that the above named Seaman was discharged accordingly, and that the character described on the other side hereof is a true copy of the Report concerning the said Seaman.

Dated this day of June 1885 AUTHENTICATED BY

Thos Allen MASTER

SIGNATURE OF SUPER! CONSUL OR SHIPPING OFFICER

OFFICE SEAL OR OFFICIAL STAMP

Signature of Seaman

OBLITERATE THESE WORDS IF THEY DO NOT APPLY

NOTE. Any Person who makes, assists in making or procures to be made any false Certificate or Report of the Service Qualifications, Conduct, or Character of any Seaman, or who forges, assists in forging, or procures to be forged, or fraudulently alters, assists in fraudulently altering or procures to be fraudulently altered, any such Certificate or Report, or who fraudulently makes use of any Certificate or Report or of any Copy of any Certificate or Report which is forged or altered or does not belong to him, shall for each such offence be deemed guilty of a misdemeanor and may be fined or imprisoned.

the ship and its registered number, port of registry, registered tonnage, description of the voyage, the name of the seaman concerned, his age, place of birth, employment capacity, and date of engagement and discharge.

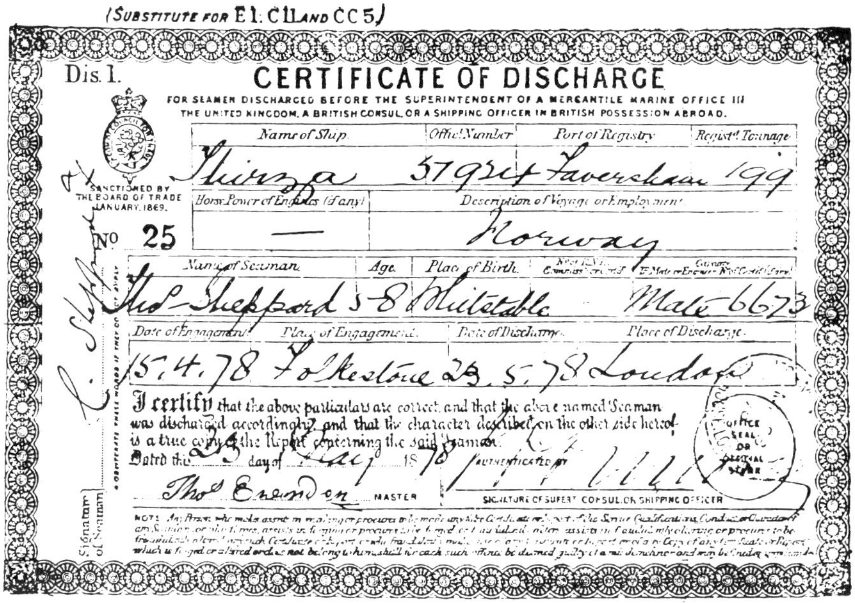
(SUBSTITUTE FOR E1. C11 AND CC5)

Dis. 1.

CERTIFICATE OF DISCHARGE

FOR SEAMEN DISCHARGED BEFORE THE SUPERINTENDENT OF A MERCANTILE MARINE OFFICE IN THE UNITED KINGDOM, A BRITISH CONSUL, OR A SHIPPING OFFICER IN BRITISH POSSESSION ABROAD.

SANCTIONED BY THE BOARD OF TRADE JANUARY, 1869.

No 25

Name of Ship	Offic! Number	Port of Registry	Regist^d. Tonnage
Thirza	57924	Faversham	199

Horse Power of Engines (if any)	Description of Voyage or Employment
—	Norway

Name of Seaman	Age	Place of Birth	No. of R.N.R. Commiss. or Certif.	If Mate or Engineer No. of Certif. (if any)
Thos Sheppard	58	Whitstable		Mate 6673

Date of Engagement	Place of Engagement	Date of Discharge	Place of Discharge
15.4.78	Folkestone	23.5.78	London

I certify that the above particulars are correct, and that the above named Seaman was discharged accordingly, and that the character described on the other side hereof is a true copy of the Report concerning the said Seaman.

Dated this 23 day of May 1878 AUTHENTICATED BY

Thos Evenden MASTER

SIGNATURE OF SUPERT. CONSUL, OR SHIPPING OFFICER

OFFICE SEAL OR OFFICIAL STAMP

Signature of Seaman

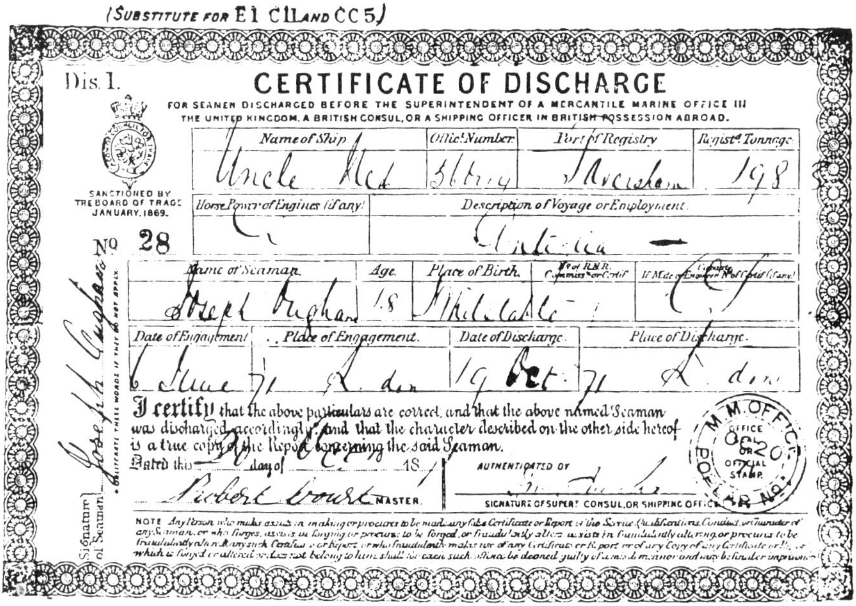
(SUBSTITUTE FOR E1. C11 AND CC5)

Dis. 1.

CERTIFICATE OF DISCHARGE

FOR SEAMEN DISCHARGED BEFORE THE SUPERINTENDENT OF A MERCANTILE MARINE OFFICE IN THE UNITED KINGDOM, A BRITISH CONSUL, OR A SHIPPING OFFICER IN BRITISH POSSESSION ABROAD.

SANCTIONED BY THE BOARD OF TRADE JANUARY, 1869.

No 28

Name of Ship	Offic! Number	Port of Registry	Regist^d. Tonnage
Uncle Ned	56634	Faversham	198

Horse Power of Engines (if any)	Description of Voyage or Employment
—	Antwerp

Name of Seaman	Age	Place of Birth	No. of R.N.R. Commiss. or Certif.	If Mate or Engineer No. of Certif. (if any)
Joseph Ingham	18	Whitstable		

Date of Engagement	Place of Engagement	Date of Discharge	Place of Discharge
6 June 71	London	19 Oct. 71	London

I certify that the above particulars are correct, and that the above named Seaman was discharged accordingly, and that the character described on the other side hereof is a true copy of the Report concerning the said Seaman.

Dated this day of 18 AUTHENTICATED BY

Robert Wraight MASTER

SIGNATURE OF SUPERT. CONSUL, OR SHIPPING OFFICER

M.M. OFFICE POPLAR — OFFICE SEAL OR OFFICIAL STAMP

Signature of Seaman: Joseph Ingham

"Raven"

Southampton
23/3/93

This is to certify that William C. Ruff of Littlehampton served with me on board the "Raven" of Faversham off. number 66357 in a sober & diligent manner – & always found him honest & obedient – and can recommend him – time from 6th Feb. 1884 – up till the present time – March 1893 –

Edwin Blaxland
Master

(E) CERTIFICATE OF DISCHARGE,

FOR SEAMEN NOT DISCHARGED BEFORE A SUPERINTENDENT.

ISSUED BY THE BOARD OF TRADE, MAY, 1855. In pursuance of 17 & 18 Vict., c. 104.

Name of Ship.	Official Number.	Port of Registry.	Registered Tonnage.	Description of Voyage or Employment.
Raven	66357	Faversham	147	Coasting

Name of Seaman.	Place of Birth.	Date of Birth.
W. C. Ruff	Littlehampton	1862

Number of Fund Ticket (if any).	Capacity.	Date of Entry.	Date of Discharge.	Place of Discharge.
–	A.B.	25/2/1884	8/1/94	Woolston Southampton

I CERTIFY that the above particulars are correct, and that the above-named Seaman was discharged accordingly.

Dated this Eighth Day of January 1894

(Countersigned) ______ Seaman. Signed E. Blaxland Master.

Witness S. Gibbens

Address of Witness Whitstable

Occupation of Witness Mariner

NOTE.—One of these Certificates must be filled up and delivered to every Seaman who is discharged otherwise than before a Superintendent.

W. B. & L. (8vo)—16111—50000-5.93

(E-1) CERTIFICATE OF DISCHARGE.

For Seaman discharged before a Shipping Master.

MARINE DEPARTMENT

COMMITTEE OF COUNCIL FOR TRADE

SANCTIONED BY THE BOARD OF TRADE MAY 1855. IN PURSUANCE OF 17 & 18 VICT. C. 104.

138

Name of Ship.	Official Number.	Port of Registry.
[illegible]	[illegible]	[illegible]

Registered Tonnage.	Description of Voyage or Employment.
[illegible]	[illegible]

		Capacity.
Name of Seaman	[illegible]	
Place of Birth	[illegible]	O S
Date of Birth	1853	

Date of Entry.	Date of Discharge.	Place of Discharge.
[illegible]/64	24/1/65	London

I Certify that the above particulars are correct and that the above Seaman was discharged accordingly.

Dated this [illegible] day of [illegible] 1865

For Signature of Seaman see back.

Signed [illegible] Master of the Ship.

[illegible] Shipping Master.

NOTE.—One of these Certificates must be filled up and delivered to every Seaman who is discharged whenever the discharge takes place before a Shipping Master.

Printed by Authority of the Board of Trade.

(E-1) CERTIFICATE OF CHARACTER.

MARINE DEPARTMENT
BOARD OF COUNCIL FOR TRADE

SANCTIONED BY
THE BOARD OF TRADE
MAY 1855.
IN PURSUANCE OF
17 & 18 VICT. C. 104.

18

Character for ability in whatever capacity V.G.

Character for Conduct V.G.

I Certify *the above to be a true Copy of so much of the Report of Character, made by the said Master on the termination of the said ~~Voyage, as concerns~~ the said Seaman.*

Dated at Fisherrow *this* 5 *day of* Sept 1868

Signed Jno Clark *Master of the Ship.*

[illegible] *Shipping Master.*

For Signature of Seaman see back.

NOTE. Any Person who fraudulently forges or alters a Certificate of Character or makes use of one which does not belong to him may either be prosecuted for a Misdemeanour or may be summarily punished by a Penalty not exceeding £100 or imprisonment with hard labour not exceeding six months.

Printed by Authority of the Board of Trade.

(E-1) CERTIFICATE OF DISCHARGE.

For Seaman discharged before a Shipping Master.

MARINE DEPARTMENT

COM. OF COUNCIL FOR TRADE

SANCTIONED BY THE BOARD OF TRADE MAY 1855. IN PURSUANCE OF 17 & 18 VICT. C. 104.

18

Name of Ship.	*Official Number.*	*Port of Registry.*
Petrel	11268	Faversham

Registered Tonnage.	*Description of Voyage or Employment.*
69	Baltic

Name of Seaman Joseph Oughams

Place of Birth Whitstable

Date of Birth 1834

Capacity. Boy

Date of Entry.	*Date of Discharge.*	*Place of Discharge.*
27 July 1868	5 Sept 1868	[illegible]

I Certify *that the above particulars are correct and that the above Seaman was discharged accordingly.*

Dated this 5 *day of* Sept 1868

For Signature of Seaman see back.

Signed Thos Clark *Master of the Ship.*

[illegible] *Shipping Master.*

NOTE.—One of these Certificates must be filled up and delivered to every Seaman who is discharged whenever the discharge takes place before a Shipping Master.

Printed by Authority of the Board of Trade

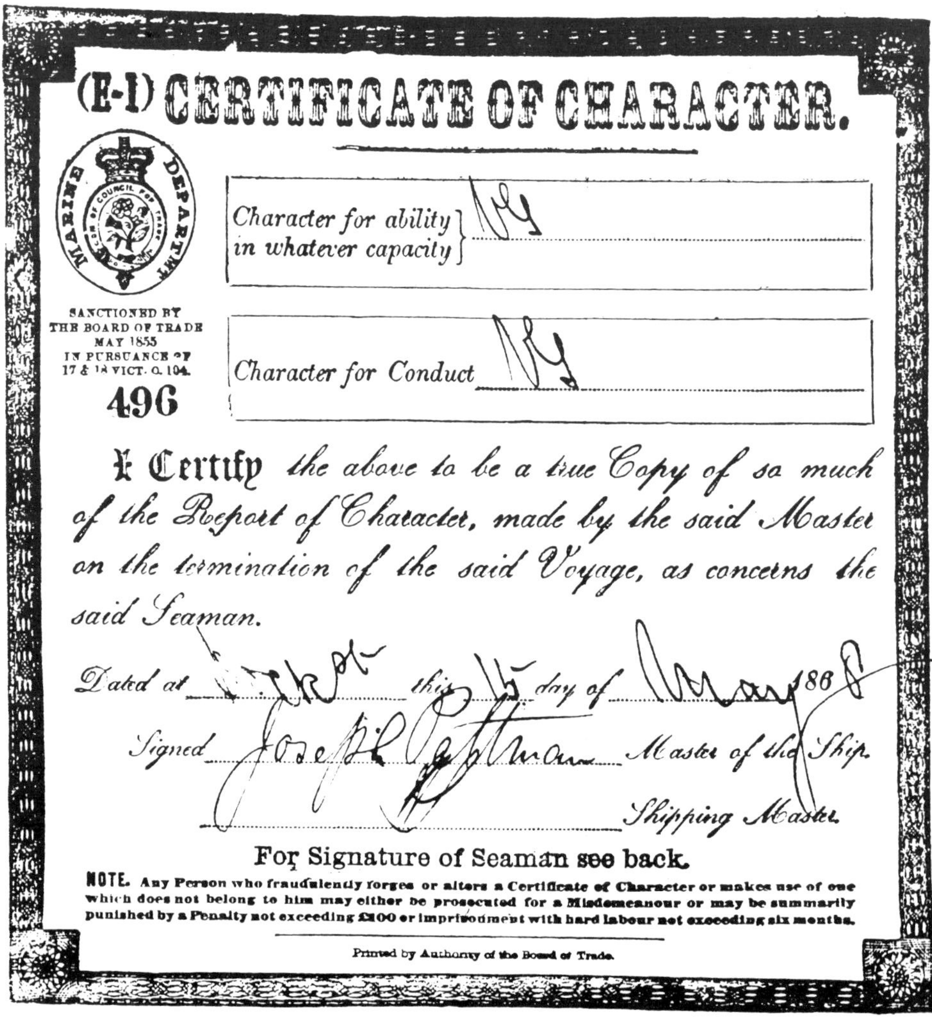

(E-1) CERTIFICATE OF CHARACTER.

MARINE DEPARTMENT

SANCTIONED BY THE BOARD OF TRADE MAY 1855 IN PURSUANCE OF 17 & 18 VICT. C. 104.

496

Character for ability in whatever capacity	VG
Character for Conduct	VG

I Certify the above to be a true Copy of so much of the Report of Character, made by the said Master on the termination of the said Voyage, as concerns the said Seaman.

Dated at [illegible] this 15 day of May 1868

Signed Joseph Pittman Master of the Ship.

Shipping Master.

For Signature of Seaman see back.

NOTE. Any Person who fraudulently forges or alters a Certificate of Character or makes use of one which does not belong to him may either be prosecuted for a Misdemeanour or may be summarily punished by a Penalty not exceeding £100 or imprisonment with hard labour not exceeding six months.

Printed by Authority of the Board of Trade.

(E-1) CERTIFICATE OF DISCHARGE.

For Seaman discharged before a Shipping Master.

MARINE DEPARTMENT — BOARD OF COUNCIL FOR TRADE

SANCTIONED BY THE BOARD OF TRADE MAY 1855. IN PURSUANCE OF 17 & 18 VICT. C. 104.

406

Name of Ship.	*Official Number.*	*Port of Registry.*
Result	47342	Faversham

Registered Tonnage.	*Description of Voyage or Employment.*
169	W Indies

	Capacity.
Name of Seaman Jos Graham	O
Place of Birth Whitstable	
Date of Birth 1854	

Date of Entry.	*Date of Discharge.*	*Place of Discharge.*
3 . 1 . 68	12 . 5 . 68	SAILOR'S HOME DOCK ST LOND[ON]

I Certify *that the above particulars are correct and that the above Seaman was discharged accordingly.*

Dated this 15 *day of* May *186*8

For Signature of Seaman see back.

Signed Joseph Pottman *Master of the Ship.*

Shipping Master.

NOTE.—One of these Certificates must be filled up and delivered to every Seaman who is discharged whenever the discharge takes place before a Shipping Master.

Printed by authority of the Board of Trade.

Lily, Alice Watts and Malvoison engaged on Salvage operations

Ship breaking

The author launches the SEA PIE at Anderson, Rigden and Perkins shipyard when Chairman of the Whitstable Urban District Council in the early 70s.

John Spenceley's Mast Yard – 1850

Spenceley's Yard – 1950

Samuel Holloway's Shipyard – 1850

Collar's Shipyard – 1899

Edward Holloway's Slipway

Anderson, Rigden & Perkins Slipway – 1950

Henry Cosby Solly's Slipway

Drawn by David Harvey

Jumping coal 1828

The Jumps. Unloading coal from a collier into railway trucks at Whitstable Harbour.

Old Whitstable Salts

The pier of the Whitstable Hoy & Trading Company that was situated to the West of the Whitstable Oyster Company Stores. Timbers from the 'Herbert' were used to construct the pier in 1913. It was demolished in August 1956.

TYPES OF WHITSTABLE OWNED VESSELS

drawn especially for this book by the late G. F. Campbell

Boomsail Barge

Prussian built Galliot

Trading Ketch

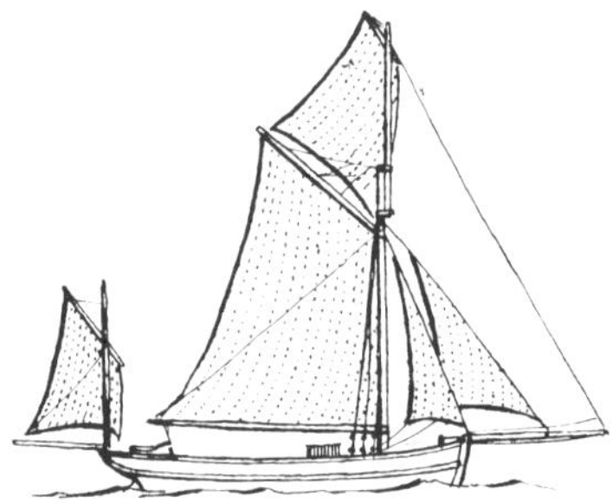

Dandy

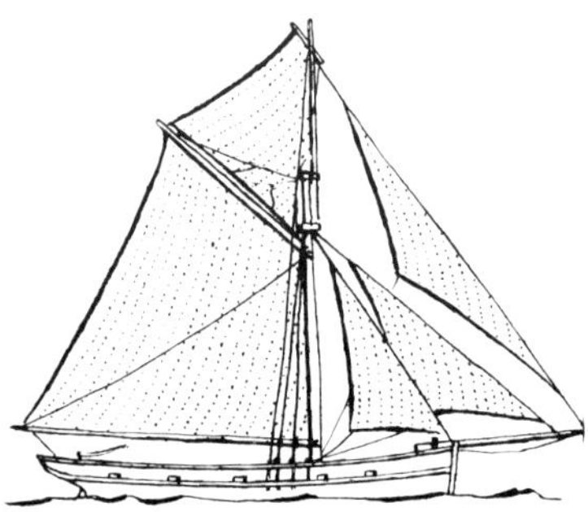

Cutter

Sloop

3 Mast Topsail Schooner

2 Mast Topsail Schooner

Brigantine

Brig

2 Mast Fore & Aft Schooner

Snow

Barquentine

Barque

G.F.Campbell.

Acknowledgements

Gratitude must be expressed to Joyce Kemp for the long hours spent in typing the full manuscript, which includes particulars of the smaller vessels, diving and shipyards, from which material for this book was taken.

To the Whitstable Museum for the use of two photographs (LOCH AWE and MALVOISON).

To John Foreman for permission to reproduce three photographs of his ancestors, a group on the HERBERT and the STAR.